The Shaping of the Foundations:

Being at home in the Transcendental Method

Philip McSh

D1328586

University Press
of America™

Copyright © 1976 by

University Press of America™

division of
R.F. Publishing, Inc.
4710 Auth Place, S.E., Washington, D.C. 20023

To those who,
like Stephen McKenna before Plotinus,
would consider it "really worth a life".[1]
in particular,
with affection and gratitude,
to Fred Crowe.

1. Confided to his private journal
   on his thirty-sixth birthday in
   1908, with two decades of interpretation, translation and
   poverty before him.

"Late in life, with indomitable courage,
we continue to say that we are going to
do what we have not yet done: we are
going to build a house".[1]

1. Gaston Bachelard,
   The Poetics of Space,
   Beacon Press, Boston,
   1969, p.61.

CONTENTS

Introduction

Paul Tillich's famous title, The Shaking of the Foundations,[1] differs only in one letter from my own, but that difference of k and p neatly symbolizes the difference in perspective. A kerygmatic focus is replaced here by a centering of attention on procedure.

But my chapters are no less exhortations than Tillich's sermons. In the sermon on "Doing the Truth" Tillich remarks that "Theology should be like a circle in which the most peripheral elements of the historical, educational and philosophical theories are directed towards the centre, the truth, which is the Christ."[2] If I make that remark on my own, I would also wish my reader to make it his or her own, but with the transformed meaning that it receives from the self-searching to which my chapters invite. The attention to be centred is the reader's; the procedure to be attended to is that procedure, procedere, emanatio, by which we bring forth our word of the Divine Word.[3] The emanationes intelligibiles of zoological truth and of musical experience belong there with the profounder emanationes that bring forth the inner word of the circle, the vortex, of theological method. Furthermore - and this is my discomforting message - without seeking to share and self-appropriate the emanationes of modern science, scholarship and art, parts of the cosmic word of revelation, the theologian risks irrelevance, an illusion of comprehension, an existential exclusion of mystery, a personal shrinkage.

It has become acceptable to consider that we are in a new age of theology.[4] But that new age is no less a precarious beginning than was the new age which died with Aquinas in 1274.[5] The new age pivots on the emergence of a community committed to the self-searching of generalized empirical method[6]: to those who struggle for that emergence this book is dedicated. "It is quite difficult to be at home in transcendental method."[7] Indeed, my thesis is that it is the task of more than a lifetime: so I make my own, and offer to others, the quotation from Bachelard with which this work begins. The work itself, as I indicate at various stages, is only a beginning, initial themes in a larger sonata form. It seeks to make manifest the personal labour involved in arriving at one's own adequate general theological categories.[8] Without such personally-appropriated categories, sets of special categories[9]

relating to religious interiority, authenticity and
redemptive history may well emerge, but they run the
danger of being a new nominalism. "The use of the
general theological categories occurs in any of the
eight functional specialties."[10] Again, theological
doctrines are "reached by the application of a method
that distinguishes functional specialties and uses the
functional specialty, foundations, to select doctrines
from among the multiple choices presented by the
functional specialty, dialectics."[11] But what is meant
here by 'use' and 'application'?[12] Clearly, it is
undesirable, even if it be possible, that techniques
emergent from general categories, or from method, be
used or applied with no more comprehension than the
schoolboy has of the technique which he uses for getting
square roots. What is required to reach adequate
comprehension, however, urgently needs existential
spelling-out.[13] Otherwise the budding theologian is
discouraged by present attitudes of theological education
into accepting facility in commonsense theological
language as basic mastery, instead of accepting human
nescience and naming as the norm, decades of questioning
and self-questioning as the way, and essential mastery
as something belonging to another life.

My spelling-out is personal. The four chapters
represent a searching over a period of five difficult
years into "the various manners of proceeding"[14] in
different realms of meaning. At the end of that period
I have reached sufficient understanding of that search
into the proceeding that is meaning to rename my search
Procedural Analysis. If I were writing a treatise I
would recast the chapters as they emerged to produce a
uniformity of style and terminology.[15] But I am not
writing a treatise: I am trying to share a search. The
sharing, too, has various symbolic levels, for, being
at home in transcendental method is a task not for the
mind alone but for the incarnate subject in the world.
My four chapters deal with issues in botany, music,
zoology and metatheology and, in counterpoint, with
the birth, life, death and resurrection of Bloom
Finnegan Joyce Dedalus. Some contemporary theologians
would consider such issues to be "peripheral elements"
far from "the centre, the truth; which is Christ." But
I would note that "the theological apprehension of
doctrines is historical and dialectical. It is
historical inasmuch as it grasps the many different
contexts in which the same doctrine was expressed in
different manners. It is dialectical inasmuch as it
discerns the difference between positions and counter-

positions and seeks to develop the positions and to
reverse the counter-positions."[16] To grasp with
metaexplanatory precision the many different contexts
requires a prolonged personal procedural contemplation
of possible sets[17] and sequences[18] of differentiations
of consciousness, and that contemplation surely requires
suci differentiations to be intrinsic to the subject.
To discern and develop in the centuries after the
twentieth a position which leaves behind the muddles of
empiricism and idealism requires that authentic
subjectivity and a fully metaphysical context[19] become
a habit of one's bones.

     Tillich, in his sermon on "The Theologian" raises
a question which surely must occur here in this wider
context of a new age: "If that be theological existence,
which one of us can call himself a theologian? Who can
decide to become a theologian? And who can dare remain
a theologian?"[20]

     I was fortunate, in my pre-philosophic and pre-
theological days, to be brought up in the hard school
of mathematical science. Most contemporary theologians
do not share that fortune, and the task of shaping the
foundations, of self-shaping, that I outline, may not
realistically be theirs. But that is not to say that
any such person is excluded from daring to be a theologian.
Whether one's education brought one into the twentieth
century or left one with a less adequately differentiated
consciousness in these latter stages of meaning[21], one
can dare to be a theologian with a commitment to the
future in the guidance of others.

     There is the hope that theology in the twenty-first
century will not be a Viconesque return to the dwarfed
reflections of the fourteenth.

                         Philip McShane

PART ONE:

PLANTS

and

PIANOS

PROLOGUE:

WORK IN PROGRESS

> Ho, Time Timeagen, Wake!
> For if sciencium (what's what)
> can mute uns nought, 'a thought,
> a bought the Great Sommboddy
> within the Omniboss perhaps
> an artsaccord (hoot's hoot)
> might sing ums tumtin[1]

"There are, in fact, two difficulties (or, rather two aspects of the same difficulty) to disconcert a reader of Work in Progress. Perplexed, he poses first the essential question 'What is it all about?' adding, sotto voce, a plaintive afterthought 'Why, anyhow, does the author make it so difficult?'

The subject of Work in Progress may easiest be grasped by a reference to Vico's Scienza nuova."[2]

That was 1929, and Finnegans Wake was still a decade away. Joyce worked, reworked, endlessly. What had been embryonically in the tail of Ulysses came forth, an enormous novelty, "a gigantic epiphany of mankind'.[3] It came forth, a mixture of chance and creativity, a mesh of particularities and dense allusions, a mosaic of puns and tongues, yet universal and all of a piece. Joyce's friends of the 1930's recorded their impression of Joyce at work and bore witness to the fact that 'he held an incredibly complex form of the Wake in his mind as a single image, and could move from one section to another with complete freedom'.[4]

It is more than thirty years now since the 'Wake's' appearance. Its appreciation has brought forth a large volume of literature, and one may remark of any chapter as William York Tindall remarks of one: 'To explain all of Chapter IX - as one could if one could - would require a book and a very big book'.[5] Primarily that explaining is orientated to mediating the deeper aesthetic appreciation of the book. But there is a deeper level of explanation that this small book treats.

"I am led to believe that the issue, which goes by the name of a Christian philosophy, is basically a question on the deepest level of methodology, the one that investigates the operative ideals not only of

scientists and philosophers but also, since Catholic
truth is involved, theologians. It is I fear, in
Vico's phrase, a 'scienza nuova'."[6]

That was 1959, with Method in Theology, still more
than a decade away. What, in a sense, was embryonic in
the tail of Insight is coming forth, a novel thing, and
it too is a gigantic epiphany of mankind. But like all
visible epiphanies, it is of essence veiled. 'Coffined
thoughts around me, in mummycases, embalmed in spice of
words. Thoth, god of libraries, a birdgod, mooneycrowned.
And I heard the voice of that Egyptian highpriest. In
painted chambers loaded with tilebooks. They are still.
Once quick in the brains of men'.[7] The dense mosaic of
meaning can fall foul of words. In recent years
Lonergan, like Joyce, has had the complex form of his
book in his mind: I recall ten minutes in 1966 when
with eight fingers he pointed out to me its basic plot,
theology as listening and talking, with its eight
specialties. In 1971 that complex form became available
in its cloud of words.

> So you need hardly spell me how
> every word will be bound to
> carry three score and ten top-
> typsical readings throughout
> the book of Doublends Jined[8]

And what of 2001?[9]

It is my hope that the dimensions of Method in
Theology will not go unminded. Of it, too, one might
say that every chapter will call for a very large book.

Yet the same may be said of the previous book
Insight. So it is that I write here of Work in Progress
in the context of work already done. The present
section has two chapters: one bearing witness to the
density of the book Insight, the other pointing to the
dimensions and relevance of the book Method in Theology.
Here I might use a Joycean portmanteau word and speak
of these two chapters or this one section as a
Blumenlied[10]; of a blumenlied given to men to mediate
the future through the metadigestion of the past; of
Bloom alias Henry Flower and Plants on the one hand
and of the musicality of the Wake on the other.

Joyce had his Tunc page.[11] Perhaps if I were to
pick a page it would be page 184 of Insight, half-
biological, half-aesthetic. What is the meaning of

that page? What does 'living' mean on that page, or
'music'? Surely what the man meant. And here we touch
on a handicap of humanity: the inevitable habituality
of our grip on the real, a handicap which is close to
the significance of Finnegans Wake. 'All we know is
somehow with us; it is present and operative within our
knowing; but it lurks behind the scenes ...'.[12] What
a man means by 'living' or 'music' may take two essays
or two books to begin to indicate.

Moreover, that indication will be an indication of
incarnate meaning, inclusive of the aesthetic. And in
this context one may raise the question, Which is the
more difficult book, Finnegans Wake or Method in
Theology? The answer is complex, but can be hinted at
briefly. First, the difficulty of Method in Theology
is of quite a different dimension than that of Finnegans
Wake; secondly, Method in Theology in its concretely-
filled heuristic may include Finnegans Wake in a manner
which cannot be reciprocated. But when I speak thus of
these two books I speak metaphorically. It is of human
subjects that we must speak. Method in Theology
expresses the possible integral attitude or orientation
of a human subject, and a component in that orientation
can be the subject's aesthetic expansion through
Finnegans Wake.

"Finnegans Wake was designed as a triumphant
reconstruction. It was in reference to this characteristic
of his last work that Joyce is reported to have remarked
during a visit to Stonehenge, 'I have been fourteen
years trying to get here'. The task of reproducing with
words the aesthetic unity of the past was an arduous
one."[13]

More arduous still the task of thematizing and
expressing a normative heuristic for present human
subjects who would listen adequately to the total human
past and mediate through human gesture a fuller future
meaning. To this task Bernard Lonergan has devoted
decades of towering silence.

> What has gone? How it ends?
> Begin to forget it. It will
> remember itself from every
> side, with all gestures, in
> each our word. Today's truth,
> tomorrow's trend[14]

PRELUDE

I shall have a word to say
in a few yards about the
acoustic and orchidectural
management of the tonehall
but, as ours is a vivarious
where one plant's breaf is a
lunger planner's byscent and
you may not care for argon, it
will be very convenient for me
for the emolument to pursue
Burrus and Caseous for a rung
or two up their isocelating
biangle.

Finnegans Wake, 165.

Chapter One

IMAGE AND EMERGENCE: TOWARDS AN ADEQUATE
WELTANSCHAUUNG

> Slow music, please. Shut your
> eyes, gents. One moment. A
> little trouble about those white
> corpuscles. Silence all.[1]

'How I would like to live on the heights. For this
is all my thinking craves for. But shall I ever work
my way upwards, if only for a little, so that I can
gain something of a free distant view? I am now forty-five
years old, and I am still a miserable beginner'.[2]

The following essay is written with a dual purpose:
there is the purpose of 'ongoing collaboration' which
brought the Lonergan Congress together at Florida in
1970; there is the hope of advancing the understanding
of the autonomy of the science of Botany. The essay,
then, is not only a contribution to the philosophy of
biology but also a contribution from the philosophy of
biology to the collaborative advancement of the study of
method.

The argument against reductionism in botany occupies
a central place in this paper. If the congress had been
one on the philosophy of biology, I would have given
much more space to that argument, for in that case the
expression of the wider significance of the argument
would seem less relevant and, furthermore, greater
biochemical and such like details would have been
appreciated more easily by the participating specialists.
Again, if specialists in the philosophy of biology
shared my basic philosophic position, the argument
could be presented to them with extreme directness.
But, since the congress was not of specialists in the
philosophy of biology, since, further, specialists in
philosophy of biology for the most part do not share
my philosophic view, the argument is presented
contortedly and in wider context.

The present expression, then, is my attempt to
reach an adequate interpretation[3] of a lengthier
expression in the same area[4], taking into account the
diversity of interests of the immediate congress
members, the general orientation of contemporary

philosophy of biology, the basic needs of ongoing
collaboration. Both ongoing collaboration and the
reorientation of philosophy of biology call centrally
for the mediation of the region of interiority. That
mediation is not a matter of some extrinsic directive:
it is a matter of the operative mediation of the
transformed horizons of the subjects who are diverse
specialists or philosophers of biology. For this reason
my expression is such as to call attention not so much
to the object of investigation as to the subjective
investigating, to the reader or the listener. That
expression looks to developed linguistic techniques,
calls for more refined reader-indicative developments
of language not unrelated to what Lonergan writes of in
another context: 'At a higher level of linguistic
development, the possibility of insight is achieved by
linguistic feed-back, by expressing the subject
experience in words and as subjective'[5]. The expression,
then, the symbolic image which is the sequence of
conventional signs, may be calculated to move the
reader to self-attention, providing an image
dispositional to the emergence of relevant self-insights
in the reader.

> But he adds: in bodies. Then he
> was aware of them bodies before
> of them coloured. How? By
> knocking his sconce against them,
> sure. Go easy. Bald he was and
> a millionaire, maestro di color
> che sanno. Limits of the
> diaphane in. Why in? Diaphane,
> adiaphane. If you can put your
> five fingers through it, it is
> a gate, if not a door. Shut
> your eyes and see.[6]

Indeed, I may note that I am touching here on a
primary meaning of the title 'Image and Emergence'.
The emergence of genuine ongoing collaboration
requires the emergence in the collaborating subjects
of a structured set of self-insights. Since, as I
believe, that emergence of a structured set of self-
insights is related to a discontinuity in the history
of philosophy, there is need for discontinuity in
image, in its expression. As the image does not
determine the insight, so even an adequate expression
of a world-subject view does not guarantee the
emergence of the corresponding network of insights.
But at all events an adequate expression should with

a certain immediacy continually challenge absence of
the corresponding insights, calling attention with
some degree of novelty to a novel gap 'between an
understanding of verbal usage and an understanding of
what names denote'.[7] Part of the adequate expression
would seem to be an indication of the slow process of
making present the adequate metaphysician. 'As an
adequate metaphysics demands sharp distinctions
between positions and counterpositions and between
explanation and description, so also it demands a
firm grasp of the heuristic and progressive character
of human intelligence'.[8] Indeed, the adequate metaphysician must grasp that the sharpness of the
distinctions and the firmness of the grasp is such as
to grow, slowly and with much labour, through a
lifetime. Prior to that firm grasp of the heuristic
character of human intelligence may be an intimation
of it through concrete witness. There is the concrete
witness provided, for instance, through the study of
the growth of understanding in a particular thinker.[9]
But there is also the concrete witness that can be
given by the contemporary thinker searching for
understanding. Certainly my own progress towards an
adequate metaphysics over the past decades has been
slow. I believe that the slowness is due, not to my
being mentally deficient, but to my being human, and
so I believe that the communal acceptance of that
human slowness is essential to authenticity of
collaboration. I give it expression here, then, as
part of the context of the more specific considerations
of this essay.

Authenticity demands that we share in a qualified
sense the orientation expressed by Husserl in the letter
cited at the beginning. In a qualified sense: one
might say that Husserl's bracketing of existence
genuinely left him in permanent puzzledom and so a
life-long beginner; what one might call Lonergan's
bracketing of existence in the book Insight is a
strategy which brings the reader to 'a breakthrough,
an envelopment, and a confinement'[10], to the stability
of an invulnerable position on the real. One may thus
be still relatively a beginner, but not miserable.
Again, as Spiegelberg remarks, 'To Husserl science
and scientific philosophy were essentially enterprizes
whose goal lay in the indefinite future and whose task
was consequently unfinishable. By contrast, the goal
of Weltanschauung was a finite one, namely to provide
the individual with the unifying perspective in which
he could live ... only in the indefinite future could

the two fuse asymptotically'.[11] On the other hand, in
so far as metaphysics is identified as 'the conception,
affirmation and implementation of the integral
heuristic structure of proportionate being'[12] and
extended to become critical method[13], it becomes an
enterprize of the subject which provides him with the
explanatory component of a Weltanschauung which may
mediate his concrete living.

In turning to the argument against reductionism in
botany we are turning to the consideration of a central
element in that Weltanschauung. For what is that
argument? In so far as a person is actually and capably
arguing against reductionism, the argument involves a
mental word expressing his understanding of the essential
conditions of possibility of levels of sciences and
things, and that understanding is pivotal in the
subject's appropriation of a world view whose philosophic
component involves a principle of emergent probability
and a sequential postulate[14]. I incline to think,
therefore, that the absence of that mental word in a
contemporary philosopher or theologian would be a
serious deficiency.

My present problem is to present, directly or by
reference, an image dispositional to the emergence of
such an understanding in the reader. Such an image
will contrast with other discussions of reductionism
in the manner in which it expresses a challenge to any
form of pseudo-objectivity, a challenge to all forms
of merely experiential conjugation, a challenge to the
existential subject.

> Every life is many days, day
> after day. We walk through our-
> selves, meeting robbers, ghosts,
> giants, old men, young men,
> wives, widows, brothers-in-law.
> But always meeting ourselves.[15]

Central, then, to our image-making is the effort
to challenge any form of theory of objectivity which
weakens on the isomorphism of structured knowing and
the real. The challenge gains expression in so far as
the reference of the print is regularly to processes
of knowing in the subject, the reader. Thus we may
speak of the different types of insight that the reader
may have in the process of doing biochemistry, botany,
etc., and our conclusions from such considerations may
appear to the reader to be an illegitimate projection

of the fruits of a study of knowing onto a real order only in so far as the reader falls short of the assumption of isomorphism which constitutes our critical position.

Secondly, there is the effort to indicate the menace of merely experiental conjugation. What is meant by the menace of experiental conjugation can be appreciated elementarily by recalling its presence in the area of natural science. Just as the Greeks in Socrates' time considered that they knew quite well what courage was, so the proverbial man in the street today considers that he knows quite well what red is, what acceleration is, what a buttercup is. Implicitly he takes experiential conjugation for adequate understanding. Moreover, when such a man takes to philosophy then he may mistake precision of experiential conjugation for philosophic refinement, a mistake indeed that seems to taint the reflections of both Analyists and Phenomenologists. But the mistake on the philosophic level is doubly and more subtly a failure. Not only may there be failure to philosophically exploit the meaning of 'red' as given by physics or the meaning of 'buttercup' as given by botany, but there can be a failure to note that there is an experiential conjugation on the philosophic level that should only be the beginning of explanation.

One may throw some light on the nature of these failures by considering the nature of experiential conjugation in its fullest sense, as also involving naming: 'Prior to the explanatory conjugates, defined by their relations to one another, there are the experiential conjugates that involve a triple correlation of classified experiences, classified contents of experience, and corresponding names. The being to be known as an intelligible unity differentiated by verifiable regularities and frequencies begins by being conceived heuristically, and then its unknown nature is differentiated by experiential conjugates'.[16] One can say, then, that experiential conjugates are 'reached by grasping the correlations between such terms as 'red as seen' and 'seeing red' or 'heat as felt' and 'feeling heat'.'[17] Now my point may best be made by noting that one can indeed arrive at saying this on a brief acquaintance with the book Insight, or at saying something equivalent in another school of philosophy. But what might one thus mean by the saying? What mental word might underpin the expression? The man in the street reaches experiential conjugates through a grasp

which contributes to identifying and distinguishing
elements in experience, and the conception proceeding
from that grasp is the peculiar one of heuristic terms.
But the man in the street does not grasp the grasp:
more precisely, one must have moved from advertence to
the type of insight involved in such conjugation,
through introspective experimentation and understanding,
to some conception of the personal procedure of
experiential conjugation. Otherwise one may well
remember or repeat the expression of an explanatory
definition of experiential conjugation, without going
beyond elementary introspective description. Then,
just as the non-physicist can identify and distinguish
the colours of the rainbow, so the philosopher may
identify and distinguish types of understanding. But
such identification by the philosopher is no more the
generalized empirical method that is generative of
scientific metaphysics than descriptive identification
of types of flowers is scientific botany.

> Wait a moment, professor
> MacHugh said, raising two
> quiet claws. We mustn't be
> led away by words, by sounds
> of words.[18]

This notion of a generalized empirical method, a
self-attentive pursuit which has the dimensions of a
science, may be unpalatable to some, incredible to
others. But on its operative admission stands or falls
the project of ongoing collaboration. One may find,
as Fr. Perego did, the projected self-attention
obscure.[19] If so, one must begin from precisely that
discovery: 'He can contrast that experience of not
understanding with other experiences in which he felt
he understood. Then he can turn his efforts to
understanding his experiences of understanding and not
understanding. Finally, when proficient at introspective
understanding, he can move to the higher level and
attempt to understand his successful and unsuccessful
efforts at introspective understanding'.[20] The entire
project is no mean task. I find it rarely spoken of as
no mean task. So it is that I emphasize here its
difficulty as part of my communication. It is
concretely emphasized, as I already noted, by indications of time and lifetime. I have spent many months
struggling self-attentively towards an understanding
of experiential conjugation. I have spent several
years introspecting my insights in physics, chemistry
and biology in order to bring me to some appreciation

of the autonomy or non-reducibility of botany.

Obviously, if there are scientific insights within this area of self-attention, they are no more communicable in brief than the insights of Quantum Theory can be communicated in a short course in physics. The contemporary scientist takes for granted this point about Quantum Theory. But, unlike physics, metaphysics as here conceived has not at present the status of an accepted scientific pursuit, and so to take its challenge and its promised possibilities seriously seems contemporarily more a leap into the dark than a leap into the light. Yet it is precisely the meeting of this challenge that is at present most relevant, not only on the philosophic level, but, as I have argued elsewhere[21], on the religious and contemplative level, to the proportionate hominization of technically-advanced man.

I have written of generalized empirical method and of its challenge to the existential subject in a manner which drew out parallels between it and ordinary empirical method[22]. A word now on a central point of difference in nature and challenge.

What one investigates when one self-investigates the intelligible which is also intelligent is most fundamentally the unrestricted questing of value which each human I is. One's investigation, one's questing of one's own questing, leads one slowly to some conception of the nuanced structure of one's embodied questing with a slowness that is related to that unrestrictness of subject and uniqueness of object of investigation. Embodied questing lies on the fringe of proper objects of human inquiry, and to raise the root question, What is Understanding? --- the question indeed of Being --- is to lift oneself into the Opaque[23]. At the early stages of the self-attentive questing, by pivoting on the pivoting of insight into phantasm, one 'is able to conceive, not without labour, the philosophic concepts of form and matter'[24]. Gradually one may reach more and more adequate heuristic concepts of the hierarchically-structured self, 'the extroverted subject visualizing extension and experiencing duration gives place to the subject orientated to the objective of the unrestricted desire to know'[25] and one may begin to operate detachedly, rigorously, within the intellectual pattern of a personal explanatory metaphysics most appropriately called Critical Existentialism. Such a reaching for an explanatory metaphysics which concretely mediates one's living is a permanent dialectic, for, 'so fine a detachment, so rigorous a disinterestedness, is a sheer leap into the void for the existential subject'[26]. Concomitant with that reaching is the personal movement into critical method which 'differs from other methods only in its subject-matter....which does not repudiate the notion of God but formulates it as unrestricted act of understanding'[27], and there is the further possibility of Faith mediating a transformation of the subject as critical methodologist and of his MetaWeltanschauung through some explicitation in questing of the image of his Trinitarian God.[28] The subject is thus slowly and dialectically revealed to himself as radically deficient image of Being and as destined for discontinuous transformation in the communal beatific realization of human intentionality. Nor, obviously, is that slow dialectic self-revelation a process merely within the intellectual pattern. Human questing is potentially integral in a spectrum of mediations. One's conception of God as Understanding is not of God as an intellectual but of God as the eminence of human attention and sympathy and affection which yet is utterly remote in Their proximity, and one's implementation of metaphysics demands that it be authentically total. So, for example, if one's Weltanschauung is one which pivots on a conception of history as God's effort to make man understanding, then one is sliding below the fringe of one's Weltanschauung if one's living, particularly with one's fellow men, is not a dialectic acceptance of that invitation to be understanding, to be an image of God. Finally, in so far as one continues to grow, and to grow in the heuristic appreciation of growth, one's questing, particularly within the field of theology, becomes ever more self-littlingly empirical[29] and, in the area of living, one's dramatic pattern ever more the expression and acknowledgement of Mystery.

What I am continually stressing is the slow growth of the subject, of you and I, in Weltanschauung, in the self-appreciative heuristic structuring of our conscious intentionality, a structuring which, if authentic, mediates a transformation of the drama of our daily encounter in a manner compatible with our psychic potential. The psychologist Maslow tells us that 'though in principle self-actualization is easy, in practice it rarely happens (by my criteria certainly in less than one per cent of the adult population)'.[30] If this is true of adult growth in general then in the specific area of philosophic growth, especially in a

period which may be called axial, one must acknowledge
the possibility of such failure, not merely as a
statistic but as a permanent personal possibility.
Spontaneously you and I dread, in varying shades of
that state, the sequence of intellectual conversions,
which are never purely intellectual, that shrinks the
dimensions of our present known. That dread breeds on
the abundant sufficiency of experiential conjugation.
In the labyrinth of language one can dissipate the
dynamism of the pure desire to know. Then the subject
can be protected from the questing potential of his
subjectivity by the environment of words. Scholarly
concern with current print can eat away the conscious
expansive potential of the scholar, and the resulting
absence of central mediation in integration leaves the
scholar fragments of a man.

> I am exhausted, abandoned, no
> more young. I stand, so to speak,
> with an unposted letter bearing
> the extra regulation fee before
> the too late box of the general
> postoffice of human life.[31]

And how can one attempt to avoid the contraction
of intentionality either in one's youth or in one's
greying years? It would seem that the continual
emergence of the subject-convert requires a continual
return to the image, and this in a threefold sense.[32]
There is the return to the image which brings one
beyond one's closed scholarly circuit to the image,
virtual, symbolic or representative, of a larger world.
It is a return which is not unrelated to the fourth
functional specialty of Fr. Lonergan's theological
method.[33] Yet the relevant image may be nothing more
than the image of a circle or of a suffering face.
Again, there is the return to the image which is not
imaginable but which is in, into, the imagined, to
insight in its preverbiality, a delicate return to our
own conscious questing intentionality that we are here
stressing. Finally, there is the return to the Image
which is imaged in our conscious intentionality--for
expansive listening and transforming conversion occur
in so far as our listening is in the Spirit.

Earlier in this essay I wrote of it as an
interpretation, that is, a second expression of
something already expressed. What is already expressed
is a lengthy treatment of the question to be treated
here briefly. But why then, one may ask, a second

expression? And how could the interpretation of my own previous expression convey more than the original expression?

Perhaps my style up to now sufficiently indicates the answer. I recall some remarks of the psychologist Maslow made prior to reading a formal paper at a conference. Those remarks regard the 'impersonality' of much conference-communication and I may quote a passage from them which can bear a heightened meaning in the present context: 'We must accept honestly and express candidly the profound truth that most of our 'objective' work is simultaneously subjective, that our outer world is frequently isomorphic with our inner world. that the 'external' problems we deal with 'scientifically' are often also our own internal problems, and that our solutions to these problems are also, in principle, self-therapies in the broadest sense'.[34]

The style of my second expression, then, is such as to indicate existentially something of what was actually going on when I was meaning the previous expression. Without the second expression one might become familiar with the entire first expression yet miss the point. With the second expression the point is perhaps less easily missed. I plead patience from the reader for the occasional eccentricities of stress, expression and allusion.

Central to the previous expression was the problem of indicating the nature of non-systematic process. I recall an occasion when I pointed out to a philosopher at Oxford that the determination of the motion of ten ideal billiard balls on an ideal table was a tedious piecemeal calculation, that it wasn't just a matter of putting initial conditions in a set of equations of motion and sitting back ready to give on demand the loci of the balls at any later time. Yet while the thing seems obvious enough, (I will return to the problem presently for the unconvinced), the chap seemed somewhat incredulous, due perhaps to my peculiarly empirical a posteriori approach to the philosophy of science - not to mention my eccentric invulnerable realism - perhaps to a certain Laplacian streak which bothers us all.

An ingenious suggestion is that
thrown out by Mr. V. Lynch (Bacc.
Arith.) that both natality and
mortality, as well as all other
phenomena of evolution, tidal
movements, lunar phases, blood
temperatures, diseases in general,
everything, in fine, in nature's
vast workshop from the extinction
of some remote sun to the
blossoming of one of the count-
less flowers which beautify our
public parks, is subject to a law
of enumeration as yet
unascertained.[35]

Before taking up the simple illustration of non-
systematic process mentioned, I will take, literally,
a more concrete example. The Oxford English Dictionary
speaks of a usage of the word 'random' in connection
with building; random is 'said of masonry, in which the
stones are of irregular sizes and shapes' O.E.D., B.3 .
Let us consider, then, the 'situation' constituted by
a wall which has been built at random. In the finished
wall the stones are situated at random, and these stones
are themselves of no particular size or shape. Their
size and shape can be said to be 'any whatever provided
specified conditions of intelligibility and not ful-
filled'.[36] How is one to investigate the detailed
structure of this wall, the sizes and shapes of its
component stones?

Were it the regular wall of a standard house there
would be little difficulty: one could, for instance,
produce a formula for the location of the faces between
the regular bricks. But here there is no short cut.
To reach an account of the irregular wall one must move
laboriously from stone to stone, taking the details of
measurement in each case. Nor is the measurement of
one stone of any consequence when one turns to the next,
apart from the shape of portions which happen to contact
each other. There is nothing to warrant the expectation
of any relationship between the measurements, and at
the end of the investigation one will have a vast
aggregate of particular measurements. The aggregate
will be coincidental, not held together by any law; it
will be a list without a formula. I pause here to
remind the reader that both 'list' and 'formula' refer
not to printed pages but to different types of insight.
One might reflect, for instance, on the mnemonic

strategies we sometimes use to retain telephone numbers or such like, to give an aggregate of insights some type of system.

We have, then, examples of coincidental aggregates on different levels. There is the coincidental aggregate of irregular stones; there is the coincidental aggregate of human insights expressed in lists and equations.[37]

Lastly, we may note that the account of the random wall is of no general value. A mason would consider it altogether foolish to carry around such an account with him, as if it were a general prescription for the construction of walls. The same point may be made regarding the next illustration, but the significance of the point will appear most clearly when we come to consider the adequate biochemical account of, say, a particular unicellular plant of the genus Chlamydomonas.

Let us pass now to the extremely simple illustration of nonsystematic process that I mentioned earlier: the motion of ten billiard balls under various ideal conditions. To present a detailed derivation of part of the motion would be tedious, yet, because the point can be missed, it is worth noting for oneself just how one must proceed by insight into the actual or imagined or symbolized motion. Consider, for instance, the problem of locating the ball A on the table after 4 seconds, given that at time $t = o$ the ball A is at position $(1,1)$ - with some convention of axes - with velocity $(1,1)$; ball B is at the position $(3,5)$ with velocity $(o,-1/2)$, and for simplicity the other balls are assumed to be too far removed to interfere in the interval of 4 seconds. If the balls have diameter of one unit, then one derives a collision position at time $t = 2$, at which time ball A is at point $(3,3)$ and ball B is at point $(3,4)$. One might proceed then to calculate the changes in velocities, etc. Evidently, the problem will involve a series of elementary, disconnected calculations. There is nothing like a systematic deduction of the motion of A: one must work tediously from individual collision to collision, determining at each discontinuity the conditions of the subsequent motion.[38]

Some readers may feel that I am labouring the obvious, but from my experience of lecturing and of philosophic discussion I honestly do not think so. Here I recall our consideration of experiential conjugation. My elementary illustrations are evidently related to the discussion in the book <u>Insight</u> of non-systematic process and coincidental aggregates.[39] That discussion in <u>Insight</u> can suffer the fate of what I would call generic experiential conjugation.[40] Generic experiential conjugation occurs when the object of discussion is heuristically conceived but the identifiable and distinguishable components of the object tend to become a set of implicit definitions without concrete reference. Generic experiential conjugation would seem to have been the fate of the human intellect in a large range of thomists and analysts. That one was talking about mind was agreed: mind was a point of departure, but also in different ways a point of no return.

So with the discussion of non-systematic process. One may agree that it is about something like the complex motion of a volume of gas molecules. But after the agreement one may fail to follow up either on the side of the object or on the side of the subject. 'The several insights by which the several parts of non-systematic process are understood form another coincidental aggregate'.[41] But has one actually tried to understand a nonsystematic process, and has one actually tried to understand one's consequent coincidental aggregate of insights? One can fail to return to the object - and of course the object may be the subject - as given in its image, representative, virtual, or symbolic in its significant sense[42], and operate with the symbolic image which is language to the exclusion of real definition.[43] Thus to appreciate the transition from arithmetic to algebra one must have 'a large dynamic virtual image that includes writing down, adding, multiplying, subtracting and dividing numbers in accord with the precepts of the homogeneous expansion'[44], coupled with the adverted-to transition insights. Similarly, one will not reach an appreciation of the gap between botany and biochemistry unless one has a large dynamic virtual image of doing biochemistry coupled with the insights which constitute the gap. Without such a personal possession one may easily repeat that 'if the non-systematic exists on the level of chemistry, then, on that level there are coincidental manifolds that can be systematized by a higher biological level without violating any chemical law',[45] but one does not explanatorily mean what one says. More generally, within a philosophic school facility in repetition and in various types of experiential conjugation is aided by the degree of coherence of the viewpoint, a coherence which topples over into the verbal expression. Thus, for example, other discussions of our present problem do not reach a basic coherent solution and so the arguments can remain somewhat problematic and elusive, with an elusiveness which both excludes facile treatment and lends an attractiveness of the erroneous or clouded solution seems to be related, among other things, to the human tendency to reject the coherent which can be experientially conjugated or talk-trapped with facility. That tendency is correct in so far as it challenges the other tendency I have criticised already: the tendency to mistake experiential conjugation for explanation, to mistake human explanation for something more than a glimpse of the mystery of Being. I recall here a part of Blondel's reply to an accusation made during his defense of L'Action as a thesis. P. Janet objected 'Votre pensée est obscure; votre façon d'écrire l'obscurcit encore. Je passe une heure sur une de vos pages, et je ne réussis pas à la comprendre; j'ai calculé qu'il me faudrait quarante-cinq jours pour lire votre thèse....' Blondel's reply included the remarks '....Il y a une certaine clarté qui, ainsi que le remarque Descartes lui-même, est souvent trompeuse et dangereuse, parce qu'elle laisse à ceux mêmes qui ne comprennent pas l'illusion de croire qu'ils ont compris, et parce que, leur voilant la complexité réelle des choses, elle les expose à tout réduire a une sort de simplisme indigent... Le style doit être un instrument de l'inévitable difficulté des choses...'[46] May I remark that I find this point relevent to the more recent works of Fr. Lonergan? Method in Theology is a more difficult and more profound book than Insight - yet it will be read with more ease, too much ease. The remedy however does not lie in introducing aesthetic obscurity but in the reader keeping the work in the context of previous writings. I would hope too that essays such as the present might provide a component of cautionary context.

> Ten Year, he said, chewing and
> laughing. He is going to write
> something in ten years.
>   Seems a long way off, Haines
> said, thoughtfully lifting his
> spoon. Still, I shouldn't wonder
> if he did after all.[47]

In the previous treatment of the problem of Emergence[48] I considered in some detail two papers[49] dealing with that problem, but repetition of that

detail would not add to this interpretation. Suffice
it to note that the two papers are illustrative of
neglect of both the object and the subject of the
inquiry. The debate in them centres on Pepper's claim
that if a function f_1 (q,r,s,t) adequately described
the interrelationships of the four variables q,r,s,t on
a given level, then there is no other adequate
description which is not identical with f_1. Meehl and
Sellars do not in fact challenge this supposition
adequately but they try to refute the reductionist
conclusions of Pepper. Pepper's basic assumption,
however, is the heart of the matter. That assumption
might more concretely be taken to be the supposition
that the biochemical processes which occur in a
particular region which I shall call Chlamydonoma[50] may
be adequately described by some particular function, f_1,
of a chemical order. My criticism of Pepper is not
simply a rejection of this assumption but a precise
empirical and metempirical determination of what the
function f_1, would be like. That precise determination
leads to an appreciation of the autonomy of botany.

From the earlier considerations of non-
systematic process one might suspect the line of the
present argument. Still, empiricality demands that we
venture into the field of plant biochemistry and into
the empirical field of our own conscious intentionality
where the range of biochemical insights occur. From
that venture should emerge an appreciation of the non-
systematic nature of the biochemical or biophysical
account of the chlamydomona-processes and of the nature
of the systematic botanical account. But the basic
principle of the venture is 'Try it and see'. As a
concrete example of such a policy of 'Try it and see'
I find convenient the work of N. Rashevski,
Mathematical Biophysics, especially the large portion
of the first volume where he discusses 'the
mathematical biophysics of vegitative cells and
cellular aggregates'.[51] Although the book is dated it
gives the methodologist a basis for appreciating the
type of account, the basic heuristic and relatively
invariant structure of any account, possible through
biophysics.

I do not intend giving here an abbreviated
expression of my previous expression of this
appreciation, but only to give such indications as
will continue to emphasize the orientation of the
investigation. It is a tricky business adverting to
the variety of insights that recur in oneself as one

tries to explain the unicellular plant in various ways
-- topologically, hydrodynamically, thermodynamically,
molecularly, etc. Rashevski remarks in his introduction
that 'only a superman could at once grasp mathematically
the complexity of a real thing'[52], but it is a further
step, a step into the science of self-attention, to
exploit the relation of that complexity to the autonomy
of the higher science. One must seek the basic
methodological reason why 'following the fundamental
methods of physicomathematical sciences, we do not
attempt a mathematical description of a concrete cell
in all its complexity'.[53] What one discovers is that
the account of the single concrete cell is multiply non-
systematic. What the reader takes as the meaning of
'non-systematic' here obviously depends on the reader's
biophysical background, but there should at least be
some elementary meaning if the earlier simple
illustrations have been pondered about: recalling, too,
S. Pepper's suggestion of a function f_1 we note that we
have in this case an aggregate of aggregates of
functions and conditions. More elaborate illustrations
might be given - of sets of integrals of equations of
motion, sets of boundary conditions, aggregates of
particle coordinates etc. - but elaborate illustrations
likely enough would be lost on the majority of readers.
Again, one ought to push on existentially to appreciate
the remark of H. Kaeser, 'It is evident that the
complete enumeration, even if it were possible, of all
the molecules within an organism would not account for
any but its most trivial aspects'[54]. Why the
triviality? Let us venture a little further in the
vague suggestive way that is possible in so far as one
is not actually labouring through the relevant physics
and chemistry.

> I declare to my antimacasser if
> you took up a straw from the
> bloody floor and if you said to
> Bloom: Look at, Bloom. Do you
> see that straw? That's a straw.
> Declare to my aunt he'd talk
> about it for an hour so he
> would and talk steady.[55]

There is the fact that a thorough investigation
of any one particular chlamydomona is singularly
worthless. What Rashevski remarks in regard to the
continuum approach to the cell holds also for the
molecular approach: 'Even granted that we could solve
exactly the differential equations of diffusion for a

large number or even for all cases, this would still
leave us with a rather serious handicap. The
distribution of the diffusion flows in every individual
case depends, among other things, on the exact shape of
the cell. A slight variation of the latter will modify
the analytic expression describing the distribution of
concentrations and flows. But, since there are no two
cells perfectly alike, the exact solution of the
problem for a given case would contain a tremendous
amount of detail which is biologically insignificant
because it applies only to the given case.'[56] How does
one get round this difficulty? Rashevski suggests two
ways. Either one solves the problem exactly in a single
case hoping that other cases will fit approximately this
solution, or one concentrates on 'such gross features as
are common to all cells of a given type, in spite of the
difference of detail.'[57] The difficulties of the first
course have been touched on above: exact solutions are
forthcoming only in so far as one simplifies the
equations enormously, thus departing from the concrete
problem. A similar departure from the concrete problem
is entailed in following the second course, for 'the
individual variations from cell to cell (in our case
from Chlamydomonas to a close relation) are so large that
it would be futile to compare exact numerical values.
But the regularities that are found in the behaviour of
cells, in spite of their individual variations, suggest
a search for relations of a general form which may
remain invariant from cell to cell despite variations
of numerical values.'[58] One thinks immediately in this
context of equations invariant in structure[59], or of
topological relations[60], or of open-system thermo-
dynamics[61]. But all of these involve evident abstraction
from the concrete process being studied. To move for
a moment into an older terminology, the common matter
of the mental word resulting from the investigation
does not include elements we are precisely keen on
including -- and indeed the form of that word falls
short of botanical correlations.

But what of the rapidly developing field of
biochemistry? Again I must insist that my expression
here is doubly at a remove from what is necessary to
bring the reader to adequate insight. My expression
does not include the array of biochemical structural
relations and reaction equations, nor does it include
adequate details of self-oriented reflection. Furthermore, contemporary talk in biochemistry, even in
respectable journals, is full of muddles about genetic
codes and such like, which presuppose for their
precipitation some degree of the self-attentive

reflection advocated here. A hint as to the line of
attack on such muddles would perhaps be appreciated,
and also will lead us on in our argument.

Thus, it is common talk that 'DNA is now
recognized as being the chemical structure that stores
the cell's hereditary information'[62]. Undoubtedly DNA
plays an essential structural role and a fundamental
role in continuity: but the role is more like the
role of resources and terrain in determining the pattern
of a battle than like the role of a general's plan.
Here, and in later sections, I would like to let the
botanists speak for themselves. While their meta-
competence is limited I find their judgment on their
own work more acceptable in general than the views of
philosophers of biology who seem to move so easily away
from the data of metabiology, the habit of biological
science in themselves. Thus my criticism of philosophic
or popular views on DNA is echoed by Mayr: '... Nor
can species differences be expressed in terms of the
genetic bits of information, the nucleotide pairs of
the DNA. This would be quite as absurd as trying to
express the difference between the Bible and Dante's
Divina Commedia in terms of the difference in the
frequency of the letters of the alphabet in the two
works. The meaningful level of integration is well
above that of the basic code of information, the
nucleotide pair'.[63] Mayr, however, exaggerates here.
In an older terminology we may speak more accurately
of the nucleotide pair as components of materia
disposita to cellular or organic form. Only components:
'While DNA, RNA, and protein are undoubtedly of major
significance, it is not entirely clear that these three
polymers (together with the necessary precursors and
energy source) represent the minimum components for a
living reproductive system, however attractive such a
hypothesis may be.'[64] I quote the latter remark out
of context and with a transformed meaning: later we
will return to what might be called the virus-problem
aspect.

Of course the cells or whatever
they are go on living. Changing
about. Live for ever practically.
Nothing to feed on feed on themselves.

To switch to subject-centred talk, one may
recall that 'the chemistry of the cell can yield an
image of catalytic process in which insight can grasp

biological laws.'[66] In this context, which indeed
should represent the reader's slant all through, it is
more precisely evident that the complete chemical
account of the components in the cell falls radically
short of an account of the organisation of the cell -
or of the unicellular plant such as Chlamydomona. 'The
plant cell, as indeed all cells, is a highly organised
entity containing within it large populations of
numerous kinds of subcellular entities: membranes,
nucleus, ribosomes, enzymes. These with certainty form
one organised system of the cell.'[67] And how indeed
would one handle that complex of systems from the
chemical point of view? It would be tedious to enter
again into the question of the non-systematic. But we
may let one who has made serious efforts to bring the
vast array of reactions into order bear witness to the
pressure on the investigator to leave behind, in one
way or another, the non-systematic: 'Biologists working
with inbred strains of mice and other homogeneous
populations have long recognized that whereas large
variations among individuals, and within the same
individual at different times, are encountered in
biological magnitudes such as levels of enzymes,
hormones, and mean blood pressure, little variation is
encountered in the structural or topological relationships among paths - endocrine, vascular, neural, and
so on - that constitute the physiological net. This
variability of magnitude and constancy of structure suggests that the responses and stability characteristics
of a physiological net, although partly determined by
numerical parameters, may be primarily determined by
structures. From this hypothesis it follows that
realistic mathematical representations of a living
organism should place structure in a central role, and
should allow for the indifference of the organism to
exact numerical values.'[68]

Let us now be more concrete and envisage, commonsensically as it were, what the adequate biochemical
account of Chlamydomona would be liked. Let us consider
'A Day in the Life of Chlamydomona'. The phrase has
the ring of a book-title, and purposely so: for the
biochemical account of a day (indeed a minute) in the
life of Chlamydomona would fill an unbelievably large
volume. The content of that volume would be an endless
sequence of reaction-equations and diagrams, and one
might envisage them being ordered through the volume
by means of space-time coordination. The non-chemist
may be helped here by recalling fading schoolday
formulae of organic compounds. The expert in biochemistry will note that space-time coordination would
not be at all adequate, that the project is on the
fringe of fantasy. Finally, having got together the

volume, one would find the title ridiculous: one would really have to settle for something like 'Detailed reaction equations of an aggregate of proteins, etc. etc. within and in the region of membranestructure ...'. Botanical correlations would find no place in the volume. Woodger puts the difficulty here in a relevant fashion: 'If from a chemical hypothesis C, containing no embriological set-designation, an embriological statement E is to be derived as a necessary consequence, this will only be possible if C is conjoined with a definition stating that the embriological set-designations E are abbreviations of C'.[69] Again, of course, our volume is of little use when we come to discuss the next day in the life of <u>Chlamydomona</u>: think, for instance, of what a tiny change in temperature does to the reaction-aggregates. Nor is the volume of much use when we turn even to <u>Chlamydomona</u>'s nearest relatives.

'I think what perhaps bothers me most is the sheer complexity of the reaction systems that are involved. For example, organic chemists, interested in plant and animal materials, have been able to demonstrate, indicate, or suggest, the pathway of synthesis of some particular growth-regulating substance from a fairly simple initial substance. Now, the chemical statement, or formulation, of this one process is often quite elaborate, i.e., it may occupy a page, or a half-page, of a text book. Yet, in any morpho-genetic process, the synthesis of the substance in question is only one of a whole system of regulated, simultaneous activities, all contributing to the eventual morphogenetic development. Even if we could tabulate the separate pieces of information - the chains of syntheses, etc. - we still have to find verbal expression for these complex dynamic, growing, differentiating systems. It is true that computers can be used to process the multitudinous accumulation of records. But, in the end, we come back to ourselves: the botanist is an individual, striving to reason inductively and intuitively, e.g. about specific organisation, or a particular organogenic development, etc.; and he can only advance his thinking if he has clear and sufficient simplified propositions on which to cogitate.'[70]

Here we come close to the crux of the matter. Wardlaw speaks of finding 'verbal expression for these complex, dynamic, growing, differentiating systems' and of having 'clear and sufficiently simplified

propositions on which to cogitate'. His expressions
parallel to some extent Woodger's talk of embriological
set-designations. Would we have sufficiently met the
situation if we arrived at a set of general biochemical
propositions? Would topological and structural statements of the type suggested by Munck suffice? Is
photosynthesis a name for biochemical processes of a
generic type?

Now let us be existential. The questions
accumulated at the end of the last paragraph call, in
the contemporary intellectual and philosophic climate,
for a semi-deductive abstractive argument with a substantial bias towards affirmative answers. I myself
have spent many hours grappling with the family of such
arguments, reluctant to concede that they were false.
Central to that reluctance is the tension between
culturally-conditioned philosophic speculation and
intellectually-patterned Critical Existentialism. In
general, if one is orientated by the former rather than
by the latter, 'the universe of being seems as unreal
as Plato's noetic heaven, and objectivity spontaneously
becomes a matter of meeting persons and dealing with
things that are "really out there"'[71] and, in particular,
in the field of cytology what is "really out there" is
a cluster of scarcely observable chemical reactions.

> Heard? Why, he could not but
> hear unless he had plugged up
> the tube Understanding (which
> he had not done). For through
> that tube he saw that he was in
> the land of phenomenon where
> he must for certain one day die
> as he was like the rest too a
> passing show.[72]

The key to breaking that culturally-conditioned
mode of pursuing philosophy of science, and to handling
in adequate dialectic the questions raised, lies in a
metascientific return to oneself as botanist. The
return must be metabotanical. The botanist indeed is
in the odd position that while he or she can regularly
make sound scientific statements about particular types
of plants, general statements about the nature and
procedure of botany are liable to be vague, descriptive,
even mythic. Why is this? It is because the question,
What is botany, What is botanical understanding?, is a
metaquestion. If the botanist does not in fact move
metareflectively towards an understanding of his

botanical insights, then he or she cannot, for example, conceive of matter and form other than as the remnants of scholastic decadence. Then the botanist, or the philosopher, can discuss endlessly the pros and cons of vitalism or reductionism but the discussion at best is restricted to the field of metaexperiential conjugation. At best: and otherwise it is only 'at worst', for, if there is no conjugation to one's experience of insight then the meaning is radically inadequate: since there is no analogue for mind outside mind.[73]

Moreover, not only is the talk about botany in general vitiated by the lack of a metahorizon: the botanist's expression of botanical science itself is liable to be a distorted mixture of mechanistic, cybernetic and anthropomorphic vocabulary. It is only within a metahorizon that such distortion can be adequately appreciated and a sufficient recasting of expression attempted.[74] I feel it worthwhile to add immediately here a substantial quotation to illustrate the need: otherwise the concrete significance of statements about the transforming power of a personally-implementable metaphysics could be missed.

'Of what then can a developmental program itself consist? We do not yet know, but we can nonetheless speculate about the matter. The program by which an apical cell or meristem grows into a stem must necessarily contain information about the proper times and planes for cell division as well as information about the size which the bud must attain before differentiation into the specialized cells of the stem occurs. It must contain information as to when and where to cut off leaf primordia, as well as directions for the making of each of the kinds of specialized cells. One general way in which such instructions might be encoded in the genome is illustrated by the concept of the developmental test. We have seen that the genome of the cortical cells of intact potato tubers maintains a posture different from that of similar cells when isolated. It is clear, therefore, that such cells test their environment to find out how many cells are about. This test might consist, for example, of sensing the concentration of some sub-stance given off by potato cells and which therefore builds up to high concentration in tubers but quickly diffuses away from simple cells. Absence of the substance derepresses - its presence represses - particular genes. In this general way, through the use of a multitude of different sensor substances and their associated genes, each cell should, in principle, be able to keep track of where it is in the developmental pathway.'[75]

This book is cited not because of its particular failings in this area. On the contrary: there are many books, especially in popular vein, with glaring deficiencies of expression. The quotation illustrates rather the best that can be done without the transforming mediation of a metahorizon. The recasting of the expression in such a text calls for linguistic inventiveness mediated by the botanist's adequate conception of form-matter and of the set of related metaphysical elements. I do not attempt a recasting here - but as an image of future philosophy one might envisage students of methodology searching for the metaphysical equivalents required by such passages!

> It had better be stated here and now at the outset that the perverted transcendentalism to which Mr. S. Dedalus' (Div. Scep.) contentions would appear to prove him pretty badly addicted runs directly counter to accepted scientific methods. Science, it cannot be too often repeated, deals with tangible phenomena. The man of science like the man in the street has to face hardheaded facts that cannot be blinked and explain them as best he can.[76]

A parallel difficulty of insight and expression becomes apparent the more directly a botanist is dealing with basic heuristic definitions, such, for example, as the definition of irritability.[77] The authors of Strasburger's Textbook of Botany[78] speak of irritability, along with metabolism and productivity, as one of the three characteristics of the plant. 'By the phenomenon of irritability is understood the capacity of an organism to react to changes in the outer and inner environments in a manner which cannot be accounted for in terms of the energy involved in the stimulus, but in which energy is supplied from the reserves of the organism itself (excitation mechanism)'.[79] Later they remark, having discussed the lack of proportionality between the pressure of a finger on a trigger and the force with which the bullet is discharged, that 'the concept of irritability is not in any way vitalistic,

but merely signifies that certain stimuli are able to
set off complex reactions in the interior of the
organism'.[80] Now, on the view presented here,
irritability is not adequately conceived of without a
metahorizon. The required definition of irritability
is a heuristic definition of a species of plant
activity,[81] reached through metabotanical introspection
and the consequent objectification in a metaphysics.
Reaching that heuristic definition, indeed, parallels
the more general effort to reach an adequate heuristic
answer to the question, 'What sort of simplified
propositions arise from my correct understanding of
Chlamydomona?' or in more modern terms 'What is the
nature of the insight which grasps the reaction-
aggregate as formally dynamic, putting itself together
but "with the blindness of natural process"[82]?', or,
in the most general terms, to the question, 'What is
plant life?'

     Here I may be relevantly existential. Some of
my richest moments in the months I spent thinking out
this paper were with Aquinas' treatment of this latter
question, in such places as the Summa Theologica, Pars
Prima, q. 18, when I reached, against a certain background of biochemistry, etc., some personally-transforming
appreciation of what Aquinas meant when he wrote of the
vivens and of plant life. Perhaps the possibility of
communicating some notion of that appreciation warrants
a slight detour through the expression of St. Thomas.

     The question of the Summa Theologica mentioned
is central to that appreciation, but without the
personal possession of the riches of St. Thomas' thought
on points such as pati communiter, motus communiter,
actus vitalis, operatio, etc.[83], the expression here
may read like a brief representation of a too-familiar
Aristotle. And indeed my own experience has been that
my small grasp of what Aquinas meant by vivens has been
reached by going all the way round through modern
science as well.

     Perhaps we might begin from a basic statement
of St. Thomas: 'Vitae nomen sumitur ex quodam exterius
apparenti circa rem, quod est movere se ipsum: non
tamen est impositum hoc nomen ad hoc significandum,
sed ad significandam substantiam cui convenit secundum
suam naturam movere se ipsam, vel agere se quocumque
modo ad operationem'.[84] The question is that of self-
movement, where Aquinas is careful to point out - and
we should be careful to appreciate - that we are here

in the field of metaphysics, of heuristics, and not in
the field of description. Self-movement, indeed, has
taken on a refinement of meaning which transcends not
only our imagination of locomotion but also the limited
category of <u>motus</u> <u>proprie</u> <u>dicta</u>. This latter transcending would seem to be the force of the phrase
following 'vel' in the quotation above, '<u>agere se</u>
<u>quocumque modo ad operationem</u>'.

Article three of the same question goes on to
specify the various degrees of realization of such
<u>agere se ad operationem</u>, and the insight directly
relevant to our reflection on <u>Chlamydomona</u> is expressed
pithily in the following paragraph: '<u>Inveniuntur igitur</u>
<u>quaedam, quae movent seipsa, non habito respectu ad</u>
<u>formam vel finem, quae inest eis a natura, sed solum</u>
<u>quantum ad executionem motus: sed forma per quam agunt,</u>
<u>et finis propter quem agunt, determinantur eis a</u>
<u>natura. Et huismodi sunt plantae, quae secundum formam</u>
<u>inditam eis a natura, movent seipsas secundum augmentum</u>
<u>et decrementum.</u>'[85] In the previous article St. Thomas
had spoken, with reference to Aristotle, of the lower
levels of life, '<u>quorum quaedam habent naturam solum ad</u>
<u>utendum alimento, et ad consequentia quae sunt</u>
<u>augmentum et generatio.</u>'[86] What could be meant by this
<u>solum ad executionem motus, solum ad utendum alimento</u>?

> He tore the flower gravely from
> its pinhold smelt its almost no
> smell and placed it in his heart
> pocket. Language of flowers.
> They like it because no-one can
> hear.[87]

A leap into quite another field is helpful.
Aquinas elsewhere[88] discusses the motion of the will by
God as not violent but natural. 'Now what does the
patient, the will moved by God, when it is moved by
God, while it is moved by God, confer or contribute?
It operates. It wills. In this case the operation is
an <u>operatio</u> <u>receptiva</u>, just as <u>sentire</u> is a <u>pati</u> of
sense and just as <u>intelligere</u> is a <u>pati</u> of the possible
intellect. The will operates inasmuch as it is the
will that is actuated. The will contributes inasmuch
as an act received in the will has to be a "willing",
not because it is an act, nor merely because of the
extrinsic mover, but proximately because act is
limited by the potency in which it is received.'[89] Let
us return to our plants: concretely we may think of
Chlamydomona and its 'use' of light, its self-motion

solum ad utendum lumine. How does this 'use of light'
self-motion - whatever that means - fit in with the
restriction solum ad executionem motus? Immediately
previous to the above citation from the Summa, Pars I,
q.18, a.3, St. Thomas speaks of a principle cause
operating through an instrument, cui instrumento
competit sola executio actionis. One may helpfully
think perhaps of Chlamydomona as an 'instrument' of
the environment, more particularly of Chlamydomona as
an 'instrument' of the light. In thinking thus, if one
is thinking correctly, what should dawn on one is a
certain lack of symmetry: Chlamydomona uses[90] the
light; the light uses Chlamydomona. We are here, so to
speak, abusing the word 'uses': saying that the light
uses Chlamydomona is a bit like saying that the tail
wags the dog. But the abuse may lead the reader
towards a central heuristic insight into the nature of
material being. What constitutes the antisymmetry?
Recall the question above regarding the will. In both
cases there is a question of operatio receptiva, of the
receiving potency determining the ontological level of
the act. In both cases there is a pati but it is not
the pati proprie of Aristotle's Physics that we speak
of: it is pati communiter.[91] But what of the question
of agere se? Here it seems to me that we are up against
a difficulty which parallels the difficulty found in
treating of self-attention, or more fundamentally still
of treating of knowledge by identity, and in order to
try and break with a tradition of misconceptions I am
led to introduce - with a meaning determined by the
entire present context - the categories of autonomic
and synnomic forms as the two basic genera of material
forms.[92] What I mean by synnomic forms might be
gathered to some extent by reflecting on Newton's law
of equality of action and reaction. I am attempting,
if you like, to categorize the non-living as being (to
borrow terms from the sociologist Riesman[93]) neither
inner-directed nor other-directed. It is helpful also
to recall here the sweep of St. Thomas' discussion of
the question, 'Quomodo accipienda sit generatio in
Divinis, et quae de Filio Dei dicuntur in Scripturis',
a discussion closely related to our total present topic,
where St. Thomas begins by specifying the lowliness of
generation on the level of the inanimate[94]: 'In rebus
enim omnibus inanimata corpora infimum locum tenent:
in quibus emanationes aliter esse non possunt nisi per
actionem unius eorum in aliquod alterum. Sic enim ex
igne generatur ignis, dum ab igne corpus extraneum
alternatur, et ad qualitatem et speciem ignis
perducitur'.[95]

Autonomic forms on the other hand pertain to the realm of the living. We are here in a hermeneutic circle: what is important is not the terminology but the insight, and that insight is reached by attending not just to such expressions as 'autonomic', 'law-to-self', 'auto-ordered', but to such processes as photosynthesis and the understanding of photosynthesis. By such attention one may grasp first - one does so by doing scientific botany - the nature of that level of being self-moving 'solum ad utendum alimento, et ad consequentia, quae sunt augmentum et generatio'.[96] By the further self-attention - and now one is indulging in metabotany - one may grasp the nature of the prior grasp, and so constitute oneself more fully - autonomically one may say - as possessor of a meta-horizon.

> What is the age of the soul of man? As she hath the virtue of the chamelion to change her hue at every new approach, to be gay with the merry and mournful with the downcast, so too is her age changeable as her mood. No longer is Leopold, as he sits there, ruminating, chewing the cud of reminiscence, that staid agent of publicity and holder of a modest substance in the funds. He is young Leopold, as in a retrospective arrangement, a mirror within a mirror hey, presto! , he beholdeth himself.[97]

Refinements to the discussion of autonomic and synnomic forms may be added here which help both to show the a posteriori nature of methodological reflection and also to raise issues of identity, thinghood, eductio de materia disposita, etc., which we have purposely avoided here and in the work Randomness, Statistics and Emergence, because present confusion calls for a lengthy treatment of these issues.[98] Such refinements would deal, for example, with forms of symbiotic living: but let us restrict ourselves to the vexed question of the nature of viruses.

First of all it is worth noting that patho-genicity, which was earlier considered to be central to the definition of virus[99] is now thought of as only secondary. An adequate contemporary description

speaks of viruses as 'sub-microscopic, infective
entities that multiply only intracellularly and are
potentially pathogenic'.[100]   The dispute about viruses
has reached at present at least nominal resolution:
'The reluctance of pathologists to change their concepts
about viruses was stiffened almost to stubbornness by
their justifiable irritation at the claims of some
chemists and physicists who, over-impressed by the
success of physico-chemical techniques in isolating
viruses and by the apparent homogeneity of purified
virus preparations, unhesitatingly called viruses
"molecules" and thereby placed them in the wrong category.
The apparently irreconcilable differences between those
who called viruses organisms and those who called viruses
molecules have now disappeared, for happily both parties
to the dispute have abandoned these names'.[101]   Still,
the question does remain: how are viruses to be
heuristically classified: equivalently and methodologi-
cally, what scientists are adequate to the investigation
of viruses? Viruses 'seem to have no metabolism of
their own and, unlike any other known kind of living
stuff whatsoever, they are crystallizable. These
substances thus seem to bridge the gap between the
living and the non-living worlds, a discovery that has
had profound effects upon biological thought. It has
been necessary, for example, to revise our ideas about
the nature and origin of life; indeed it seems that we
can no longer use the word "life" as a precise term
because we now know less than ever exactly what we
mean by it.'[102]

     What is called for is a refinement in the
heuristic categorization of material being, and that
refinement emerges a posteriori from the manner of
investigating viruses in a category such as "relatively
autonomic" - alive, one may say, only in the proximity
of a live environment. Note however that I raise more
questions here than I answer: questions regarding the
"thinghood" of the virus-aggregate both in and out of
"living context", questions about the identity in the
many possible "lives" of such an aggregate, etc. As
I remarked above, an adequate handling of these
questions presupposes a more extended reflection.
Again, the "relativity" can take on all the shades of
symbiotic etc. relations. Moreover, there seems no a
priori reason why the relativity could not be compound
("little fleas on big fleas ..."), though the virus
level itself seems to be one of necessary minimal
structure. At all events, the virus in crystalline
form falls within the category of the synnomic and so

the chemists may have their say. One may note here that parallel difficulties arise on other levels of science: one may think of the problems of bound and free electrons, or of particle-decay studies.

We have come a long way from the quotations from Wardlaw and Woodger which triggered off our discussion of vivens. At least we may have: for, as I have insisted repeatedly, the correct understanding of a discussion like the foregoing pivots on an accurate appreciation of the pair matter-form, an appreciation reached 'not without labour'.[103] Moreover, in so far as one may not have adequately conceived of the meaning of "is", "is not", of existence, occurrence, event, functioning,[104] then the sufficient context for that understanding is lacking. Again, I may note that an understanding of the foregoing expression, a sharing therefore of the mental word which subtends my expression, would carry the reader in certain points beyond Aquinas' meaning. For, in particular, the autonomic forms of material being are intrinsically genetic, and there is no evidence that Aquinas conceived with any accuracy of genetic method or development[105], though he would not be totally startled by Fr. Lonergan's discussion of finality and of principium motus in eo in quo est.[106]

The position then from which I speak and out of which I speak is a precisely and contemporarily conceived hylemorphism: not a hylemorphism which hovers vaguely between vitalism and mechanism but a hylemorphism embedded in a realism 'between which and materialism the half-way house is idealism',[107] and enriched by the abundance, precision and explanatory patterns of contemporary botany. Indeed, without the latter personal enrichment, the operative potential of one's critical realism is dammed by description, and one's grip on the heuristic meaning of "form" becomes dubious. "Form", indeed, can remain largely an addition to one's environment of words, a play object of metaphysicians, and hylemorphism continue to appear as irrelevant as Plotinus' notion of the One.

> Fed and feeding brains about
> me: under glowlamps a sloth of
> the underworld, reluctant, shy
> of brightness, shifting her
> dragon scaly folds. Thought
> is the thought of thought.
> Tranquil brightness. The soul

is in a manner all that is:
the soul is the form of forms.
Tranquillity sudden, vast,
candescent: form of forms.[108]

Yet hylemorphism as a personal appropriation of
the botanist would promise a transformation and an
integration of botanical inquiry which is sorely needed.
I have already indicated a need for transformation of
botanical expression, but the need for an integration
of botanical inquiry which would be personal to the
botanist is even more evident. Here I may recall that
my paper is addressed not only to the botanist but to
the contemporary thinker, and my expression and
references continue to be components of the effort to
provide an image of emergence, an image for emergence.
I may note then, as an image of the contemporary
emergence of man, in his meaning of plants, the fort-
nightly review Biological Abstracts, a very substantial
volume containing regularly about 5,000 summaries of
articles from current periodicals. Contemporary botany
has bred in the genus botanist a wide range of species
which express their partially-isolated meanings in
journals with such varied titles as Plant Morphology,
Plant Physiology, Palaeobotany, Radiation Botany,
Phytochemistry, Plant Pathology, Virology, Biometrics,
etc. The wealth of such detailed and clearly
explanatory discussions as 'Effects of ionizing
radiation on nucleic acids during embrionic development'
is enormous, and might well cause the contemporary
theologian to pause and reflect on the prosaic non-
explanatory nature of so much contemporary theological
writing. The list of journals, too, may be regarded
as a comment on the infant state particularly of
systematic theology. An existential question here
might be, 'Do I consider man, the mystery, to be easier
to understand than the electron, the macromolecule, or
the daisy? or that understanding less worth the effort?'

But our immediate concern is with the fragmentation of botany and botanists. It is now no longer a
question of The Two Biologies,[109] macro and micro: as
Kendrew points out, there are even two kinds of
molecular biologists with two different casts of
mind.[110] Botanists are legion, and if it is not to be
a legion of those lost in specializations there is
need for some generic transformation.[111] And the
possibility of that transformation is immanent in the
contemporary drive in Botany. What is that drive?
Here I must quote in some fulness what is for me the

centrally relevant passage from the writings of Fr.
Lonergan. It is a passage which I have puzzled over a
great deal since I first began serious work on the
philosophy of botany in 1963, and I am only slowly
coming to its meaning.

'Study of an organism begins from the thing-for-
us, from the organism as exhibited to our senses. A
first step is a descriptive differentiation of different
parts and, since most of the parts are inside, this
descriptive preliminary necessitates dissection or
anatomy. A second step consists in the accumulation of
insights that relate the described parts to organic
events, occurrences, operations. By these insights,
the parts become known as organs, and further knowledge
constituted by the insights, is a grasp of intelligibilities that

1   are immanent in the several parts,
2   refer each part to what it can do and,
     under determinable conditions, will do,
     and
3   relate the capacity-for-performance of each
     part to the capacities-for-performance of
     the other parts.

So physiology follows anatomy. A third step is to
effect the transition from the thing-for-us to the
thing-itself, from insights that grasp described parts
as organs to insights that grasp conjugate forms
systematizing otherwise coincidental manifolds of
chemical and physical processes. By this transition,
one links physiology with biochemistry and biophysics.
To this end, there have to be invented appropriate
symbolic images of the relevant chemical and physical
processes; in these images there have to be grasped by
insight the laws of the higher system that account for
regularities beyond the range of physical and chemical
explanation; from these laws, there has to be constructed the flexible circle of schemes of recurrence
in which the organism functions; finally, this flexible
circle of schemes must be coincident with the related
set of capacities-for-performance that previously was
grasped in sensibly presented organs.'[112]

Such is the condensed expression, from an
adequate horizon, of the nature of the contemporary
drive. If the meaning of that passage is elusive for
the contemporary botanist,[113] it is doubly so for the
non-botanist - though it may be less so for the

methodologist who is willing to reach an adequate set
of strategic botanical insights.

The first and second steps determine the content
of many undergraduate texts in botany, which contain two
basic sections on morphology and physiology.[114] The
third step may be regarded as programatic of the central
drive. The nature of the step might be elementarily
appreciated by introspective reflection on one's present
understanding of tropic and nastic movements in plants.
So, for example, phototropism is an easily observable
phenomenon of a functional nature and its descriptive
appreciation, including correlation with other
capacities-for-performance, belong to the first two
steps referred to by Fr. Lonergan. But what of the
third step? '... The distribution of growth substance
ceases to be uniform in unilateral lighting. Some
observations seem to indicate that the situation is
more complex, and that changes occur not only in the
amount of active growth substance but also in the
sensitivity of the cytoplasm, there being a tendency
for it to decline on the illuminated sides; for examples,
the convex side tends to be positively charged, and on
the illuminated side the concentration of sugar, the
catalase activity and the acidity are all diminished.
Little is known of the causal relationship of these
effects. Wherever conduction of a stimulus occurs, it
seems very likely that there is at first a local change
in the amount of growth-promoting substance, and that
transmission is brought about by variations in its
concentrations and activity. Hitherto, however, too
few objects have been studied for a generally valid
account of the steps in the phototropic reaction to be
put forward.'[115]

> Was there one point on which
> their views were equal and nega-
> tive? The influence of gaslight
> or electric light on the growth
> of adjoining paraheliotropic
> trees.[116]

Here 'one links physiology with biochemistry
and biophysics' but as yet one lacks the symbolic
chemico-physical images adequate to the emergence of
the insights which ground the construction of the
network of botanical recurrence-schemes.[117] Moreover,
what is lacking is not merely one "horizontal" set of
such symbolic images, but a hierarchy of symbolic
images, and the emergence of that hierarchy is dependent

on many-levelled explanatory advances. 'Cellular
physiology will expand to an unprecedented extent once
the cellular ultrastructures have been finally
resolved'[118], but their resolution is still remote.[119]
The resolution requires the invention of 'appropriate
symbolic images of the relevant chemical and physical
processes'[120], but advances in chemistry are required,
so that 'the chemistry of the cell can yield an image
of catalytic process in which insight can grasp
biological laws'.[121] Nor are there short cuts to the
adequate chemistry or to the symbolic images of such
processes. 'Living organisms possess numerous catalysts
which speed up chemical reactions to the rates achieved
in biological systems. Whether we consider digestion,
metabolism, locomotion, fermentation or putrefaction,
chemical changes are going on, and these chemical
changes are catalysed. It is the purpose of this book
to give some account of these changes and of the various
mechanisms at present known to participate in their
catalysis.'[122] And this book is an introduction 500
pages long!

        Now the plant is an aggregate of aggregates of
cells,[123] and its third step understanding can be
achieved only in so far as more integral symbolic images
of aggregated cellular processes are discovered.[124] The
advance towards that understanding can be uniform only
in the ideal order, and the importance given to one
field or another varies from decade to decade. But what
is required is the push towards explanation on all
levels - a push which in fact is present, but not
thematically present, leaving in this thematic absence a
reductionist bias. The botanist, however, is being
gradually driven into the same corner as the physicist
was driven into earlier in the century. Or rather he
is being driven into the open, the openness of the notion
of being operative in his work and leading to his non-
thematic admission that the real is not the imaginable
but the correctly verified. 'As the electron, so also
the tree, in so far as it is considered as a thing
itself, stands within a pattern of intelligible
relations and offers no foothold for imagination. The
difference between the tree and the electron is simply
that the tree, besides being explained, also can be
observed and described, while the electron, though it
can be explained, cannot be directly observed and can
be described adequately only in terms of observables
that involve other things as well.'[125] But in so far
as the admission of critical realism is non-thematic,
the push of intelligence is per accidens[126] and bothered

by philosophic crystallizations of the clouded components of infant realism, and so the field of inquiry remains fragmented and cluttered with muddles of meaning and expression.

What is contemporarily needed, and what is contemporarily possible, is the botanist's personal shift to the metabotanical horizon which would open to him a total thematic heuristic grasp of the object of his inquiry. Then for him, thematically, 'the successive, distinct autonomous sciences will be related as successive higher viewpoints. For the coincidental manifolds of lower conjugate acts, say A_{ij}, can be imagined symbolically. Moreover as the coincidental manifolds are the conjugate potency for the higher conjugate forms, so the symbolic images provide the materials for insight into the laws relating the higher forms ... The real will be existing unities differentiated by conjugate forms of various genera and species. In that case the symbolic images will have merely heuristic value, for they will serve to facilitate the transition from one science to another and to determine to what extent data are explained or not explained by either science'[127] Such areas of inquiry as molecular biology or chemo-taxonomy[128] would no longer appear as devouring the plant kingdom, and such specialized papers as 'Utilization of different carbon sources by the genus Linderina'. 'Growth responses of Pinto bean and alfalfa to sublethal fluoride concentrations' would be understood by their authors as contributing to the determination of, to use Aquinas' terms, the limits of tolerance of materia disposita for specific forms.

What I have been considering in these previous paragraphs is the movement towards an adequate Weltanschauung in the botanist as botanist. But that movement, obviously, is the movement of a person and it is relevant to the botanist as man, to the botanist in his or her possibility of adult growth and integration. It is clearly relevant as the core-contribution to that growth but it can also mediate a psychedelic transformation.[129]

O Poldy, Poldy, you are a poor stick in the mud! Go and see life. See the wide world.[130]

Again, I have been writing about the botanist in a manner which might well bewilder the botanists themselves. It is indeed evident enough to the

contemporary botanists that 'their inquiry moves off
from the familiar to the unfamiliar, from the obvious
to the recondite'[131] but the significance of that movement is largely lost on them and ignored by them.   To
anyone who has suffered his way up through the sequence
of conversions to a personally-possessed critical existentialism it is clear that 'when one is endeavouring
to explain, one is orientated to the universe of being;
one is setting up distinctions within being;   one is
relating distinct beings to one another;   and one is
relegating all the merely descriptive elements in
knowledge to particular instances of the case that arises
when some being with sense and imagination is related
through his senses and imagination to other beings'.[132]
But to the standard contemporary botanist this means just
nothing at all.   For, the contemporary botanist is
multiply handicapped.   Not only is there solidly settled
in his soul the semi-animal objectivity of his childhood,
but the present character of his education and his subject,
his living and the context of that living, are such as
to discourage consistently the emergence of an authentic
self.   One must think concretely here of the botanist
on the campus with commitments to professional reading,
publication, teaching, socializing, and, underpinning all
these, not the notion of being but the notion of surviving.

     Failure in the areas of feeling, art and exuberence
in contemporary academic life are wider topics for another
day.   But the fragmentation, personal and academic, of
the specialist botanist is evident enough.   His concrete
living and his professional work run parallel at a pace
which excludes their intertwining either in conflict or
in personal integration.   The tone of his textbooks and
biological talk is tilted by the philosophic failure of
his environment towards reductionism, and the tone of his
activities tends to accord with other-directedness.[133]
If the question of integration occurs to him, it is normally
cast into an otherdirected reductionist mould: integration
is expected to be "objectively" scientific[134], and the
relevant science is regularly physics.[135]   With such a
tempo and tonality of life the serious asking of the
question of personal integration is not to be expected,
and the issue is comfortably clouded by the fact that
the botanist, unlike his non-scientific or even some of
his physicist etc., colleagues, can straddle more easily
the "two cultures".   If he turns to the wider culture of
philosophy he is liable to seek in it, at a minimum the
possibility of intelligent interchange, at a maximum either
an aesthetically coherent world view[136] or a remote ded-
uctivist coherence[137].   If he seeks more in it, he is
liable to be seeking in vain.   And if he turns authenticall
to theology he is liable to find it speaking to men of
another age.

It would be a giant step of authenticity, then,
a leap into an unknown, were he to face into the task
of self-attention, the fruits of which lie deep and
come forth only slowly. But should the botanist take
that leap, he has in fact within his own consciousness
a central core of data, a pivotal image in the widest
sense of that word, from which his self-insight might
generate an adequate Weltanschauung.

> Wait.   Five months.   Molecules
> all change.   I am other I now.
> Other I got pound.
> Buzz.   Buzz.
> But I, entelechy, form of forms,
> am I by memory because under
> everchanging forms.[138]

But a central point of the present chapter is
that this shift to an adequate methodological Weltanschauung is essential to the contemporary thinker in
any field.   Indeed one may note that, while the metabotanical horizon is, in a sense, extrinsic to botany
as botany, the metahorizon is intrinsic and most
profoundly essential to anyone in the area of human
science: for the objects of such science have minds.
From another point of view one may note that if the electron and the tree transcend imagination, much more so do
you and I, and you and I as objects of human wonder, human
inquiry, include an intelligibility which is also
intelligent,an intelligibility which in its obediential
potency[139] and in the present order[140] draws the category
of Mystery into the human sciences[141].   But leaving aside
inverse-insightwise this category, in so far as you and
I attain an adequate horizon, "I" and "you" can become
symbolic images, and 'it is only in an extremely remote
and general fashion that we can include our own sensitive
acts within an explanatory view'.[142]

But, one may ask, can it be that the cultivation
of the adequate contemporary Weltanschauung requires the
contemporary thinker also be a botanist, not to speak of
chemist, sociologist ...?   An immediate answer to the
objection implicit in this question would point out that
one can reach first degree level standard in any of these
fields in a few years, which is not long compared to the
normal lifetime of the philosopher or theologian.   It
is not then a great sacrifice for the enormous benefit
of coming intellectually into the twentieth century.
Still a more basic answer would point to the axial nature
of the present period.   Rollo May in a recent book
remarks that 'our human responsibility is to find a plane

of consciousness that will fill the vast impersonal
emptiness of our technology with human meaning'[143]
and the transforming possibilities of that plane of
consciousness in the human subject are not to be
underestimated. As Colin Wilson remarks, 'man is not
yet equipped for long excursions into the noosphere'[144]
a noosphere which I would identify with the second time
of the temporal subject referred to already. But if
all this seems remote one may recall the lesson of
lesser transformations in the history of education and
science. Much of what was done as postgraduate stuff
in my days of mathematical science two decades ago is
now undergraduate work. Not long ago physicists were
bewildered by the introduction into physics of tensors,
eigenfunctions and the like, just as contemporary interpreters of documents may be bewildered by canons of
hermeneutics and resist their challenge. "Still, this
is the minor resistance, and it should cause no greater
difficulty in the field of interpretation than its
analogue does in physics'.[145] Again, the contemporary
liturgical expert or the music critic may well be
dismayed by advances in musicology and in metamusic I
indicate in chapter two,[146] but they are advances which
in the long run cannot be ignored. There is, finally,
the fact that one must expect within the new context a
significant transformation of education on all levels,
leading to the possibility of fuller human living and
continued adult growth.

Nor, indeed, should the transforming adequate
horizon be less significant when we enter into philosophic
dialogue. Indeed, it should mediate that dialogue, and
all our dialogue. Just as the psychotherapist's
accumulation of science is operative in his non-scientific
therapeutic discourse with his patient, mediating that
discourse, so might it be for the philosopher. Nor am
I speaking here of some disembodied discourse, with
meaning packaged up in Reason and shuttled back and forth
from mind to mind. I speak of human talk which, in
treating of method, may touch the marrow of the bone.[147]
What philosophic discourse needs above all is authentic
embodiment. Contemporarily much philosophic discourse,
particularly in the field of analytic philosophy, is
carried on with a pseudo-detachment that secures it from
the dialectic of performance and content. And what is
required to undermine such deficient discourse, to open
the way to authenticity, may be, not a clash of metaphysical words, but refinements of feeling and aesthetic
exuberance.[148] 'Aesthetic liberation ... generates in
experience a flexibility that makes it a ready tool for

the spirit of inquiry'.[149] Moreover, the expansive
influence is two-way: good philosophy liberates; bad
philosophy makes man a ready tool of the disorientated
economy.   "... What I want to communicate in this
talk on art is the notion that art is relevant to concrete
living, that it is an exploration of the potentialities
of concrete living; that it is extremely important in
our age when philosophers for at least two centuries,
through doctrines on economics, politics and education,
have been trying to remake man and have done not a little
to make human life unlivable'.[150]

> Cityful passing away, other
> cityful coming, passing away
> too: other coming on, passing
> on. Houses, lines of houses,
> streets, miles of pavements,
> piledup bricks, stones.
> Changing hands. This owner,
> that. Landlord never dies they
> say. Other steps into his shoes
> when he gets his notice to quit.
> They buy the place up with gold
> and still they have all the gold.
> Swindle in it somewhere. Piles
> up in cities, worn away age
> after age. Pyramids in sand.
> Built on bread and onions.
> Slaves. Chinese wall. Babylon.
> Big stones left. Round towers.
> Rest rubble, sprawling suburbs,
> jerrybuilt, Kerwan's mushroom
> houses, built of breeze. Shelter
> for the night.
> No one is anything.[151]

     Aesthetic liberation, obviously, should not be
entirely absent when philosophers come together to commune.
In so far as the communing is entirely functional, exclus-
ive of sociability[152] a psychedelic contribution to that
communing and to the possibilities of ecumenical listening
has been lost.   Ecumenical listening is no mean achievement - indeed I doubt if it is a mere human achievement
at all - and its possibility is increased for the normal
run of men by the various shades of the actual presence of
incarnate meaning.[153]   I touch here on something of what
Cardinal Newman meant when he spoke of 'personal influence,
the means of propagating the Truth', in an Oxford sermon.[154]
Clearly too the Blessed Trinity are not unappreciative of
Incarnate Meaning.   And so I am led to put expansive
ecumenical listening in its total context.   I would note
the fullness of both Cosmic word and Incarnate Word.[155]

I would note that 'man is nature's priest and nature is God's silent communing with man',[156] and I would recall the words of Carl Stumpf, 'To me a man who does not contemplate hardly seems to be living, and a philosopher who does not cultivate and practice contemplation is not worthy of his name: he is not a philosopher but a scientific craftsman and among the philistines the most philistine'.[157]

But I would note all these things as requiring appreciation in the new context. Central to that appreciation is the appreciation of the human subject's own solitude. "We are all condemned to solitary confinement within our own skins', to quote Tennessee Williams.[158] Yet that confinement, linked with the appreciative confinement[159] of critical realism, reveals itself as a limitless openness to Being. That solitary openness can be grasped adequately only within the horizon of critical existentialism. In a basic sense it is true that the only image available to the subject is the emergent subject. It is only in radical subjectivity that genuine objectivity is appreciatively found, the subject's openness to all. Was it this, perhaps, that Husserl, the tireless beginner, was groping towards in those solitary afternoons in his seventies? At all events I would like to make my own what he wrote at an earlier age: "In the way the sciences of the spirit are at present developed with their manifold disciplines, they forfeit the ultimate, actual rationality which the spiritual Weltanschauung makes possible. Precisely this lack of genuine rationality on all sides is the source of what has become for man an unbearable unclarity regarding his own existence and his infinite tasks. These last are inseparably united in one task: only if the spirit returns to itself from its naive exteriorization, clinging to itself and purely to itself, can it be adequate to itself'.[160]

I have touched in this chapter on a variety of meanings of "image" and "emergence" which I hope are suggestive. I have written existentially, since I have no other viewpoint. What I have written about, Fr. Lonergan meaning, is profoundly relevant to a global on-going collaboration in the emergence of man. What I would like to see emerge, from the growing interest in Lonergan, is not a group of "Lonerganists" gathered round the 'plausibility structure'[161] of a common vocabulary and the writings of the later Lonergan, but a globally-orientated attitude of critical and self-critical existentialism which would exploit the density of heuristic meaning of the early Lonergan.

There is then the challenge of solitude, of a
withdrawal from synnomic 'with-it-ness'[162] to the deepest
removes of creativity to guarantee the reaching of a
meaning which may eventually be embodied in the total
clothed, built-up, cultured image of man.   And there is
the challenge of a deeper dialogue, not a dialogue which
has the obviousness of exchanged words in face-to-face
encounter, but a dialogue which is a fragile sharing of
opaque images by incarnate questings of infinite emergence
of mattered-mind and its technicoaesthetic objectification,
towards the Omega where Image and Emergence coincide in
the triply-relative dynamic serenity of self-appreciative
Autonomy.

> I am getting along nicely in the
> dark. My ask sword hangs at
> my side. Tap with it: they do.
> My two feet in his boots are at
> the end of his legs, nebeneinander.
> Sounds solid: made by the mallet
> of Los Demiurgos. Am I walking
> into eternity along Sandymount
> strand?[163]

INTERLUDE

"The birds sang in the wet trees
And as I listened to them it was
    a hundred years from now
And I was dead and someone else
    was listening to them.
But I was glad I had recorded for him
    The melancholy".

Patrick Kavanagh,
"Wet Evening in April",
Collected Poems,
Martin Brian and O'Keefe,
London, 1972, 140.

Chapter Two

METAMUSIC AND SELF-MEANING

> Sobs they sighdid at Fillagain's
> chrissormiss wake, all the
> hoolivans of the nation, pros-
> trated in their consternation and
> their doudisimally profuse plethora
> of ululation [1]

    'What is needed to clear the air is first an exposition of the nature of and relations among theory, analysis and criticism, then secondly, an examination of the pertinence of all this to compositional procedure'.[2]

    My task here is, not to attempt the required exposition, but to indicate with some adequacy what is needed and the context sufficient for the meeting of that need. My indication of need will be impressionistic, drawing heavily on the statements of those who best appreciate it, those actually engaged in the field. My indication of context will scarcely go beyond noting that the functional specializations outlined by Fr. Lonergan[3] are not restricted to theology, that 'listening and talking' occur in parallel complexity in the world of music. If my writing here about those contemporarily talking about music is critical it is so not because I consider these thinkers and talkers to have failed - they talk from the horizon of their time - but because I have some glimpse of the possibilities of transformed talking through the mediation of metamusic. Transformed listening as well as talking: where by listening I mean not only the listening of critical debate but aesthetic listening, and by talking I mean not only theoretical talking but the talking of man which is musical composition and performance.

    The quotation I began with is taken from an article by David Lewin which takes issue with the previous article by Mr. Cone.[4] Lewin's article is followed by Cone's reply. Cone's first article had to do with such things as the effect of mirror-inversion on twelve-tone composition. Lewin in his article seeks to define Theory, Analysis and Criticism. He considers that Cone has confused theory and analysis and indicates a like deficiency in Schenker, the theoretician of tonal music.[5] Cone, on the contrary, considers Schenker's methodology exemplary and points out Lewin's error in saying that when a theoretician approaches music he makes only a partial and selective analysis, 'for every analysis is partial and selective'.[6] Again, the authors do not agree on what theory examines; is it actual composition; or abstractions from compositions; or does it make use of a process of abstraction? But both authors make good poinds throughout, regarding the interplay of theory, analysis, composition, listening and criticism, and both agree on the relation of analysis to criticism, and on the significance of criticism. 'The artist must be a critic. The observer must be a critic'.[7]

> ... inharmonious creations, a captious critic might describe then as, or not strictly necessary or a trifle irritating here and there, but for all that suddenly full of local colour and personal perfume and suggestive, too, of so very much more and capable of being stretched, filled out, if need or wish were, of having their surprisingly like coincidental parts separated don't they know, for better survey by the deft hand of the expert, don't you know?[8]

But what, one may ask, is it to be a critic, particularly in the act of creation or in aesthetic reception? Is it perhaps to have one's artistic and aesthetic expansion mediated by a thematically-transformed horizon? And what might be the nature of that horizon? Ernst Krenek says that 'by "educated" musician I understand an individual who has absorbed knowledge of music theory and history on the graduate level'.[9] But is this a sufficient transformation of horizon? Later in the same article Krenek remarks: "After assiduously studying Babbitt's essay "Twelve-tone invariants"[10] I have covered several sheets of music paper with experiments, exercises, and examples trying to penetrate the meaning of his discourse, and finally I approached my learned friend by letter for more information. It was of no avail, and I gave up in frustration since I do not wish to encroach further on his time. I am afraid that the use of this language in Perspectives has reached a point of diminishing returns: the possible increment of scholarly prestige (not to speak of snob appeal) is compensated by the loss of communicability'.[11]

I am not judging the issues between Krenek and Babbitt: but who is to judge? David Lewin concludes his essay by pointing to the present social state of professional music as tending to 'discourage rational critical thought. But this only makes the task all the more important. Hence the critique'.[12] From what horizon could the critique come? Is it a horizon of theory? Is it a horizon of criticism that pronounces on theory and criticism?

This the way to the musey room.[13]

Here I am at a loss. I can give my basic answer to the previous set of questions in the brief statement that the horizon adequate to transforming talking and listening is the horizon of critical existentialism offered by a personal appropriation of the works of Bernard Lonergan. But what can that minute-read statement mean what it is year-thick with meaning? I can only hope that it carries through a faint plausibility. I cannot reasonably expect much more of the contemporary musicologist, musician, etc. Nor can I do much more here than increase the plausibility of my claim by indicating more fully the need for a basic and novel investigation. That novel investigation of art in general has been touched on elsewhere,[14] and only within that appropriated context could further refinements of the investigation have adequate meaning. 'In the first place, either one pursues this investigation through the well-defined scientific method of introspection or one does not, and if one does not then one is liable to be tied to refined description if not to a mere use of words. In the second place, the investigation and its conclusions must be consistently taken in the context of the structured critical realism dealt with in the earlier chapters. The real is still, let us recall, what is reached by correct understanding. It is far from easy to pursue a discussion of art within that critical horizon. There is a constant gravitation towards taking the discussion to the obvious "realistic" level of the already-out-there-now. Thus we might write here, with Susanne Langer, of the piano as a living presence in a room.[15] We write thus, meaning the real piano in the real room and its artistic import. But perhaps you find that spontaneously you think about the large brown object out there in the corner?'[16]

The correct understanding of this essay and the solution of the problems it poses presupposes that context, and indeed the wider context of an adequate Weltanschauung indicated in the first essay. For those

possessing a critical existentialist viewpoint the essay
will be a programme for the transformation of an area
of human science and human living. For those whose
interest is, rather, musical, it will be, not an init-
iation, but an invitation.

> Take thanks, thankstum, thamas.
> In that earopean end meets Ind.
> There is something supernoctural
> about whatever you called him it.
> Panpan and vinvin are not alonety
> vanvan and pinpin in your Tamal
> without tares but simply-soley
> they are they. Thisutter followis
> that odder fellow. Humkim kimkim.
> Old yesterloaves may be a stale
> as a stub and the pitcher go to
> aftoms on the wall. Mildew, murk,
> leak and yarn now want the bad
> that they lied on. And your
> last words todate in comparative
> accoustomology are going to tell
> stretch of a fancy through strength
> towards joyance, adyatants, where he
> gets up.[17]

Immediately then I turn to the need for an adequate
Weltanschauung. Does this not seem an exaggerated need
when taken in the full sense of the previous essay? It
is plausible, of course, in a restricted sense: in this
sense, that western music in the last centuries was, to
twist a phrase of my fellow countryman, 'Earopean from
end to Ind', that it moved towards the exhaustion of
partially-arbitrary tonalities and sound-sources, that it
needed and still needs an expansive orientation which would
be global not only geographically but also sonically. But
in so far as one enters more fully and thematically into
these questions, the wider need is revealed. I have indeed
found no area of inquiry into music which would not be
transformed by the presence of an adequate horizon in the
investigators. Those working in these areas themselves
bear witness to the need of transformation, but its
dimensions escape them.

So, for instance, in the field of ethnomusicology
all is not well. Alan P. Merriam continually points to
the need to 'revise our own thinking'[18] if the apparent
gap between anthropology and musicology is to be bridged,
and elsewhere he touches on the deeper question: 'It is
clear that only through the fusion of these aspects of
knowledge, and probably in single individuals, that the
problem will be solved. If this is the case, and if the

fusion is the goal, are not the problems insurmountable?
Is there any hope of putting together the humanities and
the social sciences, areas of study which are considered
planes apart?   Is there any means of treating the social
sciences humanistically, or the humanities in terms of
social science?'[19]   He himself tries to contribute to
the solution of such problems, central assumptions being
that field method, as opposed to field techniques 'remains
essentially the same in over-all structure no matter what
society is being investigated'[20],   and that music sound
is an integral objectification of human meaning.[21]
Within that context he moves through topics ranging from
the physiology of hearing music[22] to music as a factor
in cultural stability and dynamism.[23]   But we may return
here to a question raised in regard to Lewin's critique.
What precisely is Merriam doing in this work?   What is
his procedure? As Bruno Nettle notes, 'The members of
most non-western cultures, especially the non-literate
and folk-societies, have difficulty in verbalizing about
music'.[24]   Western man through the mediation of developments in Hebrew and Greek culture, has been long capable
of talk about himself and his music.   But in books like
those of Nettle and Merriam the talk raises the problem
of talking about talking, and that in a particular area.
To talk intelligently is to mean: talking about talking,
then, somehow is a reaching towards the meaning of meaning.
But meaning is a process found only in the intelligent
subject: the meaning of meaning thus raises the question
of the roots of the expression of the human subject.
Furthermore, meaning is not restricted to intelligent
talk, and so expression here is not restricted to talk.
The question of the meaning of the meaning of music is
therefore a complex question which takes in thematically
all the objectifications of the human subject, from the
most elemental musical expression or the refined expression of musical analysis to the total musical event.[25]

>Our wholemole millwheeling
>vicociclometer, a tetradomational
>gazebocrototicon, autokinatonet-
>ically preprovided with a clapper-
>coupling smeltingworks exprogressive
>process, receives through a portal
>vein the dialytically separated
>elements of precedent decomposition
>for the verypetpurpose of subsequent
>recombination so that the herotic-
>isms, catastrophes and eccentricities
>transmitted by the ancient legacy of
>the past, type by tope, letter by
>litter, word at ward, with sendence

of sundance, since the days of
Plooney and Columcellas when
Giacinta, Pervenche and Margaret
swayed over the all-too-ghoulish
and illyrical and innumantic in
our mutter nation, all, anastomosi-
cally assimilated and preteri-
dentified paraidiotically, in fact,
the sameold gamebold adomic structure
of our Finnius ...[26]

In what sense does the complex question 'take in'
all these processes of objectification? Clearly it is
the human subject, the incarnate complex question, that
takes in. Nor is that 'taking in' a restriction on the
symbolic: rather it may mediate a liberation and a
transformation of the symbolic. It is a non-interfering
but transforming mediation that is called for: 'It is
natural that in the conduct of our daily work we avoid
direct and interfering contact with its fundaments. But
it is clear, too, that there must come times of reflect-
iion about the goals that are defined and the ways that
are marked'.[27] That time comes when in some vague way
goals have begun to reveal themselves, ways have already
been marked, and both have reached sufficient complexity
to be problematic. Activity must be prior to reflection
and appreciation - yet somehow that appreciation is
expected to go beyond present performance, to be normative,
to be non-interfering. And who, what, is to be the
source of that appreciation? The composers, perhaps,
who are after all the central subject-source of the
universe of patterned sound? 'The most verbally articulate
composers are dominated by ultimate allegiance to
expression in the non-verbal medium and should welcome
someone else to represent their viewpoints, to help solve
their problems: the theorist, for example, who has
special insight into the creative process without being
a practising composer himself. Such a theorist, alas,
is rare'.[28]

Indeed, such a theorist would seem to be only a
proximate potentiality of the present situation in music.
Charles Rosen remarks pessimistically that 'we are all
to blame for the present state of music: composers,
performers, musicologist, and public alike.[29] But one
should also see that situation in more positive light.
If composers are isolated, one from another and from
the public,[30] if standards are absent or confused, if
the musical event has been trapped in commerce and convention and concert hall and approval narrowed to ritual
handclap or 'earopean' critique, if technology has

enlarged our too-tight notion of 'instrument of music'
beyond the bounds of present sympathy and control, and
our notion of patterned sound beyond the bounds of
present hearing, if the level of contemporary noise
needs that enlarged musical context for audiosurvival,[31]
still all this may be regarded as pointing towards a
creative effort. With Boulez, we may expect an expansive
transformation of techniques, methods, scripts, etc., we
may expect a transformation of listening and talking on
all levels of the universe of music.[32] 'The present
musical situation is a unique one, and not only requires
unique compositional solutions, but also engenders a
unique consciousness about the fundamental implications
of every aspect of musical perception, structure and
relationship. And this, in turn, manifestly necessitates
the development of equally unique and particular modes
of examining and theorizing - about everything that has
been traditionally regarded or that we wish to regard
as a musical phenomenon or object'.[33]

Our basic question recurs: the question of a
unique mode of theorizing. How is one to go about such
theorizing? It is the theorist 'who has special insight
into the creative process' that is significant. Indeed,
it is the creative process which is the core of the range
of human expressions I already mentioned. The creative
process is an expansion of human questing[34], and it is
the structure of that expansion that is the issue of
our times.

In what sense, structure? It must be a structure
that touches goals and ways, that criticizes without
being a critique, that theorizes without being merely
another theory, that transforms, integrates, orientates.
We asked regarding Merriam's work or procedures in
ethnomusicology, What is his procedure? And this
precisely is the key-question: the structure in
question is the structure of creative procedure, whether
that procedure be composition, performance, listening,
theorizing, criticizing. As remarked already, the
appreciation of that structure must spring from present
performance in these areas, yet point beyond it to
further performance: it must be heuristic, methodological in a fundamental sense. Finally it is not 'it' but
you and I as incarnate quests. What is called for is a
methodology of music rooted in self-appreciation.

Since it is only in the context of such a self-
appreciation, as programmed in Insight, that a reader
might appreciate Fr. Lonergan's treatment of art as
the objectification of a purely experiential pattern,

I pass over that treatment here and continue the policy
of problem-indication and invitation.[35] So I turn to a
central problem of self-appreciation: the problem of
avoiding metaphysical mythology or deductivism, the
invitation to be adequately empirical.

> ... And you then took down in
> stereo what took place being tunc
> committed?
> -I then took my takenplace lying
> down, I think I told you. Solve
> it!
> -Remounting aliftle towards the
> ouragan of spaces. Just how
> grand in cardinal rounders is this
> preeminent giant, sir Arber? Your
> bard's highview, avis on valley!
> I would like to hear you burble to
> us in strict conclave, purpurando,
> and without too much italiote
> interfairance, what you know in
> petto about our sovereign being-
> stalk, Tonans Tomazeus. O dite![36]

It is fairly commonly said, among philosophers
and critics and musicians, that music is an image of
experienced time. But what does this saying mean? That
depends on who says it or who hears it. In so far as
the person making or hearing the statement is self-
appreciative in a scientific sense and adequately self-
empirical in musical experience and reflection, the
meaning is enormous and elusive. But anyone can repeat
the phrase: and so there is man's permanent problem of
falling short of meaning.[37] The usage of verbal schema
balanced on vague heuristic insights can pass at times
for mastery. 'To effect an agreement between general
concepts and specific details is one of the most difficult tasks of human understanding. In order to reduce
the world of appearances to only a few concepts,
knowledge must seek general truths. At the same time,
one must examine the particulars to the last detail,
in all their secrets, if one wishes to grasp correctly
these general concepts, which are, after all, supported
by particulars. The task is difficult because
generalities, however arrived at, easily mislead man
into a premature satisfaction which spares any further
effort concerning specifics. Through continuous dis-
regard for detail, knowledge of general truths is
impaired; it does not ripen into truth, but remains
limited to a schema'.[38]

Furthermore, even if one pushes on through
scientific self-attention to a thematic appreciation of
music as an objectification of temporality-patterns, one
must resist always the temptation to mistake the generic
heuristic for an axiomatics of future achievement. The
best one can humanly reach is something akin to what
Aquinas reached, 'a position of dynamic equilibrium
without ever ceasing to drive towards fuller and more
nuanced synthesis, without ever halting complacently
in some finished mental edifice, as though his mind had
become dull, or his brain exhausted, or his judgment had
lapsed into the error of those that forget man to be
potency in the realm of intelligence'.[39]

As in metascience, so also in metamusic, one must
faithfully cling to a deep empiricality.[40] 'Loss of
contact not only means that metaphysics ceases to play
its integrating role in the unity of the human mind but
also exposes the metaphysician to the ever recurrent
danger of discoursing on quiddities without suspecting
that quiddity means what is to be known through
scientific understanding'.[41] So, to grasp heuristically
that music is expressive of forms of human temporality
should be to open oneself to permanent enlargement of
that grasp and to enlargement not only in thematic and
heuristic viewpoint but to 'the enlargement of the
boundries of the permissible in the empire of sound'.[42]

As Eternity is the 'now' of a being that is
dynamically unchanging, so time is the 'now' of a being
that does change, where time is not clock-time but the
complex hierarchic dynamico-static patterns of incarnate
questing's living in the unfinished symphony of history's
times and places. And that time's aesthetic objectification, suggestive of an ever-richer human 'now', is no
less complex. Furthermore, the enlargement of the human
subject, and in particular of the metaphysician, is
through a multiply symbiotic dynamism of mediations.

'If music is to me an "image of our experience
of living as temporal" and however unverifiable, I
suppose it is , my saying so is the result of a
reflection, and as such is independent of music itself.
Anden means "Western" music or, as he would say, "music
as history"; jazz improvisation is the dissipation of
the time image and, if I understand "recurrence" and
"becoming", their aspect is greatly diminished in serial
music. Anden's "image of our experience of living as
temporal" which is also an image is above music,
perhaps, but it does not obstruct or contradict the
purely musical experience. What shocks me, however, is

the discovery that many people think below music. Music is merely something that reminds them of something else - of landscapes, for example'.[43] The reflective experience and the musical experience can transform the spontaneous human subject, each opening the subject to fuller experience of the other. But the problem is to think "above" the music. We will touch later on an aspect of this problem in dealing with music criticism. Here the relevant "aboveness" is the expansive opening of the heuristic subject to wider musical experience and a continually more nunanced thematized heuristic. So, for instance, it is true enough, as Stravinski says, and commonly admitted, that serial music diminishes the "becoming" component in the form of the musical image. But one may fail to exploit that expansion of the world of sound. One may, for instance, think "below the music", not in terms of landscapes, but in metaphorical terms, of "spatialization", thus moving away from the challenge of more refined specification of the objectified 'now'.[44] Or one may think of that sound-expansion out of the context of an adequate <u>Weltan-schauung</u>, and so settle for a blanket description of the shift from 19th to 20th century music which has become 'one of the slogans of the avant-garde: The new music aspires to Being and not to Becoming'.[45] Not that I deny the suggestiveness of the metaphor of "spatialization"[46] or the element of truth in the slogan. But it requires an altogether more refined introspective empirico-aesthetic effort to specify adequately and humanly contemporary forms - I use "forms" in a technical sense - of music. And that refinement is possible, in my view, only in so far as the theoretician of music achieves an adequate methodological horizon. So I might make my own the remarks of Benjamin Boreth: 'Without such fundamental methodological tools, it becomes all too easy to fall into the kind of error most frequently associated with uninformed discussion of twelve-tone structure, in which it is assumed that resources fundamental to tonal musical coherence - hierarchization, for example - are absent in the instances - and more fundamentally are unavailable within the resources - of the newer system. It is precisely this sort of egregious misconception, rooted in the ignorance, it must be said, of a considerable body of both musical and music-theoretic literature, that one would hope to avoid by developing standards for verbal responsibility to accuracy in writing about music ... in short, an awareness of musical structure at a level of depth all too prevalently unavailable in contemporary forms of musical thought'.[47]

> every crowd has its several tones
> and every trade has its clever
> mechanics and each harmonical has
> a point of its own, Olaf's on the
> rise and Ivor's on the lift and
> Sitric's place between them.
> But all they are all scraping
> along to sneeze out a likelihood
> that will solve and salve life's
> robulous rebus, hopping round his
> middle like kippers on a griddle,
> o.[48]

Still, if the depth of a methodological level is unavailable to contemporary musicology this is not to say that the growing body of detailed work on questions of form in music is not significant. The emergence of a methodological horizon in the human subject does not replace science and common sense but transforms them.[49] Moreover, the pressure towards developing that methodological horizon is found precisely within the complexity of the contemporary detailed discussion. To the musicologist that complexity becomes more manifest by the month - his learned journals oscillate between higher mathematics and problems of objectivity in history. But some instances of detailed effort to understand may be of help to the non-musicologist.

The composer Varèse discusses musical form as being the result of a process: 'There is an idea, the basis of an internal structure, expanded and split into different shapes or groups of sound constantly changing in shape, direction, and speed, attracted and repulsed by various forces. The form of the work is the consequence of this interaction. Possible musical forms are as limitless as the exterior forms of crystals'.[50] As Milton Babbitt remarks, Varèse himself does not fit easily into a category as a composer, 'an important reminder that one of the fundamental aspects of the musical revolution in which Varèse was so primary a figure is that it was a struggle to create a world of musics, not a struggle between one music and another, serial and non-serial, tonal and "atonal".[51] I recall here my earlier quotation from Schenker regarding the problem of general categories: neither composer nor composition can ever be trapped in a single category. The meaning of the composition is a multilevelled human complexity and if one thematizes that hierarchic meaning, part of the density of the mental meaning is an acknowledgement of its limitations.

Again, one might consider Stockhausen's view of Carré: 'To quote the composer, "the work is composed in moment-form: each moment, in itself static or in process, is a personal, central fact that is to exist for its own sake. The musical events do not have a precise course from a determined beginning to an inevitable end; a moment is not only the consequent of the preceding and the cause of the succeeding; the concentration on "now", on each "now", on the contrary, is incised, so to speak, vertically through a horizontal notion of time ending at the negation of time that I call eternity: an Eternity that does not begin at the end of Time, but in each moment must be attained'.[52] Stockhausen seems to consider the problems of macro-form here as non-existent. Yet his talk bears witness to his idea and sensibility of the work:[53] if it is composed in moment-form, that is its form; if the end is not inevitable, that is its form of ending. I recall here Pierre Boulez' discussion of contemporary music in the context of his interest in Joyce and Mallarmé, where he quotes aptly from Mallarmé: 'A book neither beings nor ends: at most it pretends to'.[54]

Here I am only giving the vaguest impression of the complexity of the search for form, generic and specific, in contemporary music.[55] That effort to thematize experienced form can be either posterior to composition, or it may be prior and thus mediate composition. One may recall Schoenberg's search for a compositional a priori and the later extensions of his method to the serialization not only of pitch but of timbre, time-value, etc. Indeed, some further reflection on this question of total serialization would help to intimate the various dimensions of the methodological horizon required to break through the range of contemporary problems.

Henri Pousseur, in "The Question of Order in New Music", analyses two passages from Boulez' Structures I.[56] He notes the difficulty of making a precise comparison between the two figures as heard, a difficulty traceable to the fact that each passage is organized in the most irregular, least periodic fashion. He likens the passages to the statistical "Brownian Movements" of physics. The root of the irregularity is found in the rigorous serial procedures, which, far from establishing perceptible symmetries, seem instead to hinder all symmetry.[57] Moreover, he confirms from the writing of Boulez that the divergence between serial procedures and the perceptible result is sought after. A similar problem of levels is treated by

Philip Batstone in his "Musical Analysis as Phenomenology", where he means by analysis the attempt to
describe musical composition as aural phenomena.[58] 'A
genuine work of art has different levels of significance,
and evokes response at different levels of awareness. A
highly complicated Bach fugue follows a harmonic design
which can be grasped quite intuitively. The subtlest
twelve-tone construction would be mere empty mathematics
if the composer did not imbue it with life on levels that
are immediately accessible to the listener'.[59] But what
are the relations between these levels, unaccessible and
accessible? In an adequate theoretic context it will not
be enough to say that 'there can be no twisted thought
without a twisted molecule',[60] that 'the relationship
between a work of art and its audience is the sum of
complex aesthetic, psychological and social conditions'.[61]
For, the sum is a structured sum[62] linking mediately
molecule and mind, and a methodological appreciation
should bring into integral perspective every level from
that of physical and physiological response[63] to that
of the mediation of mind.

> if one has the stomach to add the
> breakages, upheavals distortions,
> inversions of all this chamber-
> made music one stands, given a
> grain of goodwill, a fair chance
> of actually seeing the whirling
> dervish, Tumult, son of Thunder,
> self exiled in upon his ego, a
> nightlong a shaking betwixtween
> white or reddr hawrors, noonday-
> terrorised to skin and bone by
> an eluctable phantom may the
> Shaper have mercy on him!
> writing the mystery of himsel
> in furniture[64]

And it is only within that perspective that
there can emerge adequate principles of criticism and
interpretation, a sufficient consideration of
creativity, a basic viewpoint on music advance. Let
us touch in turn on these few areas of musicology.

All would not seem to be well in the field of
musical criticism and hermeneutics.[65] What Kostelaneth
remarks regarding the writing of Mellers, 'his criticism
seems curiously informed by literary notions'[66] may be
said of a wide range of writings descriptive or
critical of musical composition. I recall Stravinski's
remark, quoted earlier, regarding those who wrote

"below the music". Moreover, the writing tends to be restrictively european, heavy with culturally-conditioned allusions: not that allusions are unwanted, but they restrict in proportion to the lack of appreciation of cultural conditioning.[67] What is needed is a more basic set of categories akin perhaps to what Durand seeks when he categorizes symbolism not in virtue of Freudian or Jungian psychology but in relation to basic reflexology.[68] But more fundamental still is the need for the critic to return to himself. 'There are three overlapping ways of writing about music. One is to write about music. The second is to write about performance. The third, the most popular among writers and readers alike, is to write about oneself. It is the least popular, though, among the people written about, and among those who understand their work. It is also the one way never yet fully realized. At the same time, we only need one simple logical step to become aware of it - though psychologically, the step may not be all that easy, since it has not yet been made: a step into the unwillingly, half-consciously known is, perhaps, more difficult than a step into the unknown'.[69] The step is the subject's reflective withdrawal into the roots of his or her horizon, to ensure a thematic transcultural expansive component in that horizon. That transcultural component would both give perspective to culturally-orientated criticism and given openness to personal expansion required by new music.[70] Also it would make the task of thematizing musical meaning less remote, and ground a comprehending openness to the technological enlargement of artistically-transformable sound sources.[71]

> the memories of the past and the hicnuncs of the present embelliching the musics of the future from Miccheruni's band[72]

These latter points are obviously relevant to an adequate consideration of creativity. There is no need to recall here the witness of a host of composers to the centrality of personal creativity in the concrete emanation of the composition. That creativity has been variously described but has never with any adequacy been self-attentively appreciated. Furthermore, that describing can reach enormous detail without there being a clear transition to a sufficient thematic: I think, for instance, of Hanson's description of Kepler's struggles,[73] or of Koestler's Act of Creation. Or, in the field of music, one may instance Schenker's discussion of highpoints of Beethoven's Sonata Op. 109.

'The manner in which Beethoven suddenly abandons the
high g#^{3} in m.21 and jumps down to d#^{2} has puzzled
everyone. What could this leap, this sudden change,
signify? Even if one grapples with the problem of
discovering a relationship between such widely separated
highpoints- namely the ascent from g#^{3} to b^3 (m.42)
which is to be the main note of the recapitulation, one
has not yet gained the highest degree of insight.
Understanding result much more from the following connection: the improvisational fantasy of the master pursues
both tones of the upbeat in the development of the
coda! He must drive after them. They signify to him a
motive - the key to a world of unity and coherence.
What does the theory of sonata-form care about such a
miracle? And yet, the substance of this movement develops only through the miracle'.[74]

    Again, there is such work as that of Robert
Craft's "The Rite of Spring: Genesis of a Masterpiece",[75]
in which he investigates the emergence of the final
composition through the sequence of manuscripts: 'if
we cannot actually invade the creating mind, we are able,
as we watch its leaps of logic and the sharpening of
its images, to follow the minds footsteps. To anyone
interested in musical embryology, these facsimile pages
are a major document'.[76] But such studies as these at
present do not get beyond a descriptive appreciation
of insight. The shift to the adequate context of self-
understanding is necessary. The creative insights must
be not only reproduced in an adequacy of aesthetic and
thematic context but also attended to with a self-
attention of scientific dimensions. Nor need one be a
musical genius to pursue such an investigation. Undoubtedly it seems a strange and tall order to anyone
who has not been introduced correctly to this axial
human enrichment. And I cannot dispel that strangeness here. As I remarked at the beginning, in this
short essay I can only issue an invitation. Again, my
remarks on creativity are not an effort to communicate
insight into creativity - they merely indicate how one
might begin to undertake the understanding of the
creative process.

    Furthermore, it seems to me that one must have
much more than begun that investigation to handle
adequately the problem of creativity in the fields of
electronic, concrete, computer and aleatoric music or
in the area of free performance. Recall the earlier
remarks about the meaning of the real piano for a
critical existentialist. One cannot, for instance,
discuss, with a theoretic adequate to our times, the

problems associated with John Cage's prepared piano or
with his inkbattle in Silence while remaining personally
rooted in the naive philosophic view that would hold
that the prepared piano and the inkmeaning are "already-
out-there-now".[77]

> Kuskykorked himself up tight in
> his inkbattle house, badly the
> worse for boosegas, there to stay
> in afar for the life, where, as
> there was not a moment to be lost,
> after he had boxed around with
> his fortepiano till his whole
> bach bamp him and bump him blues,
> he collapsed, carefully under a
> bedtick from Schwitzer's, his
> face enveloped into a dead
> warrior's telemac, with a
> lullobaw's somnbomnet and a
> whotwaterwottle at his feet to
> stoke his energy of waiting,
> moaning feebly, in monkmarian
> monotheme[78]

    But what then of the contemporary literature on
such subjects? Clearly, the shift to a methodological
horizon does not eliminate or render null and void one's
prior insights. That shift purifies, transforms,
integrates. In the companion essay[79] I concretely
illustrated this possibility and need by quoting a
botanical text. Here I may quote Varèse's expression of
a view on electronic music which, though worthwhile,
requires an enriching sublimation into a metacontext if
it is to mediate wholesome expansion in the aesthetic
sound-world: 'Babbit certainly represents a completely
different view of electronic music from mine. It seems
to me that he wants to exercise maximum control over
certain materials, as if he were above them. But I
want to be in the material, part of the acoustic
vibration so to speak. Babbitt composes his material
first and then gives it to the synthesizer, while I
want to generate something directly by electronic
means. In other words, I think of musical space as
open rather than bounded, which is why I speak about
projection in the sense that I want simply to project a
sound, a musical thought, to imitate it, and then to
let it take its own course. I do not want an a priori
control on all its aspects'.[80] Obviously, when I talk
of the transformation of such expression and the puri-
fication of its meaning, I am talking of a future
musicological dialogue which may be remote. But it is

the methodologist's task to appreciate and indicate
with heuristic wholeness the deep potentialities of
man, to point with both incarnate and thematic meaning
towards the possibilities of ever-richer human living.

Present histories of music do not point in that
direction: and here I come to the third aspect of the
adequate context that I already mentioned: its contribution to an appreciation of the advance of music. I do
not intend to try and express briefly Fr. Lonergan's
view on the method of history as available in Method in
Theology: I wish only to indicate its need.

I centre my attention on a recent essay by Leo
Treitler, "The Present as History".[81] In this essay
Treitler reviews four recent books on the history of
music.[82] He begins by considering Ranke's slogan,
"... telling it as it was", and points to its weakness
by directing it at the present where 'there are fewer
mysteries posed by lost documents and forgotten
traditions',[83] for, '"there is still so much we don't
know" has been part of a grand self-deception'.[84]

Treitler's basic thesis concerns a "covering
law" model of historical explanation, and notions of
causal sequences and of 'logic and necessity in the
history of music'[85] which go with it. He contrasts
this model-use with a search for pattern, not merely
within history but within things, where the subject
is placed not under covering laws but under what he
calls 'covering concepts'[86] - I would have used here
rather 'heuristic structures'. This second view he
would associate with such thinkers as N.R. Hanson[87]
and Michael Polanyi.[88] While the search for pattern is
an open one, the covering-law approach is dogmatic and,
for example, tends to reduce the role of the composer
to grasping the necessary consequence of the historical
development that he has inherited and to being midwife
to it.[89] He notes that the covering-law or nomological
model for explanation is designed to circumvent the
problem of "subjective" standards in history[90] and
points out that 'the problem of the present in musical
history is a formal (linguistic, epistemological)
problem, rather than a research problem. By reflection
this might suggest that the problem of past history is
far more a formal problem, and far less exclusively a
research problem, than we have generally allowed. And
what that suggests, in turn, is a reversal of the
objectivist priorities. It is problems of theory and
interpretation that most urgently require our
attention'.[91]

Treitler himself does not offer a basic alternate position on the nature of objectivity or of historical method. In passing, however, he does give two interesting cases relevant to Lonergan's critical perspectivist view of history from the history of "tonality": how Heinrich Schenker's general notion, "directed motion within the framework of a single prolonged sonority", contributes to the study of Medieval and Renaissance polyphony, and how David Lewin's notion of "total centre"[92] provides a framework for contemporary studies. But his main effort is directed to exposing the presence of a dogmatic assumption regarding history in the authors under review, and he does so in convincing fashion. Not only is there dogmatism regarding evolution towards the present, but all the authors are found to contribute in their own way to what Treitler calls 'The Crisis Theory of the History of Twentieth Century Music'.[93]

> Time: the pressant.
> With futurist onehorse ballet-
> lattle pictures and the Pageant
> of Past History worked up with
> animal variations amid ever-
> glaning mangrove-mazes and
> beorbtracktors by Messrs Thud
> and Blunder[94]

It would be out of place to review here Treitler's lengthy criticism of these histories of music. Sufficient has been said to indicate that within this field of inquiry all is not well. It would be equally out of place to try to indicate the nature of thematic historical consciousness or the relation of historical method to the functional specializations of Lonergan. But perhaps it is clear that in moving our considerations of the problems in the field of music to this level of history we have also given our invitation to critical existentialist reflection its full dimensions. Those dimensions are the dimensions indicated in the previous essay: the dimensions of a self-appropriated Weltanschauung, a thing not to be expected merely through the writings of the later Lonergan. Without the self-appreciative grasp of emergent probability[95], the sequential postulate[96] and a fundamental hermeneutic[97], those writings cannot possibly convey the man's meaning.

Finally, let us turn to consider discussion of the function of music. The reader perhaps has tired of my weaving about in different special fields: but at

least he or she has not had to bear with the discontinuous sonatonality of a James Joyce. The reader
tires too, perhaps, of the mere promise of transformation of various components of human meaning. But, even
if I had realized adequately such a transformation in
myself I could not briefly communicate it, even to
those who are past the introductory stage of methodology, no more than I could communicate briefly Advanced
Topology to an undergraduate mathematician. When,
therefore, the communal methodological effort remains
to be made in later generations, an invitation to that
effort cannot but be unsatisfactory, if not unwelcome.

Views on the function of music are brought
together by Alan P. Merriam in chapter eleven of his
work, The Anthropology of Music. There he lists ten
major functions: the functions of emotional expression,
of aesthetic enjoyment, of entertainment, of communication, of symbolic representation, of physical response,
of enforcing conformity to social norms, of validation
of social institutions and religious rituals, of contributing to the continuity and stability of culture,
of contributing to the integration of society. Some
of the points raised in this chapter are treated in the
four concluding chapters on symbolic and aesthetic meaning, music and cultural history, music and cultural
dynamics. I list the topics purposely. Merriam does
not claim that his list is exhaustive or coherent or
that his discussion is adequate. Indeed his whole
message is the need for method, for more adequate
context, for an orientation in fieldwork towards meaning:
'Ethnomusicology in the past has devoted itself primarily to fact-gathering rather than to the solution of
broadly-based problems couched in terms of the study of
music as part of human culture'.[98]

But, on Professor Llewellys ap
Bryllars, F.D., Ph.Dr's showings,
the plea, if he pleads, is all
posh and robbage of a melodeon-
tic scale since his man's when
is no otherman's quandour[99]

The need for an adequate orientation towards
meaning is what we have been dealing with all along.
The present question of determining the function of
music raises the issue more precisely in the area of
the human sciences. The various functions listed by
Merriam may be inadequately separated into two classes:
those centering on the individual and those centering
on the group. Elsewhere something has been said
about the psychic liberation of the individual,[100]

but a great deal remains to be done, through the mediation of the neurosciences, to determine sufficiently
psycho-musical correlations. The question of group-
function raises larger issues which at present bother
anthropology and sociology. 'Every sociologist, of
course, dreams of being the possessor of some sort of
abstract framework which will enable him to study the
system of social forces in an objective and disinterested manner. But this has not always been possible,
and many sociological contributions to our present
subject have tended to be superficial, unmethodical'.[101]
The required framework, alas, has all the dimensions of
the heuristic worldview mentioned at the end of our
reflections on the history of music. Here I would
like to note the relevance of works such as those of
Peter Berger and Gibson Winter in helping to specify
more fully that framework and the special problematic
of the human sciences; Berger's sociology succeeds in
bringing together Weber's understanding of social reality
as ongoingly constituted by human signification and
Durkheim's view of that reality as having the character
of chosiété, thingness as against the individual. The
key issue in the entire field of the human sciences is
the issue of human meaning. 'The "stuff" out of which
society and all its formations are made is human meanings externalized in human activities ... sociological
thinking should always be humanized, that is, brought
to refer back the imposing configurations of social
structure to the living human beings who have created
them'.[102] Or as Winter notes, 'Regularities of gesture,
symbolic meaning, action, and expected forms of behaviour
furnish the coherence of the social world; this sedimentation of meaning makes possible a science of human
action'.[103] That sedimentation is related to what
Berger would speak of as the plausibility structure of
a group's orientation, or in Winter's term the 'project' -
the word 'project' will recur in a later and illumin-
atingly-related context - 'the project is the total
intentionality with which subjectivity as a totality
is stretched towards the world as possibility'.[104]
I speak of the work of such authors as filling out
the framework. Without the framework of a critical
realism such factors as subjectivity, empiricality,
normativity, indeed truth, will remain problematic.
Again, Berger's discussion of signals of transcendence
clearly requires a thematic consideration of the subject's
creativity and expansiveness for its adequate development,[105] and Winter, in the latter half of the book
cited, raises questions of distinctions within the field
of sociological endeavour which could be handled adequately only through the appreciative and specificative
use of Lonergan's functional specializations.

Returning to the book by Silbermann already
cited, it is not surprizing to find it falling short of
these large demands. I recall again my initial remarks
regarding the inevitable limitations of present writers.
The first half of Silbermann's book serves to bear
witness to the existence of the range of problems I have
tried to indicate in this essay, the second half bears
witness to his own behaviouristically-tinged sociology,
and a remark such as 'we can only gain insight into
human beings from their behaviour'[106] leaves little room
for an empirical science of methodology pivoting on
insight into insight. Still, there is a value in the
book in that Silbermann repeatedly returns to the fundamental problems in the field: 'In so young a science
as the sociology of music, we must take nothing for
granted, and must therefore remind readers of theoretical
elements at every opportunity'.[107] My repeated return
here to basic issues echoes his on another level.
Self-attentive methodology is an infant science. I have
taken every opportunity to indicate the need for it in
contemporary musicology. I have taken for granted that
to the majority of at least my musicologist readers the
science was till now an unknown and so I have avoided
consideration of its theoretical elements.

> how minney combinaisies and
> permutandies can be played on
> the international surd!
> pthwdndxrclzp! hids cubid rute
> being extructed, taking anan
> illitterettes, ififif at a tom.
> Answers, (for teasers only).
> Ten, twent, thirt, see, ex and
> three icky totchty ones. From
> solation to solution. Imagine
> the twelve deaferended dumbbawls
> of the whowl abovebeugled to be
> the contonuation through regen-
> eration of the urutteration of
> the word in pregross[108]

I have endorsed Treitler's criticism of certain
views of progress or eternal return. Nevertheless I
write with a viewpoint of human progress as the dialectical expansion of man, the complex hierarchic unity
of ultimoquaerozoobotanicochemicophysico-levels. I
write too with a viewpoint which expects deeper returns
through the mediation of mind, such as a return to the
core of primitive mystery through the expansion of man
into noösacrality. But these are larger topics.

There is in human progress a continual interplay
of levels.   Most evident perhaps in this context is
the interplay of developed physics and chemistry -
embodied in technology - and aesthetic developments.
Here the progress I have been stressing is progress on
the level of mind, or the need for that progress for
the total advancement of incarnate questing.   But one
might also write at length of the mutually-fostering
interplay between aesthetic change and the growth of mind.
Boulez wrote of Joyce, particularly of <u>Finnegans Wake</u>,
'It is not only that the way the story is told has been
upset, but also that the novel, if one dares put it this
way, observes itself as a novel, reflects on its own image,
becomes aware that it is a novel;   and this results in a
logic and cohesion of this prodigous technique that is
constantly on the alert, creating new universes.   It is
in this way that music, as I see it, is not destined solely
to "express" but must become aware of itself, become an
object of its own reflection'.[109]

It would take more than the conclusion of an essay
to deal with these vague insights of Boulez.   There is,
for instance, a dual advance in such a novel: an advance
towards deinstrumentalization of e.g., language or human
speech-structure from levels of reductive meaning, an
advance connected with the general problem of derepresent-
ationality;   an advance towards a higher ambivalent
mediation of memory-mind, where there may be higher-level
representation.   It is the latter advance that primarily
interests me here.

Clearly, there has always been a mediation of mind
in human talking and listening - where that talking and
listening cover all forms of human expression and response, including the talking of musical composition and
performance, and the correlative listening.   That mediation, in a partially developed culture, may be enormously complex yet scarcely adverted to.   Here I may
hark back to the problems raised regarding ethnomusicology
and history and human meaning, and in that context recall
the subtleties of Burmese musical tradition.   It is one
of many oral traditions of the East.   Field work and
reflection have revealed the nature of the modes of this
tradition, where mode is not defined in the restricted
meaning of a scale but as a system of melodic formulae
which provide the material and structure for oral composition.   Within that structure tones are combined into
segments, into patterns, into verses, into songs, making
Burmese music 'a multilevelled hierarchic system.   How
the Burmese musician manipulates the various levels of the
hierarchy to create a song has eluded objective investigation and remains within the mysterious realm of the

intuitive.   But with sharper, more effective tools of
investigation this mental operation itself should begin
to be revealed'.[110]

> While they paddled away, keeping
> time megnetically with their eight
> and fifty pedalettes, playing
> foolufool jouay allo misto posto,
> O so jaonickally, all barely in
> their typtap teens, describing
> a charming dactylogram of noctures
> though repelled by the snores of
> the log[111]

I have tried to indicate in this essay the orientation of the effort required to mediate that sharpened
investigation.   T he immediate point, however, is to note
that, as Becker remarks, neither musician nor listener
could be articulate about these things.   'How does the
rice farmer sitting on a mat in the open courtyard watch-
ing a traditional musical drama know immediately the song
type of the aria sung by the princess?   The villager has
never had any musical training and has not formally
learned the song classification.   It is doubtful if he
could tell you how he knows one song type from another,
but he knows.   Likewise how does the musician playing
the harp for friends gathered in his home create a new
song within a given song type, clearly related to every
other song of the same type?'[112]   The Burmese musician
operates within this oral tradition which, for all its
complexity, and within its complexity, allows freedom
of personal inventiveness and includes creation within
performance and guarantees songtypes recognizable by the
audience.   If there is a parallel here with contemporary
liberations and structurings of music, there is also a
world of a difference.[113]   That difference relates to
the centuries-slow emergence of self-reflectivity,[114]
which in our own times has reached a turning point in
the possibilities of human control of emergent human
meaning.   Put simply, one may note a reversal of priorities: the complex Burmese tradition emerged prior to
its thematization by Becker and operated in that tradition
without thematization;   on the other hand, the thematization which is Schoenberg's method and its extensions
enjoyed and enjoys a certain mediative priority in
composition.

But beyond that mediation of the musical theoretic,
a mediation which is paralled in all other areas of the
development of man,[115] there is the possible mediation of
the adequate self-appreciative horizon discussed in this
essay.   The basic question of that self-appropriation

as complex human project is, Who am I?, What am I? To
have faced that question personally and prolongedly and
to have reached a meaning for oneself as project with
other human projects within history, clearly this should
give rise to a higher mediation of talking and listening.[116] And in this sense one might expect, with Boulez,
that music 'become an object of its own reflection':
whose reflection, if not the reflection of the transformed human subject? And, inversely, an invitation
to that memory-dense self-reflective historico-atemporal
consciousness may itself be immanent in and mediated by
the contemporary 'enlargement of the boundries of the
permissible in the empire of sound'.[117]

> We just are upsidedown singing
> what ever the dimkims mummer
> allalilty she pulls inner out
> heads. This is not the end of
> this by no manner means[118]

Our thesis here is far removed from Professor
Meller's view of music's history as movement from Revelation to Incarnation and back to Revelation again with
a reborn Caliban: 'We cannot "know outselves" unless
we can first recognize and accept the fish-like Caliban
within us, who was (we recall) an offspring of the
Moon-Goddess'.[119]   Tristan was not the end of a phase
in human consciousness, nor are we in the presence of
a new primitivism. Still, a demythologizing of Mellers
would yield elements of our own metempirical and scientific
thesis. If one considered new primitivism more tech-
nically as a transformation and expansion of patterned
temporality and considered the strife as the integral
dynamism of a hierarchic structured consciousness, one
might well agree with him when he writes 'In so far as
the new primitivism, whether as manifested in the work
of Boulez, Cage and Stockhausen, of Britten and Stravinski, of Ornette Coleman, or of the Beatles and Bob
Dylan, may evade the strife inherent in consciousness,
it may evade too our human responsibilities'.[120]   But
it is not 'it' but we that may evade the question inherent not only in music as problematic - our topic throughout - but in music as aesthetic.[121]

Music in general is not only a liberation of
the audio-kinesthetic in man - and mediately a general
synesthetic liberation - it mediates too an expansion
of the memory-mind of man. The unity of a temporally
structured composition challenges our 'disposition to the
present', to use a phrase of Schenker: 'We know how
difficult it is to grasp the meaning of the present if
we are not aware of the temporal background. It is

equally difficult for the student or performer to grasp
the "present" of a composition if he does not include at
the same time a knowledge of the background.   Just as
the demands of the day toss him to and fro, so does the
foreground of a composition pull at him.   Every change
of sound and figuration, every chromatic shift, every
neighbour note signifies something new to him.   Each
novelty leads him further away from the coherence which
derives from the background'.[122]   If, as is generally
remarked about present composition, the unity is more
elusive, the structuring more "static", and the rhythm
less somatically isomorphic, then the challenge to 'our
disposition to the present' would seem all the greater
and more refined.   And the adequate listener or performer should live to some extent in the realization of
these refined possibilities.   To use terms coined in
the previous essay,[123] that adequacy represents a radical
shift from synnomic stress in consciousness to an autonomic self-possession.

For the inadequate listener the masterpiece
remains remote.   Schenker remarks that 'even if we
must let the unwilling and incapable move about in a
chaotic, superificial day-to-day existence, at least
we can force him to realize that a true masterpiece has
no connection with his superficial mindless life'.[124]
But force is too harsh.   All men have a reach beyond
the day-to-day.   Few men are closed from that reaching.
History and circumstance may leave the masterpiece beyond
that reach.   But within their grasp may still remain
a glassful of memory-laden melody or the silent echoes
of a song.

What I have written here lies, too, beyond the
reach of these many little people.   Yet it is of
significance to them.   It remains as a challenge to those
who might be willing to face the self-reflective transformation of man that it indicates, so that there might
be a richer reaching in the life of man, mighty or mitey,
whose true pattern is one of aesthetic exuberance.

What I have written must surely also lie beyond
the reach of a single reading, of many readings.   Its
twisted unity flowed forth with a certain inevitability of
form and at times my scribbling pen was silenced through
the accumulation of insight.   Stravinski remarked in
his maturity 'I use the language of music, and my statement in my grammar will be clear to the musician who has
followed music up to where my contemporaries and I have
brought it'.[125]   I cannot be so optimistic.   My grammar
is the grammar of critical existentialism, and my language has twisted and turned through the chaos of

contemporary problems that cry out for the communal
emergence 'of a springtime of philosophy. Still, there
is room for optimism. Stravinski's remark would have
rung hollow in the Paris of 1913. Perhaps then, 'in
a hundred years or so', to recall Kavanagh's stance,[126]
what I have written here may be seen in <u>Perspectives</u> as
a part of the write of spring.

> End here. Us then. Finn, again!
> Take. Bussoftlhee, mememormee!
> Till thousendsthee Lps. The keys
> to. Given! A way a lone a last
> a loved a long the[127]

INTERLUDE

'I am, at 47, more interested in
work built on foundations wherein I
have laboured, than in that produced
by Mr. J's imitators, and feel that
this is justified on human and critical
grounds.

Awareness to the present is indis-
putably part of a great writer's
equipment, it is a dimension to be
measured, or a component in his
specific gravity to be judged and
computed, and if you ask me whether
I believe that Joyce in 1933 is alive
to the world as it is, a world in
which technocracy has just knocked
out all previous economic computations,
and upset practically all calculations
save those of C.H. Douglas; a world
in which the network of french banks
and international munition sellers is
just beginning to be expressable on
the printed page; in which class-war
has been, or is as I write this, simply
going out of date, along with the
paddle-wheel steamer, and being replaced by a different lineup or conflict,
I must answer that Mr. Joyce seems to
me ignorant of, and very little concerned with these matters'.[1]

1. Ezra Pound on James Joyce, Pound Joyce, The Letters of
Ezra Pound to James Joyce with Pound's Essays on Joyce, edited
by Forest Read, Faber and Faber, London 1967, 251-52. The
extract is from "Past History", The English Journal (College
Edition), Chicago, XXII, 5 (May 1933), 349-58. I recall here
my comment at the end of page v above. This book is a set
of initial themes. This bridge-interlude is a totally undeveloped pointer to a keystone neglected by theologians, as
well as by Joyce and, even more amazingly, by economists. I
share at present Fr. Lonergan's preoccupation with economics.
He is now working towards a book Economics and the Religious
Dialectic which will sublate his own remarkable work of the
thirties and early forties.   (See below, pp 80-1, 212)

PART   TWO:

FUTURE   PHILOSOPHERS

and

FOURTH-LEVEL   FUNCTIONAL   SPECIALISTS

PROLOGUE:

WORK IN PROCESS.

> "...between my eyes and heaven a
> dark golden bee is hovering and
> humming - I care about that. It
> is humming the song of happiness,
> humming the song of eternity. Its
> song is my history of the world."[1]

The change of mood, the change of key in the
prologue titles' from g to c, is not representative of a
transition to the second half of a completed work, but
rather to a second theme in a longer sonata-form struggle
which is also an invitation. Joyce's Bloom is not the
all-round man, nor is Finnegan, and "the tale of the
tribe", as Pound called his epic Cantos, must concern
itself "With Usura".[2] If, for example, "money has been
called 'the promise men live by'",[3] then shaped foundations ought to provide a thematic context adequate to
the meshing of such promises with eternal promise of
life. Nor can the shaper of foundations omit from that
thematic an adequate heuristic answer to the question,
"What is sensibility, what is sensible life?" The
mystic may withdraw or be withdrawn, but the foundational
theologian must twine his ultimate concern with finite
metaphysical care. Even if he should stand looking up
to heaven, as in the beginning of The Acts of the Apostles,
the reality of his seeing is of photons and the flight of
birds and bees and international threat: his turn to
the foundational idea cannot authentically leave such
seeing unmediated by a mind procedurally illumined. In
medieval times, "there was the need for a unified apprehension of things: the search of faith for understanding
could not be a merely partial understanding; it had to
be coupled with an understanding of nature; else divine
grace would be perfecting an unknown nature, and divine
faith would be illuminating an unknown reason."[4] In our
own times this is more profoundly true, with the pro-
foundity of an axial shift and the possibility of a
knowing of reason which initiates a new control of meaning.

More elementarily one may note that "a theology
mediates between a cultural matrix and the significance
and role of a religion in that matrix".[5] The cultural
matrix includes the presence of animals and the science
of animals, the schemes of their survival, cultivation
and economy, as well as the symbolic of whale and lamb,
of sculpted horse and dove. The foundations of that
theology can afford no abstraction, and the dialectic

reshaping of those foundations, as Louis Zukofsky wrote
of Pound's Cantos, should "proceed towards a· living
museum of facts about man and his world which displays
the validity of his successive positions as against the
unwieldly detail of all his story".[6] The possibility
of such proceeding lies precisely in the focus of the
subject's work in process, in the process which is his
or her own deepest emergence. Philosophy, Dialectics
and Foundations emerge in axial adequacy only in so far
as the self-attending subject seeks continually to make
more luminous to self the intelligible intelligent
processes in self. The shift from possibility to
probability of such seekers in present academic populations is a key crisis of our day.

No doubt the economy of both man and God could
be rethought in these decades by enlightened common
sense supported by disorientated science in a manner
that may keep decline at bay. But such rethinking is
neighbour to Real Politik and strange to what I would
term Sargawit,[7] Kondratieff thinking, or the thinking
forward to a million years.[8] But what is this thinking,
this Sargawit, and what new perspective in economics,
zoology, theology can it support? Reaching the answer
demands the degrees of sympathy with work in process
that are to be determined in this second part, particularly in the conclusion of the final chapter, and
in the epilogue.

My prologue, a minor bridge between themes for
a larger form, cries out for development beyond these
themes. There is Narziss' intimation of the single word
as epiphany,[9] and the epiphany of Joyce's Ballast Office
clock.[10] There is Pound's figure of "words as electrified cones, charged with the power of tradition, of
centuries of race consciousness, of agreement, of
association", expressive of Vorticist aspiration to
digest and bring forth the past.[11] There is "the man
on giant stilts" of Proust, raised up by the lived
living self-digestive memory.[12] And there is the
personal vortex of each of us which, by digestion of
self and history, can underpin the gift[13] in the un-
veiling of boy or Bible, butterfly or bee.

> There the butterfly flew away over
> the bright water, and the boy
> flew after it, hovering brightly
> and easily, flew happily through
> the blue space. The sun shone on
> his wings. He flew after the
> yellow and flew over the lake

and over the high mountain, where
God stood on a cloud and sang."[14]

PRELUDE

                    that   storm

        it

              one   the

                         Mystery[1]

                                    the
        is
                    can

                              name   of

        only

                                             eye

              in

                         the

1.   My vortex merges, in a manner suggestive of
foundational transformation, two titles only seemingly
unconnected: Patrick White's The Eye of the Storm, and
Langdon Gilkey's Naming the Whirlwind. Much of White's
work meshes elderly hardening and epiphany: 'his body
was hardening ... there was no obvious sign that his
soul too might not harden ...' (The Tree of Man,
Penguin, p.42). Gilkey's book spells out a search for
foundations and the Whirlwind's Name. My own efforts
are towards the specification, in myself and for others,
of the maturing and growing old of foundations persons.
There is the eye, intentio entis, at the centre of the
vortex of method and at the centre of any person's storms
of finitude. And there is the same eye in Faith for
whom the ultimate name is Mystery. (One may link here
Method in Theology, 341-42 with the treatment of Mystery
and inverse insight in Lonergan's De Deo Trino Pars
Dogmatica, Rome, 1964, 274).

CHAPTER 3

ZOOLOGY AND THE FUTURE OF PHILOSOPHERS

"As I read through these chapters for the purpose
of making this summary, I realize how little I have
succeeded in doing justice to the greatness and importance
of the phylogenetic phenomena whose workings I think I
really understand myself, but which are so difficult to
explain, and I am overcome by the discouraging feeling
of helplessness".[1]

Konrad Lorenz, from whose book on aggression I
have just quoted, has been described as the Father of
Ethology.[2] The original English meaning of the word
'ethology' was 'the interpretation of character by the
study of gesture' and the orientation of the ethologists
has been towards a precise scientific study of the
'motorpatterns' of animals with a view to accurate
interpretation. It is not my hope here, however, to
introduce the reader to a particular branch of the study
of animals - a branch which I consider of central significance in the development of that science. My hope,
rather, is to move the general philosophic reader towards a more precise appreciation of his or her own
nescience - and therefore of his or her own humanity -
and also to introduce the animal psychologist to the
possibility of transforming that science, where by
science I mean not the content of laboratories or
libraries but primarily the content of the scientific
mind. The quotation from Lorenz with which I began
serves to focus my task.

To read seriously the works of Konrad Lorenz is
to meet a man who laboured for many years to understand
animals both with an enormous delicacy of perception,
and with scientific precision. There is a loneliness
in the achievement of such understanding - a loneliness
intimated in that page from which the quotation was
taken. For, achieved understanding cannot easily be
shared - indeed, one is tempted at times to take
seriously the question, Can it be shared at all?
Certainly, in so far as that understanding is of any
serious dimension - be it scientific or affective -
it can be shared perhaps only by a decade of delicate
attention. But can a man speak for a decade to a
disciple, work with him, walk with him, teach him?
And would the disciple remain in authentic listening?

The peripatetic method does not seem to belong to our civilization.[3] A man now is normally required to place his meaning in the Gutenberg Galaxy. He must trap himself and his thought in print.

Now I am no opponent of print. The printed word indeed lends a permanent precision[4] to our human efforts to reach out towards one another. But a culture can misrepresent radically the significance of the printed word, and, in precise terms that I used elsewhere[5] a culture can be crippled by the unquestioned acceptance of experiential conjugation as adequate human knowing. Experiential conjugation, one may say, is the power to identify what is being talked about, without knowing in any serious way what is being talked about. "Do you know Smith?" "Oh yes, I know Smith - I was introduced to him last week". Smith can be identified.... but is he known? Known as perhaps his wife knows him after decades of loving depth? Indeed, to anticipate our concluding point, even to his wife Smith is unknown, and rightly unknown, and should remain unknown, if their marriage is to retain its depth of meaning.

And the possibility of experiential conjugation, of a mastery of names, is a central element in what renders Lorenz's task hopeless. Generations of teenaged students may read his books - or their equivalent - master his words, mime his meaning. But do they understand? One can pass graduate and post-graduate examinations by a mastery of print and an adequate descriptive familiarity. The mastery of printed definition or description can be the work of minutes; understanding and real definition may take a genius a decade. Nor can the genius, or the serious scientist, communicate such real definition with the facility that our culture seems to demand. Furthermore, a culture is sick if there is no subgroup within it which respects on some thematic level the remoteness of real definition.

A little autobiographical aside may help to make the point. I recall an experience of mine which relates to an element of the meaning of Bernard Lonergan's Insight. During the summer of 1970, before I began the present essay, I took to the study of a particular unpublished 130-paged typescript of Fr. Lonergan, completed in 1944, on Circulation Analysis. I found the study very exacting, and on a third work-through began to appreciate its unique precision. The interplay of the velocities and accelerations of goods and monies was analysed in a way which I did not find elsewhere

in the literature. But the experience I wish to relate
occurred later, when I was perusing parts of the eighth
chapter of Insight and came upon a sentence which spoke
of capital and the acceleration of goods. Upon reading
it I could only pause and close the book - for now it
seemed to me that I had some understanding of what the
man meant, having laboured through the background, the
lengthier expression of the inner word, over the
previous months.

Yet what can a man do who settles down to
summary printed expression of the fruits of his labours?
Should he not rather write an autobiography? I have
often thought that it might be worthwhile to take some
small point and tease it out over a thousand pages.
But who would print or publish it? I recall now
spending twenty odd pages and many days working out a
particular problem and eventually putting the results
into a sentence of an article. What could it have
meant to the reader? Again I am reminded of the months
I spent trying to understand - I would say, not with
great success - the particular insights of the concluding steps of Godel's Theorem, and eventually all I
could give it in print was a footnote indicating a
problem area.[6] I write personally here not because of
anything privileged about the experience; indeed, my
precise claim is that my difficulty in understanding
and in communicating are mine not because I am a moron
but because I am human. The loneliness of which Lorenz
writes is centrally the loneliness of being human. But
the loneliness of being human is a variable ranging
from the thin loneliness of which men like Riesmann
write[7] to the self-attentively cultivated loneliness of
the critically existential metaphysician, and beyond to
some modern equivalent of the mystic Carmelite loneliness. And, to return to the problem of cultural
sickness, the presence of the adequate relevant
authentically-nescient sub-group in our time requires the
mediation of self-attention within the horizon of Critical Existentialism. That presence is not only the
presence of an understanding of the human condition of
nescience but also a concomitant presence of a tonality
of mystery which may radiate into the wider community.[8]

Let us be so prosaic as to return to the problem
with which Lorenz dealt at such length: the problem of
animal aggression. The verbal expression of the methodological context of such a discussion is worth recording
here, but I will return to it later:

"The study of animal behaviour, of stimulus and response,

would reveal at any stage of development a flexible
circle of ranges of schemes of recurrence. Implicit in
such a circle of schemes, there would be correlations
of the classical type. Implicit in such correlations,
there would be the conjugate forms that

(1) account for habitual perceptiveness of determinate
types and habitual modes of aggressive and affective
response, and

(2) would seem to be emergent in underlying neural
configurations or dispositions as insights are emergent
in images and functions in organs".[9]

      Aggressive response is conceived of adequately
only in the large coherent context of an account of
the animal's behaviour pattern. Indeed, as both
Lonergan and Lorenz would agree, it would require the
wider context of ontogenetic and evolutionary considerations.[10] Yet, again, there is the oddness of being
human in that we can ask, and answer with some ease,
the question, What is aggression? I recall the introduction to a scientific symposium on the nature of
aggression: "We do not attempt to define 'aggression',
nor, with the exception of Veness, did our contributors.
Nevertheless, at least in relation to aggression by
individuals, it became clear that they were all talking
about the same thing. An animal acts aggressively when
it inflicts, or attempts to inflict, or threatens to
inflict damage on another animal".[11] In that sense we
all know what aggression is. But it is so easy to forget, and to live integrally in that forgetfullness, the
qualification 'in that sense'. To yield to the
perennial illusion that we understand when we do not,
in this instance or in any instance, is to orientate
ourselves towards thin loneliness and trivial living.
It is to belittle abominably ourselves and - what
should be most precious to us - our friends.

      And if we did claim to know what aggression was,
what might we say of the labour of Lorenz? Was he just
adding footnotes and precision to our essential knowledge? Rather, does he not mark a basic transition
from implicit heuristic conception to at least partial
explanation? "The being to be known as an intelligible
unity differentiated by verifiable regularities and
frequencies begins by being conceived heuristically,
and then its unknown nature is differentiated by
experiential conjugates".[12] As I have noted already,
the problem of appreciating this gap[13] between
experiential conjugation and real definition is not

merely an intellectual one, but a problem of the total human subject in community. It is a problem which Fr. F. Crowe touched on when he wrote of the exclusion of the uncanny in human living.[14] It is a problem that cannot be tackled merely in print: it calls for artistry, for music and architecture, to intimate to man his heuristicality, his loneliness.

Yet the present contribution is a printed one, and while it hints at other modes, it appeals to scientific effort. It asserts that what the scientist is searching for is understanding, be it of electrons, or atoms, or dahlias or dogs; that the scientist searches for what the majority of us do not have, nor will have; that each scientist searches and contributes in the feebleness of print some sign of his contribution to man's ongoing collaboration towards the understanding of the universe.

Lorenz writes in his introduction, "I hope that the territorial fight of the coral fish, the 'quasi-moral' urges and inhibitions of social animals, the loveless married and social life of the night heron, the bloody mass battles of the brown rat and many other remarkable behaviour patterns of animals will engage the reader's interest up to the point when he reaches an understanding of the deeper connections between them".[15] Yet could one claim, even with attentive reading and re-reading, to have reached up to the mind of Lorenz on the subject? Perhaps here I lay myself open to undergraduate mockery: Lorenz's work, after all, is only a corner of their examination concerns. Still, I hesitate to yield to such mockery, and if I shift my attention momentarily to the field about which I am most concerned here, philosophy, my hesitancy vanishes. Where is the undergraduate who can manage to authentically trap the meaning of Aristotle, Aquinas or Kant?

Lorenz's painstaking work carried him to an appreciation of what he called "The Great Parliament of Instincts",[16] and to a contextual understanding of animal aggression, correlating it with various other sources of behaviour, particularly with what he calls the four central drives of animal behaviour: feeding, reproduction, flight, aggression.[17] I cannot help recalling here his comments on the term 'reproductive instinct'. "We are all familiar with the term 'reproductive instinct'. However, we should not imagine - as many vitalistic students of instinct did - that the invention of such a term provides the

explanation of the process in question. The conceptions
corresponding to such labels are no better than those of
nature's 'abhorrence of a vacuum' or 'phlogiston' which
are only names for a process but 'fraudulently pretend
to contain an explanation of it', as John Dewey has
bluntly put it".[18] In his discussion he succeeds in
initiating the correlation of the various drives in
patterns of behaviour - schemes of recurrence, as
Lonergan would say - indicating compatibilities and
incompatibilities, e.g. "...in the male (ciclid) the
motivations of flight and sexuality cannot be mixed.
If the male has even the slightest fear of his partner
his sexuality is completely extinguished. In the
female there is the same relation between aggression and
sexuality",[19] showing "how different the relations between the 'big' drives can be even in males and females
of the same species".[20]

But it is not my purpose here to spell out, as
Lorenz has done, the subtleties of animal behaviour, such
as the zig-zag dance of the male stickleback before the
female, where three 'drives' are coordinated in a scheme
of behaviour. I consider it enough if I have drawn
attention to the already dense meaning of Lorenz in the
context of Lonergan's brief characterization of the
goal of the investigation of psychic phenomena.
"Accounting for habitual perceptiveness of determinate
types and habitual modes of aggressive and affective
response" is a short phrase - yet the accounting has
filled, and will fill, an enormous number of volumes
and periodicals in our times. Should this not awake in
us some expansive depth of intellectual humility, of
awe? Yet it scarcely seems to - unless one has some
feel for being and mystery in one's bones.

Furthermore, Lorenz's understanding of animal
behaviour was not an end but a beginning. In technical terms, a great deal of Lorenz's work was only a
first or second step in the pursuit of the understanding of animals. "A third step is to effect the transition from the thing-for-us to the thing-itself, from
insights that grasp described parts as organs to insights that grasp conjugate forms systematizing otherwise coincidental manifolds of chemical and physical
processes. By this transition, one links physiology
with biochemistry and biophysics. To this end, there
have to be invented appropriate symbolic images of the
relevant chemical and physical processes; in these
images there have to be grasped by insight the laws of
the higher system that account for regularities beyond
the range of physical and chemical explanation (and

also botanical, in the case of animals); from these laws
there has to be constructed the flexible circle of schemes
of recurrence in which the organism functions; finally,
this flexible circle of schemes must be coincident with
the related set of capacities-for-performance that previously was grasped in sensibly presented organs".[21]
This third step inevitably transcends a good deal of
Lorenz's work: one does not expect a man to be altogether
beyond his time in a particular science. The topic,
aggression, has since become a complex of specialized
fields. In a recent symposium already referred to,
Arnold Klopper gives indications of these developments
in an article entitled "The Physiological Background to
Aggression".[22] Undoubtedly earlier works such as W.B.
Cannon's Bodily Changes in Pain, Hunger, Fear and Rage
gave indications of physiological changes. But past
decades have seen the development of extremely refined
techniques of investigation. These refined techniques
however only serve to reveal the complexity of the
problem of precisely defining aggression. A difficulty
that lends confusion to the results in this field is
the ignorance of scientists as to the significance of
the shift involved in what Lonergan calls 'the third
step'. So, Klopper records the work of Elmadjian who
published in 1955 an account of investigations of
urinary steroid excretion and protein catabolism in
soldiers in various battle situations in the Korean
war. He concluded that each of the groups studied -
the controls, those in acute battle situations, chronic
combat situations, and those who became psychiatrically
disturbed - showed a different "biochemical profile".
But how would Klopper or Elmadjian correlate the biochemical profile with the psychological state? Would
they perhaps consider the biochemistry as someway
'explaining' the psychology, or even explaining it
away? We will return to this point shortly.

        We may turn aside for the moment from the ques-
tion 'What is aggression?' to parallel questions
such as 'What is hunger?', 'What is thirst?', in the
animal. Here there is a forest of specialized papers.
The philosopher would do well here to peruse such a
work as S.P. Grossman's A Textbook of Physiological
Psychology (New York, 1967). Indeed, I seriously
consider that it would be of considerable philosophic
and personal profit to the philosopher to be surrounded
for a time by the endless volumes of biophysics and
biochemistry which bear witness to the efforts of contemporary scientists to answer such apparently simple
questions. The experience, for one thing, might move
him to some glimpse of the significance of the "rule of

explanatory formulation. It is a rule of extreme
importance, for the failure to observe it results in
the substitution of a pseudo-metaphysical myth-making
for scientific inquiry. One takes the descriptive conception of sensible contents and without any effort to
understand them, one asks for the metaphysical equivalents. One by-passes the scientific theory of colour
or sound, for after all it is merely a theory and, at
best, probable; one insists on the evidence of red,
green, and blue, of sharp and flat; and one leaps to a
set of objective forms without realizing that the meaning of form is what will be known when the informed
object is understood. Such blind leaping is inimical
not only to science but also to philosophy. The
scientific effort to understand is blocked by a pretence
that one understands already, and, indeed, in the deep
metaphysical fashion. But philosophy suffers far
more..."[23] Philosophy has indeed suffered from such
phenomena as non-scientific thinkers speaking learnedly
on 'the concept of red'. And what of the concept of
hunger or the concept of thirst? Despite the efforts of
zoologists over half a century one finds regularly in
their writings the plea that they are only beginning to
understand. "Thirst cannot be defined in terms of water
deficit, absolute dehydration, or negative water load,
for these states do not necessarily lead to water in-
gestion. Conversely, water consumption is not a
reliable index of water deficit. If subjective sensations cannot be trusted, what precisely do we mean when
we say an organism is 'thirsty'? These persistent
problems of definition are only too common in almost all
areas of physiological psychology. They reflect the
present state of our ignorance about the complex interrelationships among the many physiological variables
that affect as basic a regulatory mechanism as fluid
exchange. It can only be hoped that our definitions
will improve as additional data become available. This
can occur, however, only if we can proceed with relevant
research projects..."[24] And the philosopher may learn
a lesson from this for his own field: if the understanding of animal thirst is a remote goal of the zoological
enterprise, the philosopher should hardly consider the
understanding of human understanding or human thirst
for understanding as some youthful achievement preliminary to doing his own thing. To be more specific,
let us return to the question of the understanding of
aggression. It would be useful to ponder over the
simple statement made at the end of one of the two
papers submitted by R.P. Michael and D. Zampa to the
journal Animal Behaviour: "Aggressive interactions
between pairs of adult rhesus monkeys of opposite sexes

were studied quantitatively during 1019 hours observation
extending over 2.5 years".[25] Undoubtedly the philosopher
will complain that the philosophic pursuit cannot be
compared to the study of aggression in monkeys. But
one may ask the more precise question, what of the
understanding of the understanding of monkey aggression?
For, this understanding should belong in some part to
the adequate metaphysician who conceives heuristically
(if he lives long enough!) of monkey aggression in his
integral heuristic grasp of proportionate being.[26] And,
to come full circuit to Lorenz's helplessness, it would
seem probable that that conception of aggression is the
conception, the inner word, expressed by the words
'aggressive response' as they occur in Insight.[27]

I have dwelt already, mainly in a botanical and
musicological context, on the philosopher's difficulty
of developing over the years an adequate Weltanschauung.[28]
Here I wish only to add some complementary points and a
zoological perspective.

The contemporary zoologist has no precise
methodological conception of what he is at. He is
carried forward by the dynamism of his implicit metaphysics towards an understanding of a particular range
of being, while at the same time he is bedevilled in his
thinking and in his expression by his own naive realism
or by popular conceptions of philosophy ranging from
vitalism to total reductionism. Even in his efforts to
avoid philosophic dispute the zoologist's perspective
is liable to be distorted: "We have studiously avoided
the problem of conscious experience by phrasing our
definition in terms of physiological mechanism. To
pursue a parallelistic philosophy, we might assume that
the conscious sensations of thirst are correlated with
variations in some or all of the neural and/or hormonal
mechanisms that participate in the regulation of water
intake. This problem is currently not open to scientific investigation, and an answer to this question is
not demanded for the purpose of our research efforts.
We can proceed to theorize about the physiological
aspects of thirst without being enmeshed in philosophical
discussions."[29] Moreover, the perspective tends to be
increasingly distorted as one moves from the ethologist
through the physiologist to the biophysicist, where
"The Unity of Science as a Working Hypothesis"[30] - the
relevant unifying science being physics - may be more
than implicitly operative. In the limit one may reach
thin statements about the analogy between computers and
minds[31] which do little credit to the minds of their
authors and little to help in the integral advancement

of behavioural science. I am no opponent of biophysics
and cybernetics: indeed the entire point of "the third
step" already discussed is that the explanation of the
animal requires that one move into these fields. But
unless one's perspective is adequate the fruits of one's
special research will require extensive critical re-
appraisal and re-expression before it can contribute to
wholesome scientific progress.[32]

I have already claimed that the contemporary
zoologist, whatever his specialty, lacks this perspective. My claim is based both on some familiarity with
the field of zoology and on the view that the possibility
of that adequate perspective is only of recent emergence:
scientific self-attention alias methodology as a communal possibility marks what Jaspers calls an axial
period.[33] It would seem then that the entire science
of zoology requires critical appraisal. It is not a
matter of liquidation but of critical reconception and
re-expression, and what I am trying to indicate here is
the dimensions of that required "reorientation and integration".[34] That reorientation and integration requires
the emergence in the community, and in the university
in particular, of a collaborative effort of methodologists and zoologists to move authentically into the
field of interiority. Nor, as I have repeatedly emphasized, is this move contemporarily achieved with any
ease. To put the point popularly, both the zoologist
and the methodologist find it hard to admit, either
unthematically or thematically, that from the explanatory
viewpoint the animal disappears!

Less popularly, and as an illustration of a
generic need for the rethinking and re-expressing of
zoological knowledge, one may note the effect of the
absence, in present culture, of what I may call the
hylemorphic mentality on the efforts of scientists.
The hylemorphic mind is one which has conceived of
matter and form "not without labour"[35] in such a way as
to have it habitually mediate a pressure towards the
emergency of hylemorphically-suggestive outer words.
The animal is a four-levelled hylemorphically-related
hierarchic unity, but the contemporary zoologist does
not thematically appreciate this and so his efforts to
retain and express an integral view of his scientific
efforts to understand the animal are continually frus-
trated. So, for example, in Tinbergen's very fine book
The Study of Instinct[36] there is a chapter entitled "An
Attempt at a Synthesis" where he comes to "tentatively
define an instinct as a hierarchically organized nervous mechanism which is susceptible to certain priming,

releasing and directing impulses of internal as well as
external origin, and which responds to these impulses
by coordinated movements that contribute to the main-
tenance of the individual and the species",[37] and he
goes on in an effort to relate the levels of integration, from those revealed by the ethologist to those
revealed by the neurophysiologist and neurophysicist.
The effort concludes with a diagramming and discussion
of a seven-levelled hierarchy of 'centres' underlying
a major instinct, viz., the reproductive instinct of
the male three-spined stickleback. As Tinbergen
remarks, "it should be emphasized that these diagrams
represent no more than a working hypothesis of a type
that helps to put our thoughts in order".[38] But the
working hypothesis falls axially short of the viewpoint
which would conceive "the successive, distinct autonomous sciences related as successive higher viewpoints.
For the coincidental manifolds of lower conjugate acts,
say A_{iy}, can be imagined symbolically. Moreover as the
coincidental manifolds are the conjugate potency for
the higher conjugate forms, so the symbolic images provide the materials for insight into the laws relating
the higher forms...".[39]

   That axial shortcoming reminds me of the earnest
plea of H.S. Sullivan, at the beginning of his book, The
Intersonal Theory of Psychiatry,[40] that his audience
take not for granted that they shared his meaning of the
word "anxiety". He was, one might say, staking a claim
for the world of theory. Here I am trying to stake a
claim for the world of scientific interiority, and I am
tempted to have recourse to a stratagem adopted by
Carnap in handling the two meanings of probability -
the stratagem of subscripts.[41] Then I would be in-
clined to write such words as "aggression$_1$",
"aggression$_2$", "aggression$_3$", where "aggression$_1$" meant[42]
aggression as commonsensically conceived, "aggression$_2$"
meant aggression as scientifically conceived, and
"aggression$_3$" meant aggression as heuristically conceived
within the context of the Weltanschauung of emergent
probability, the conception being linked with symbolic
images of the lower manifolds involved. I would contend,
moreover, that the book Insight was written from the
perspective of subscript 3 and that the subscript 3
should thus recur regularly. I would contend, further,
that to reach its meaning it is not sufficient to read
the book Insight even with serious introspective attention. "The metaphysician has to raise proximate questions and seek their answers from scientists".[43] I
have already tried to indicate this in relation to some
lower sciences and to the conception of randomness,

emergence, recurrence-schemes, etc.[44] In the present
zoological context I might draw attention to the difficulty of conceiving, subscript 3, of "the flexible
circle of ranges of schemes of recurrence"[45] in which
the animal lives. To reach that conception one must
reach insight into one's own relevant zoological insights: one must thus transform from a heuristic viewpoint such understanding as that expressed in Tinbergen's
discussion of the reproductive behaviour of the male
three-spined stickleback.[46] Again, if one has not
reached this conception of animal behaviour as well as
such conceptions as randomness3 one will be hard put to
it to indicate with precision how it is that from the
botanical point of view the organic performance of the
animal is random. And this brings me to a final major
point relevant to the reorientation of the science of
zoology. "The animal pertains to an explanatory genus
beyond that of the plant; that explanatory genus turns
on sensibility; its specific differences are differences
of sensibility; and it is in differences of sensibility
that are to be found the basis for differences of organic structure, since that structure, as we have seen,
possesses a degree of freedom that is limited but not
controlled by underlying materials and outer circum-
stances".[47] The significance of the scientific development of ethology is to have implicitly stressed this
specific difference, but in so far as there is a shift
in discussion to neural, hormonal and lower levels,
deficiencies of conception and expression emerge.

As illustrative of this problem one might consider the work of Joseph Altman, Organic Foundations of
Animal Behaviour.[48] The author seeks to take a biologically orientated view of psychology which "obligates
us to describe, analyse, and if possible systematize
psychological findings in terms of biological concepts
and categories, rather than in terms of philosophical
ones (which is the traditional approach) or in terms of
unrelated physical or mechanical ones (which is a common
modern trend)".[49] He combines, in fact, an organismic
approach with a cybernetic viewpoint and expression.
So, while the word "consciousness" scarcely occurs in
the book, the vocabulary draws regularly on that of
information theory. Here I would like to quote at some
length from Altman to illustrate the nature of the
problem of reorientation and integration of science and
common sense through the mediation of an integral
hylemorphic viewpoint: "If animative activity is
analysed into its functional constituents, three basic
processes may be distinguished. One process, not
necessarily the first in sequence, is concerned with

the gathering of information about the conditions of the
body and its environment. This process is dependent on
physical and chemical influences on the organism, which
can serve an environmental stimulus. The utilization of
stimuli by the organism as sources of information requires transducer functions, and the various organic
transducers are collectively known as receptors.
Another process is the control or coordination of animative activities, and it consists of two major aspects,
the transmission and processing of information. The
transmission of information from one part of the body
(or the nervous system) to another is dependent on the
conductile property of nerve fibres; the neural processing of information is based on complex synaptic functions
with the aid of which impulses are sorted out, amplified,
inhibited, biased, or otherwise modulated, then integrated
and channelled along various transmission routes. The
third process, not necessarily the last in sequence, is
the effector or motor process, consisting of various
adjustments produced by the body. This accomplishment
is to a large extent dependent on the muscular system,
which is capable of producing mechanical work".[50]

From this it may be seen that the concrete and
detailed task of conceiving the animal non-mythically
as "a solution to the problem of living in a given
environment"[51] and expressing that conception in adequate
external words is deeply hindered by obscurity on the
nature of intelligibility and objectivity and by the
absence of an adequate meaning of "form", particularly,
as I have indicated elsewhere, of "autonomic form"[52].

It is of some value to consider further Fr.
Lonergan's contention that "an explanatory account of
animal species will differentiate animals not by their
organic but by their psychic differences"[53] in relation
to the special field of taxonomy.

In the introduction to his book Taxonomy: A
Text and Reference Book,[54] Richard E. Blackwelder
indicates "great dates" in the history of taxonomy,
such as 1859 (Darwin's Origin of Species), 1900 (The
rediscovery of the work of Mendel), 1940 (The publication of The New Systematics) - great dates, however,
which did not see any significant transformation of
taxonomy. "It has not been so clear why there was no
change after Darwin or again after Huxley. It was not
because taxonomists rejected any particular part of
the evolution or speciation theories or directly rejected genetic knowledge and population ideas. The
simple fact seems to be that the sort of change

expected is not possible in the taxonomic system. A
second likely reason is that the system worked so
effectively for taxonomists that they had no wish to
alter it. Whichever reason has been dominant, there
has been very little real change in the system in two
hundred years. There is no reason to think that it
will change in the future, although it is quite con-
ceivable that it might be replaced with some other
systems".[55] Briefly, taxonomy as it stands is, with
qualifications, adequate to the differentiation of
zoological species. That classification has been based
mainly on scientific description of morphological
characters - characters easily observed in preserved
specimens. Now in so far as the science advances
clearly into an explanatory pattern through evolutionary
theory and through advances in ecology and ethology, the
chasm between a taxonomy which centres attention on
materia disposita and one which focuses on conjugate
forms emerges. One appreciates that the prior classification remains convenient in so far as one appreciates
the meaning of materia disposita, and it is to some
extent this convenience that tempts some taxonomists to
claim that the function of a classification is to provide an easy-to-use filing system. But, E. Mayr notes,
"as important as this function of classification is,
it is not the only one. To reduce the taxonomist to a
filing clerk is to misunderstand his role. This would
be even more true if the filing-clerk taxonomist were
asked to file the items by superficial resemblance
rather than on the basis of a thorough understanding of
the contents. It would mean not only reducing taxonomy
to a service function for other branches of biology,
but also causing it to do this service badly".[56] Later,
Mayr lists the various types of taxonomic character,
ranging from the morphological to the geographical, and
remarks that "behaviour is undoubtedly one of the most
important sources of taxonomic characters. Indeed,
behavioural characters are often clearly superior to
morphological characters in the study of closely related
species, particularly sibling species. Yet there are
two major technical drawbacks. Behaviour cannot be
studied in preserved material, and it is intermittent
even in the living animal. Certain types of behaviour
occur only during the breeding season or during part
of the 24-hour period. The comparative study of related
species has become an autonomous discipline, comparative
ethology. It has already made major contributions to
the improvement of classifications of birds, bees, wasps,
orthopterans, frogs, fishes, and other groups".[57]
    Now, what the student of behaviour normally
focuses attention on is the flexible circle of schemes

of recurrence at some stage in the animal's development.[58]
Taxonomy would require that a further step be taken, for
"implicit in such a circle of schemes, there would be
correlations of the classical type. Implicit in such
correlations, there would be the conjugate forms that

(1) account for habitual perceptiveness of determinate
types and habitual modes of aggressive and effective
response, and

(2) would seem to be emergent in underlying nerual configurations or dispositions as insights are emergent in
images and functions in organs".[59]

          In such a manner one may move, through decades of
zoology, to a taxonomic determination of the conjugates
C_{jx}, C_{jy} of the cellular and the multicellular animal.[60]
The reader may note how different this manner of facing
the generic question of the nature of sensibility is
from the normal approach of books on the senses. Usually
discussion tends to waver round "the third case" mentioned in Insight, page 81, with excursions into the
lower sciences. Moreover, it tends to bog down in
epistemological problems. So, for instance Wyburn et
alii spend the last 100 pages of their book on the
senses surveying views on perception, present a further
possible view, and conclude: "even if the suggested
solution is unacceptable, one thing at least is clear:
the bankruptcy of the orthodox theories shows only that
by some such radical revision of fundamental concepts
can success be obtained".[61] It is clear that one cannot
handle the senses with scientific clarity without an
accurate personal position on objectivity and extrover-
sion.

          To the non-zoologist, perhaps, the emergence of
a definitional spectrum of sensibilities may seem beyond
the bounds of possibility. But one might reflect, for
example, on the range of vestibular receptors, which
have to do with the animal's position with respect to
gravity, from the statocyst - the simplest type involving a small spherical sac partly covered with sensory
hair and containing a mobile granule - to the complex
vestibular sensitivity of the mammal; or again, on
the variability of the underlying neural aggregate from
the peripheral nerve plexus of coelenterates to the
primate's complex nervous system. The zoological conjugates to be reached will "vary with variations in the
type of aggregates of processes E_{ijx}, E_{ijy}",[62] and of
structures. So it is that a discontinuity with the old
taxonomy is not to be expected, yet a quite different

level of explanation in terms of sensitive conjugates
is reached. Moreover, on that level of explanation
"measurement loses both in significance and in effi-
cacy",[63] and in this context I may remark that I do not
see the recent development of numerical taxonomy as
anything more than a peripheral advance.[64]

As I come to the end of this brief essay opening
up the field of metazoology I might well echo the helplessness of Lorenz regarding communication. The essay
can be read in less than an hour - but if its sources
are not sought out, both in the literature of zoology
and methodology and in the science and common-sense of
the reader, then little new insight may be communicated.
The essay was an experiment in philosophy, where by
philosophy I mean precisely self-attentive methodology.
The title related that experiment in metazoology with
the future task of present philosophers, and something
more should be said on this point.

Most evident from the essay is that the zoologist is in need of methodological assistance, as are
all scientists at present - not merely indeed as
scientists but as men. But equally important is the
fact that the philosopher cannot ignore zoology - an
integral heuristic grasp of proportionate being cannot
be reached without some explanatory grasp of the animal
kingdom. The philosopher indeed cannot afford to ignore
any major area of science or art if he is to make his
proportionate contribution to the axial transformation
of man. In a certain sense, precise specialization and
methodology are incompatible. A philosopher indeed may
be a specialist e.g. in metalogic, or chemistry, or in
the philosophy of Jaspers,[65] but such specialization is
only in focus when it falls within one's own adequately
developing Weltanschauung. Nor is that Weltanschauung
developed in the first decade of one's philosophizing.
Indeed, one remains always in this life little more
than "potency in the realm of intelligence".[66] Present
philosophers may argue that I spell out an impossible
task. In one sense I do: for, what I describe is the
possible philosopher of the future, a type of philosopher
not concretely communally possible at present. Yet, my
title indicates that I speak of the future of present
philosophers. That future is the task of cultivating
much-needed authentic methodologists. Undoubtedly such
a cultivation would require a transformation of education, not merely at university level, where a methodological component is now indispensible, but at all lower
levels. Still, each one can contribute in a basic
existential sense, by acknowledging the slow growth of

personal and communal understanding and by seeking to
win respect for remote meaning.[67] That respect must be
won above all within oneself, so that through a nurtured
growth of awareness of this (I use awareness in its
widest sense), one becomes an incarnate acknowledgement
of the mystery of man, where to the complexity of the
animal is added the elusive intelligibility of human
intelligence and the opaqueness of the absolutely supernatural. In a certain sense, what matters for the contemporary philosopher is not achievement but the acknowledgement, intellectually and feelingly, that we do not
know what being is, nescimus quid sit ens.

INTERLUDE

"Who killed James Joyce?
I, said the commentator,
I killed James Joyce
For my graduation.

What weapon was used
To slay mighty Ulysses?
The weapon that was used
Was a Harvard thesis.

How did you bury Joyce?
In a broadcast symposium.
That's how we buried Joyce
To a tuneful encomium.

. . . .

. . . .

Who killed Finnegan?
I, said a Yale-man,
I was the man who made
The corpse for the wake man.

And did you get high marks,
The Ph.D.?
I got the B.Litt.
And my master's degree."[1]

1.   Patrick Kavanagh, "Who killed James Joyce?",
     Collected Poems, Martin Brian and O'Keefe, London,
     1972, 117.

CHAPTER 4

INSTRUMENTAL ACTS OF MEANING AND FOURTH LEVEL
FUNCTIONAL SPECIALIZATION

> "-Have you a new book in process
> of ... incubation?
> -Are you writing something new?
> Joyce gave a short, brief smile.
> -Writing is not quite the word.
> Assembly, perhaps is better - or
> accretion. The task I have set
> myself could probably be termed
> the translation into language of
> raw spiritual concepts. I stress
> here translation as distinct from
> exposition. It is a question of
> conveying one thing in terms of
> another thing which is ... em ...
> quite incongruous."[1]

"Without fantasy, all philosophic knowledge remains in the grip of the present or the past and severed
from the future, which is the only link between philosophy and the real history of mankind."[2]

For the person who has seriously faced the
existential discomfort of Lonergan's methodology, neither
fantasy nor the Frankfurt school, to which Marcuse owed
some allegiance, can be considered foreign to the self
searching for foundations. And it is the dialectic
search for foundations that is our concern here. According to Martin Jay, the historian of the Frankfurt
Institute, "The role of the intellectual, the Institute
came to believe with growing certainty, was to continue
thinking what was becoming ever more unthinkable in the
modern world."[3] Nor is this far from a view of doctrines
of economics, politics and education in these past centuries as making human life unlivable.[4]

That unlivability is all around, but it is manifest only to those who succeed in escaping it in the
mode of mind and with a resonance of feeling. I will
not enlarge here, then, on the deprived recurrence-
schemes of school-children and subway-people, of the
bewildered aggressions of generations and the dwindling
days to death. "What should a society be, so that in
his last years a man might still be a man? The answer

is simple: he would have to have been treated as a man
... It is the whole system that is at issue and our
claim cannot be otherwise than radical - change life
itself."[5]

     I speak of "manifest" and I think of Heidegger's
Being and Time, for the unlife is manifest only to one
who is mindful of being, and this indeed not merely in
the pattern of Maslow's peak experiences, but in the
plateau fashion of which he later wrote.[6] I speak of
"escape" and I think of something like the personal
spiralling towards the Absolute Idea programmed in
Hegal's Phenomenology of Mind. I add "a resonance of
feeling" and I recall such different symbols as Assisi
and Marcel Proust,[7] but in our present focussing on
foundational unlife I may specifically recall Husserl's
comment on "the ardent desire for learning, the zeal for
a philosophic reform of education and of all humanity's
social and political forms of existence, which makes
that much-abused Age of Enlightenment so admirable. We
possess an undying testimony to this spirit in the
glorious 'Hymn to Joy' of Schiller and Beethoven. It
is only with painful feelings that we can understand
this hymn today. A greater contrast with our present
situation is unthinkable."[8]

     However, my question must be, Do you have
painful feelings about being?[9] Are you thus in
existential discomfort, even if it be meshed with
ultimate serenity? Does the over-optimistic statistic
of one per cent of professional theologians who adult-
grow in that profession not raise a personal dis-
quiet?[10] And does it not cause you to pause reflectively
- Bachelar writes of "inducing in the reader a state of
suspended reading"[11] - on meeting my suggestion that
foundation persons, persons operating within the two
functional specialties of dialectics and foundations,
have greater need of such growth than those of other
specialties?

     The previous paragraph points in unaccustomed,
perhaps unwelcomed, fashion towards my reader. I would
recall here, then, the pages of Insight dealing with
expression, simple interpretation and reflective interpretation,[12] and would further link that treatment of
interpretation with the comment in Method in Theology:
"At a higher level of linguistic development, the
possibility of insight is achieved by linguistic feedback, by expressing the subjective experience in words
and as subjective."[13] In the present stage of the
axial shift[14] to which Method in Theology belongs we

are a long way from adequate signs and symbols of
studied interiority, but that very point cries out to
be made.[15] The critic and writer Anthony Burgess speaks
of Flann O'Brien's talent for counterpointing myth,
fiction and actuality:[16] would that I had the talent to
counterpoint expression, simple and reflective interpretation to reach an inevitability of horizon-expansive-
ness. But the reader is spared the Joycean horror.
Instead, I will try, with a balance of clarity and unclarity,[17] to make some points contextual to the central
problem of the emergence of authentic foundations persons
in whom the four functions of meaning adequately fructify
the anthropological turn in theology.

I cannot resist, however, a passing salute to
Joyce in the words of Samuel Beckett who was commenting
at the time on the blending of form and content in
Joyce's Work in Progress. The quotation, I fear, is food
for thought for more than the readers of Joyce, for more
than those for whom "sufficient for the day is the news-
paper thereof."[18] Beckett writes: "Here is direct
expression - pages and pages of it. And if you don't
understand it, Ladies and Gentlemen, it is because you
are too decadent to receive it. You are not satisfied
unless form is so strictly divorced from content that
you can comprehend the one almost without bothering to
read the other. This rapid skimming and absorption of
the scant cream of sense is made possible by what I may
call a continuous process of copious intellectual sali-
vation. The form that is an arbitrary and independent
phenomenon can fulfil no higher function than that of
stimulus for a tertiary or quartary conditioned reflex
of dribbling comprehension."[19] It seems to me that
the further one moves away from the reading of prayer
or poetry or higher mathematics, the more evident is a
massive inauthenticity in the tradition of reading. In
this sense - and does Finnegans Wake escape? - "There
is no document of civilization which is not at the same
time a document of barbarism."[20] But before turning to
the topic of such instrumental acts of meaning as wakes
and cakes[21] and documents, let me state my concern in
more recognizable terms.

"As will be observed the writer
of this still believes in the
people; he knows that there is
virtue in race; he believes that
there should be a virtue in
religion and that men who purport
to hold a transcendent belief in
the Communion of Saints, the

Resurrection of the Dead, etc.,
should be wild with a spirit of
imaginative adventure and love
of life. There is something of
that in the country (i.e. Ireland)
but it is either blotted out by
the tradition of society or grows
out of its faith and hope into
what makes our political and
business leaders."[22]

I am concerned, then, with the possibility of
New Mandarins,[23] of adequate foundations persons, at a
time when the schemes of recurrence of education, pro-
motion and living within academy and ecclesia are
such as to yield unfavourable statistics of their
emergence. I am concerned about the second million
years: "the most ironical of all the unintended consequences of Man's achievements during the first million
years of his existence is that his struggle to become
master of his situation, instead of continuing to be its
slave, has resulted in his exchange of one servitude for
another."[23a] That servitude would require a lengthy
tracing, more profound than Toynbee's, moving through
the upside-down emergence of mind in the mesh of history, with mind's more recent upside-down rating of the
various levels of science in difficulty and importance.
One must surely grant that in the emergence of mind
the most elementary science, physics, would show and
grow first, with its corresponding technology. But
one must also suspect that emergent mind would fail to
appreciate the hierarchization of the sciences implied
here,[24] so that modern man, far from coming of age,
lives largely under the illusion that a big car is more
precious than a big laugh, than a grain of wheat.
Changing our focus mightily we might take in view the
four centuries, 1776-2176, bracketing our own time,
beginning with The Wealth of Nations. But where ending?
Robert Heilbroner gives his own well-informed descriptive indications, in a mood of factual gloom, weighing
up adversely problems of energy and fertility, food and
conflict, economic and social organization.[25] Such
descriptive indications must needs be sublimated[26] in
the foundation person's perspective[27] on being, so that
he or she might envisage, not without fantasy and within
an explanatorily-patterned emergent probability,
probability schedules of schemes of recurrent-responses
to the long-term[28] challenge: "What values and ways of
thought would be congenial with such a radical reordering
of things we also cannot know, but it is likely that
the ethos of 'science',[29] so intimately linked with

industrial application, would play a much reduced role.
In the same way, it seems probable that a true 'post-
industrial' society would witness a waning of much of
the work ethic that is also intimately entwined with
our industrial society ... It is therefore possible
that a post-industrial society would also turn in the
direction of many pre-industrial societies - towards an
exploration of inner states of experience rather than
the outer world of fact and material accomplishment.
Tradition and ritual, the pillars of life in virtually
all societies other than those of an industrial
character, would probably once again assert their
ancient claims as the guide to and solace of life."[30]

But do we have to wait for this? Does it take
starvation and conflagration to bring us - eastern,
western, anonymous religious thinkers - "a little
breathlessly and a little late,"[31] to pause on the rub-
ble of Adam's and Smith's world and seriously question
our questioning selves, seriously analyse those proceedings in our own intimate minds of which the Proceedings
of Whatever Association are, in our days, such pale
unworthy images?

When I was asked in Autumn 1973 to make the contribution of this paper to a meeting in Boston in June
1974, I selected instrumental acts of meaning as my
zone of interest. I selected it because it had been an
area of my questioning ever since, in the late sixties
I had spent hours and months in seeming idiot-staring
at the green of library-lamps and trees, searching out
the axial meaning of experiential conjugation: "What
is it to name green?" Later, what I called at Florida
"the menace of experiential conjugation in the field of
interiority"[32] became a focus of consideration and concern, and remained so in the months of writing, as I
tried to listen to the universe under this formality.

I am here, of course, deliberately autobiographical as deliberately too I twist and turn uncomfortably
in these instrumental acts of meaning. If our interest
is incarnationally dialectic, then we are to meet as
persons, "our arms and legs full of sleeping memories
of the past"[33] which may well, any one, surprise us as
a luminescence of being. Centrally, I would like to
pose my candid position on the slow growth, in any
finite subject,[34] of luminous procedural meaning. I do
not do so in the form of a treatise, or within the context of well-defined dialectic, or with the precision
of the objectifications suitable to a community of
foundations persons with some established zone of common

meaning.[35] I take a stand on the view that we are
"always future hollows,"[36] that to envisage the meaning
of that hollow as infinitely elusive is not a transcendental illusion,[37] that procedural analysis is axial,[38]
focusing and illuminating the mystery,[39] always opaque.
And in the present paper I would cry out that the human
power of naming is not only a triumph but a trap.

Am I merely echoing an accepted view? I do not
think so. As I remarked elsewhere, too many people consider the book Insight as a springboard to doing one's
own thing.[40] I know a man, not more than averagely
stupid, who has spent fifteen years reading Insight and
five years reading Method in Theology, slowly coming to
grasp their axial seminality, their beyond-him-ness,
their further-pointing. Is there, then, some magic in
the aggregates of instrumental acts called Insight and
Method in Theology? Certainly not. The problem is "to
discover oneself in oneself."[41] And the self one is
to discover is the self of ultimacy in the twentieth
century seeking liberating control of the inner and outer
words that both do or do not dominate the twentieth century. Without that twentieth century quest, reflective
ultimacy is not mediating twentieth century culture: it
is in the twentieth century like animal bones in a museum,
locally and very dead. And the self to be discovered is
inclusive of the self of potentially refined sensibility,
the self benumbed and bewildered by interpersonal
opaqueness of sensibility[42] or threatened by the abundant
instrumental acts of techno-inner words of those elementary sciences, physics and chemistry.[43] The question,
then, of the inner gentle control of the twentieth century meaning of persons finite and infinite is of large,
perhaps frightening, dimensions. But the catastrophe
of shirking, shrinking, the foundations that question
requires could be of parallel dimensions. "It is a
central lesson of biological evolution that increasing
complexity of organization is always accompanies by new
levels of hierarchic controls. The loss of these controls at any level is usually malignant for the organization under that level. Furthermore, our experience
with many different types of complex systems, both
natural and artificial, warns us that loss of hierarchi-
cal controls often results in sudden and catastrophic
failure."[44] But no one surely, if failure writ large
should come, will claim that it is sudden? The electron
and molecule instead of leading us like the Ascension
"ad invisibilium amorem"[45] have gradually been made to
mesh the globe with a net that strains.

"-If you hit a rock hard enough
and often enough with an iron
hammer, some mollycules of the
rock will go into the hammer and
contrariwise likewise.
-That is well-known, Mick agreed.
-The gross and net result of it
is that people who spend most of
their natural lives riding iron
bicycles over the rocky roadsteads
of the parish get their personalities mixed up with the personalities of their bicycles as a result
of the interchange of the mollycules of each of them, and you
would be surprised at the number
of people in country parts who are
nearly half people and half
bicycles."[46]

The foregoing are instrumental acts of meaning
relevant to the emergence in human persons of procedural
analysis.[47] The previous sentence is an aggregate of
instrumental acts of meaning drawing attention to something I have in mind which escapes the serious attention
of either conceptual analysts or Whiteheading theologians:
that something is a grasping of intelligible process
which is both ultimate in mystery and paramount for ongoing process.[48] The present Goedelian sentence draws
attention to the hope - it says, too, "I am not a
communication" - that this and other paragraphs will
have made you pause, that my paragraphic gestures might
have something of the re-collective effect of Marcel
Proust's little madeleine. But let me ask you: did
you pause, will you pause, are you reading loud and
clear? Or is there no element of drama, of Poor
Theatre,[49] in our philosophic discourse? Is a workshop
in interiority merely a convention? Like Jerzy
Grotowski,"We are concerned with the spectator who has
genuine spiritual needs and who really wishes, through
confrontation with the performance, to analyse himself.
We are concerned with the spectator who does not stop
at an elementary stage of psychic integration, content
with his own petty, geometrical, spiritual stability ..
but with him who undergoes an endless process of self-
development, whose unrest is not general but directed
towards a search for the truth about himself and his
mission in life."[50] Might it not be the reader's conviction, then, that "the author's text is a sort of
scalpel enabling us to open ourselves, to transcend
ourselves, to find what is hidden within us...?"[51]

> Hamm: "...Moment upon moment,
> pattering down, like the millet
> grains of ... (he hesitates) ...
> that old Greek, and all life long
> you wait for that to mount up to
> a life. (Pause. He opens his
> mouth to continue, renounces) Ah
> lets get it over!...
> Clov: "...Sometimes I wonder if
> I'm in my right senses then it
> passes off and I'm as intelligent
> as ever...[52]

But let us continue, if not to get it over. My
title clearly invites the question, what have instrumental
acts of meaning and fourth level functional specialization
to do with one another? And if the question has in fact
occurred I invite the reader to the tricky task of trans-
posing it into subject-centered explanatorily-heuristic
terms.[53] Just how tricky a task it is may gradually
show through.

Instrumental acts of meaning certainly recur, in
the four functions of meaning, in a theologically relevant fashion and in residual fashion of possible later
relevance, within any functional specialty. The same
may be said of the interlocking in meaning of different
functional specialists. Also, there is that region of
meaning linking first level functional specialization
with zones of possible theological relevance in the
past and zones of probable religious relevance in the
future. And other complexities we are passing over.[54]
Problems of expression, then, lurk everywhere, calling
for procedural analysis, and within[55] the general bent
of procedural analysis there must occur an objectification of position procedure, in regard to expression,
coincident with a piece of foundations.

It would be helpful, I think, to take bearings
at this stage in relation to the aggregate[56] of expressions on pages 286-287 of Method in Theology and in the
twist of lines 24ff. of page 250 of that book. Just how
helpful this suggestion is, however, depends on where
"one is at" with regard to procedural analysis and to
a precise personal position on knowing and being.

So, for example, only a maturity for whom such
an event as a graduation day is a memory[57] can enjoy
serious comfort in the challenge of the dialectic programme of page 250. The reality intended by lines 24ff.
resembles Marechal's five-volume effort but successfully
goes beyond it.[58] Again, in that same context, positional

debates which tend to be merely "present tense"[59] appear
as pre-methodological, pre-procedural. As illustration
of the context of pages 286-287 of Method in Theology
one might consider "instrumental acts of meaning" as a
multivalued variable over the nine specifications of
the differentiation of basic relations, and one might
go on to grapple with heuristic categories for that portion of the second specification involving instrumental
acts of meaning in music.[60]

Obviously such indications of elements of
dialectic and pieces of foundations can, and will, be
multiplied into volumes. But instead of scattering ourselves on proleptic illustrations which may well be lost
on the younger reader let us focus a question on the core
issue of the emergence and maturation of intellectual
conversion.

You may, then, have sympathy with Lonergan's
position on the isomorphism of knowing and being. But
does your sympathy extend to a personal general explanatory heuristic of the universe? Or does your sympathy
at least reach back to a "clear memory of its startling
strangeness"?[60a] Or perhaps your sympathy goes no further than the admission, say, that chapter seven of
Insight is a rather readable account of features of the
sociology of prejudice, but not strange?

The three questions touch on three levels of
sympathy. Let us start with the last question, calling
Hegel to our aid. Then we will return to the question
of memory and in that ambience treat of the question of
general heuristics.

> Things inside things endure
> Longer than things exposed;
> We see because we are blind
> And should not be surprized to find
> We survive because we're enclosed.
> . . . .
> The real is rightly intolerable,
> Its countenance stark and abrupt.
> Good souls, to survive, select
> Their symbols from among the elect -
> Articulate, suave, corrupt.
>
> But from corruption comes the deep
> Desire to plunge to the true;
> To dare is to redeem the blood,
> Discover the buried good,
> Be vulnerably new.[61]

First, then, let us glimpse the possibilities of the Proustian strategy of meshing, on our desks, in our sensibilities, and eventually in another larger book that someone surely must write, the two aggregates Insight and The Phenomenology of Mind. Recall the conclusion to chapter seven of Insight: "Our account of common sense related it to its neural basis and relates aggregates and successions of instances of common sense to one another." Recall the beginnings of Hegel's dialectic of Lordship and Bondage: "Self-consciousness exists in itself and for itself, in that, and by the fact that it exists for another self-consciousness; that is to say, it is only by being acknowledged or 'recognized'." Next, bring my comment on the reading with limited and insufficient sympathy of chapter seven of Insight into imaginative symbiosis with G.A. Kelly's comment on readings of Hegel's Lordship and Bondage: "Many modern readings - inspired by Kojève's artful exegesis in his Introduction à la lecture de Hegel - tend to distort lordship and bondage in the total Hegelian structure. Though every student of Hegel is deeply enriched by Kojeve, this experience is not without its dangers. In the present case, the difficulty seems to me chiefly twofold: the subjectivity of the scenario is largely ignored, and the master-slave relationship is made an unqualified device for clarifying the progress of human history."[62] Brief expression of the book-length suggestiveness of this symbiosis is obviously out of the question. What I have in mind is a new mode of the "personal spiralling" I mentioned at the beginning, a new way which would carry subjects such as you and me, not primarily towards a reinterpretation of Hegel, or a reinterpretation of Lonergan, but what, after all, they both point to, a reinterpretation by us of the subjects that we are: yet not just a reinterpretation; more, if you like, a reincarnation. I would like to have us feel our way to the position on being through a labyrinth of instrumental acts of meaning that parallel but transform the guide-lines of those first xxx + 385 pages of Insight, so that page 386 would "find" the reader not only in the position but housed[63] in the position. My present expression is summary and only distantly points. Perhaps another parallel may help, and widen the pointing: "We are no longer required to regard as fortuitous the fact that the hero of Proust's novel is named Marcel. Within the last two decades English and American poets have programmatically scuttled the sacred doctrine of the persona, the belief that the poet does not, must not, present himself to us and figure in our consciousness as a person, as a man speaking to men, but must have exclusively aesthetic

existence."[64] Must the theologian have exclusively
theological existence? A Hegelian subject-indicative
expression of Lonergan's Way[65] would be no less exacting
in regard to the elementary sciences of physics and
chemistry,[66] but it would be in a new mood, with Jack
and Jill in dialogue spiralling out of naive humanity,
contemplating the precise talk of kittens and dogs[67] and
burnt-out houses and typewriters of Lonergan's Way with
new dimensions of meaning:[68] "Place the smell of your
hand between my short-sighted face. Sway my Jill? Am
I all right Jack? Taste the feel of my life-line: it
isn't there at all."

Jack and Jill must, too, face a parallel transforming of Method in Theology if they are to mean it as
more than a document of barbarism. In the solitude of
basic authentic subjectivity, generated by such self-
digestion as a book like Insight indicates, he or she
must, at least in memoried fantasy,[69] pause on the
campus to look before and after asking "to whom shall I
turn?", slowly thus discovering the eightfold Way.
"Such an objectification of subjectivity is in the style
of the crucial experiment."[70]

These are, no doubt, impossibly brief hints.
What we need perhaps is someone to play Fichte to
Lonergan's Kant, searching out continuously for a "Sun-
clear Statement to the Public at large concerning the
true nature of the Newest Philosophy. An attempt to
force the reader to an understanding."[71] It is, of
course, an impossible dream. Sun-clarity is not given
to him or her who emerges from Plato's Cave in temporality, and a house for the position is a matter of
beatific ultimacy.[72]

> Cogito ergo sum. I close my eyes
> and go back seventeen years.
> Mother Marie-Therese writes it on
> the blackboard. Her arm is bare
> to the elbow: the sleeve of her
> habit is rolled up to avoid chalk
> dust. "I think, therefore I am,"
> she says. Where the Latin was
> just something to translate, the
> English jumps and my hand is up
> (unlike me, that,) and when
> Mother sees me I ask wouldn't it
> have been more correct for him to
> have said "Memento ergo sum?"[73]

This essay, obviously, is no more than a set of

indications of the opening out of procedural analysis,
especially of that dimension of procedural analysis
which coincides with fourth level specializations.[74]
And, as my title indicates, there is the more particular
interest in the transfigured manifestation of the metaphysical equivalents[75] of truths regarding procedural
analysis and its growth. Here, then, I must move on to
yet another indication, an indication of what now appears
to me to be focal to our personal struggle against the
menace of experiential conjugation within the study of
interiority. I write "now," although for a decade it
has, so to speak, been staring me in the face. For a
decade I have lectured here and there on that key paragraph in Insight with its bracketed statement, "...the
discovery (and one has not made it yet if one has no
clear memory of its startling strangeness) that there
are two quite different realisms..."[76] Yet it was only
while working on this paper's topic that I awoke, or
began my awakening[77] to what I am about to "reveal" to
you. And you will "have it" then, and you will have no
difficulty in remembering it. And there precisely is
the difficulty. Perhaps you will find, like Proust,
that it is a matter of a certain type of reading over
and over: "And I continued to read over the invitation,
until the letters which made up the name, so familiar
and yet so mysterious, rebelled, declared their inde-
pendence and seemed to outline before my weary eyes a
name that was strange to me."[78] Perhaps, too, if your
religion includes a sacred book, you have experienced
a meditative reading such as Proust's, or such as the
Carthusian monk who wrote, "I read somewhere that
books are of more value for what they do not say than
for what they do. The reader is like a man gazing at
a horizon. Beyond the outlines that he sees, he seeks
perspectives he barely discerns, but which draw him
precisely because of the mysteries he senses in them.
So, the books one loves are those which make one think.
One seeks in them that silence whence the words were
born, which is these depths of the soul which no language can express, for they are beyond expression. It
is here we touch what is measureless, eternal and divine
in us."[79]

But what is this name, this invitation, to which
I awoke? As far as I recall (and that word points a
Viconesque ricorso at the centre of this paper) it was
about the time of my reading of Bachelard's remarks on
reading.[80] Certainly it was before I read Proust, for
it was the awakening that led me to Proust and to an
enlargement of that awakening. To discover, further,
that Herbert Marcuse agrees with me is not so much an

enlargement as the provision of a quotable quotation
with which I introduce you to the name and the invitation: "The restoration of remembrance to its rights,
as a vehicle of liberation, is one of the noblest tasks
of thought. In this function remembrance (Errinerung)
appears at the conclusion of Hegel's Phenomenology of
Spirit: in this function, it appears in Freud's theory."[81]

The name is memory, the invitation to remember.
Years previously I had "read" Eros and Civilization, but
had I read these words?[82] But, then, as I remarked, the
little phrase,[83] "no clear memory of its startling
strangeness" had been "read" long before, had been for
years a slogan, and again Bergson's distinction between
two types of memory had been a favorite weapon against
the power of naming. And here I have named something
akin to Bergson's "memory which relives" in a new
context: and will the naming effect you any more than
the reading of the word "memory" in the little phrase
from page xxviii of Insight previously effected me?
Writing of Ruskin's influence on Proust and through him
on his literary descendents, Andre Maurois remarks, "a
single copy of a book, transplanted by chance and fallen
upon a mind that was receptive ground for that particular
way of feeling, is enough to introduce to a patch of
ground a plant that did not previously exist and that
suddenly thrives and overruns it."[84] The problem centres
fantastic[85] fertility of feeling knit into quest. The
problem relating to another context, is to feel the
"large and commonly obscure gap in which the heuristic
anticipation of insight can pass muster for the occurrence of insight and the partial insight for mastery."[86]
The problem, one might say, is conversion-poise, where
I give conversion a meaning broad enough to include
Debussy's reaction to Stravinski's Le Sacre du Printemps
with his gratitude for "the enlargement of the boundaries
of the permissible in the empire of sound,"[87] and by
"poise" I mean something equivalently broad, something
also remote, of adult-growth, and belonging to a position on being. Maslow remarks: "Very important today,
in a topical sense, is the realization that plateau
experiencing can be achieved, learned, earned by long
hard work. It can be meaningfully aspired to. But I
don't know of any way of bypassing the necessary
maturing experiencing, living, and learning. All of
this takes time. A transient glimpse is certainly
possible in the peak experiences which may, after all,
come sometimes to anyone. But, so to speak, to take
up residence on the high plateau of Unitive consciousness, that is another matter altogether. That tends
to be a life-long effort. It should not be confused

with any single experience. The "spiritual disciplines"
both the classical ones and the new ones that keep on
being discovered these days, all take time, and work,
discipline, study, and commitment."[88]

The poise I speak of is still more remote, for
it is a plateau-poise of integral heuristic perspective[89]
which, despite that integrality and because of it,[90]
incarnates an expectation of, a listening for, infinite
surprise, when a previous plateau may fall away to yield
another[91] integral perspective, from which one views and
feels a bank, a book, a friend, in a new-toned way.   In
this perspective - or should I say one of these remote
perspectives? - the problem becomes to-self-manifest
(think again of Heidegger) in all patterns of temporal
subjectivity, in the modes of address[92] of age by youth,
of art by common sense,[93] and it becomes in temporality
individually stumblingly soluble only through a self-
correcting process of learning, living and belief
mediated by ultimate fleshed concern.[94]

Let me turn back here to the early stages of
that learning, to the "startling strangeness," to what
I have elsewhere called the Bridge of Asses in philosophy.   That stage itself is not easily reached, and
when it is reached it remains indeed clear in recall.
But I ask for self-digestion[95] within that startling
strangeness.   While it is true of the subject in a
pattern of self-affirmation within the position that
"no man is born in that pattern; no one reaches it
easily; no one remains in it permanently; and when some
other pattern is dominant, then the self of our self-
affirmation seems quite different from one's actual
self, the universe of being seems as unreal as Plato's
noetic heaven, and objectivity spontaneously becomes a
matter of meeting persons and dealing with things that
are 'really out there',"[96] still, there is the possibility of countering opposing patterns by the cultivation of supporting, sustaining, patterns of cultivation
of "a transformation of sensitivity and intersubjectivity
penetrating to the physiological level."[97]   There are
possibilities for a "philosophic space,"[98] there are
possibilities for integral position symbols,[99] there
are possibilities for a sensitivity[100] to the position,
and these possibilities can become probabilities through
sustained digestive memory.   Without such strange-made
strange-making memory and sensitivity, even foundational
position-dialogue, where subjects sharing elements of
the position on being seek to move towards common
objectifications, can be shot through with the distor-
tions of the habitual naive view of meaning of our

first decades of life. Habitual achievement in this
zone, however, is so rare as to be impossible: the gap
between _intentio entis_ that is each of us at core, and
our temporal sensibility, is infinite. Still, there is
the goal: to provide the position on being, literally,
with a house. Mind and, strangely, sensibility are in
integral infinite potency,[101] and fidelity to the position would seem to require a continued repentant[102]
incarnate stretching: "Late in life, with indomitable
courage, we continue to say that we are going to do what
we have not yet done: we are going to build a house."[103]

Proust spelt out his inspiration, his special
way of evoking the past through a reinforcing coincidence
of present sensation and memory, over thousands of pages
and thousands of days - it is a way of sustaining,
spirally, attention, of _ricorso_. A short paper can only
point, but it points no less to thousands of the reader's
days.

In speaking of memory I have also touched on
fantasy, and would now recall my initial quotation in
this richer context. Sensibility digested in flexed
affective memory opens out to the future in further
fantasy. But by fantasy I do not mean free flights of
fancy. I do not mean Daniel Bell's advice to the
Commission on the Year 2000 to "think wild".[104]

I mean the stretching of the total imagination
(think of the possibilities of fuller living as they are
embedded in the range of arts) within the fleshed-out
intention of being.[105] Without such stretching of the
foundational imagination what substance can there be
to concrete-intending categories for doctrines on eternal
life, for systematic analogues of what "hath not entered
into the heart of man," for an effective communication
to scientists and artists "that the splendour of the
world is a cipher, a revelation, an invitation, the
presence of one who is not seen, touched, grasped, distinguished by a difference, yet present"?[106]

> "Confidently Vico looked forward
> to a panetymological dictionary
> of thought-words, a sort of
> theoretical counterpart of
> Leibnitz's dreamed-of universal
> and symbolic language. 'Such a
> lexicon is necessary,' said Vico,
> 'for learning the language spoken
> by the ideal eternal history
> traversed in time by the histories
> of all nations'."[107]

Our procedure in these past sections has been determined by the three questions regarding sympathy with Lonergan's position, and now we have reached back to the question of a sympathy which extends to an adequate Weltanschauung. But whether the reader is with me at this stage depends on where the reader "was at" from the beginning, whether the counterpointing footnotes controlled adequately the pace, the pauses, and so on. The essay is a map to a way: if the reader has already traversed a similar way then he or she has a habitual understanding and memory and strangeness.[108] But if the way has not been travelled then what the reader has is a vague description of an enterprize. We are back of course at the old problem of words. Let us push on, however, to the question of a general heuristics of words.

One of the troubles of the old Thomism was the easy descriptive derivability and nameability of its elements. So, for example, out of change - more graphically, say, the death of a dog - one could arrive at the need for form and matter (...plus la même chose!), and whatever tricky talk might occur about the nature of the distinction between essence and existence, the distinction was made. And, as in the Black Theatre of Prague, the real actors, the intelligible proceedings in the subjects, were nowhere in sight. I have long puzzled over the problem of such facile nameability. For one thing one might ask whether it be a property of a correct view on being that it be trivializable?[109] Certainly it has the traversibility of a city as opposed to that of a maze. And what is one to do, then, to prevent immediate post-everything[110] nameability, whether it be for acceptance or rejection? Realize Vico's dream in a new Joyce, so that Lonergan's Way becomes Finnegan Sway? Perhaps, indeed, we need a topology of truth such as will make it as indescribable as a Klein bottle, or an obscure inept symbolism like Woodger tried in biology,[110a] or something like C. S. Peirce's Existential Graphs with their meshing of containing curves suggestive of complexity and hierarchic integration.[111]

A beginning of useful symbolism certainly might be had from mathematics. So, for example, one may symbolize a heuristic definition of man as $F(p_i, c_j, b_k, z_e, u_m, r_n)$, where the main letters in the function stand for levels of conjugages, b= botanical, etc., and the subscripts indicate the range of conjugages on that level e.g. z_{6_2} might refer to a particular form of animal aggression.[112] Certainly it gives more symbolic feedback than animal rationale, and it raises the problem of level-linkage in evident fashion: the commas in the expression are like small question-marks hovering over

the issue of randomness of sets of lower acts and the
presence of higher forms.[113] Moreover, it points to
the need for a scientific "filling out" of the heuristic
form,[114] and continually more so as the filling out
modifies the symbols towards expressing, for example,
subfunctions of chemical aggregates relevant, within
limits,[115] to certain forms of feeling. Again, more
complex symbolization would be required to control
one's insights into, for example, Betcherevian reflexology as underpinning Durand's categorization of symbols.[116]
But here we are touching on a much more tricky and basic
complexification, for u_m is not merely a level of integrated zoological acts, it involves the twist of the
feature of being named meaning. Here is no place to
struggle with the problem of a possible symbolic expression of an explanatory heuristic of meaning, but an
illustrative problem may be raised relating to our main
topic.

Let us consider words, spoken words say. Recall
Chomsky and his followers in linguistics, or any other
group known to you which seeks to specify words as words
and words as meant.[117] If you are operating within the
suggested general explanatory heuristic of man, then you
will find yourself carrying forward Aquinas' discussion
of products of the respiratory tract[118] into a contemporary context, and casting into that same explanatory
heuristic such indications as that of "a triple correlation of classified experiences, classified contents of
experience, and corresponding names."[119] Such a heuristic would, I think be enormously valuable to the Chomsky
school. Unfortunately, that value is conditioned by a
twofold handicap under which linguistics, and with it
structuralism, functionalism and systems theory, all
labour: the lack of any explanatory thematic resembling
the position on being and the further lack of what I
would call an aggreformist perspective.[120] Piaget
remarks of Chomsky: "Chomsky sees only two alternatives
- either an innate schema that governs with necessity,
or acquisition from outside (cultured and therefore
variable determination such as cannot account for the
limited and necessary character of the schema in
question) - there are in fact three possibilities. There
is heredity versus acquisition from outside, true; but
there is also the process of internal equilibration."[121]
Piaget goes on to advocate the retention of Chomsky's
theories while dropping his innatism, the latter to be
replaced by Piaget's own constructivist hypothesis.[122]
But this entire debate does not take on serious
epistemological dimensions,[123] nor can it without an
adventure in interiority. Again - to indicate explicitly

the second lack - systems theory has its epistemological problems:

"Although the world appears to function as a whole, our best representations come out piecemeal. If the world is a whole there should be some complex, multilevel representation possible. The design of such a multilevel construct depends on a methodology for the valid organization of systems into suprasystems. Whereas the inverse problem of analytic resolution of a system into subsystems is readily treated by such top-down approaches as deduction, and single level systems are amenable through induction or statistical procedures, there is no corresponding technique for vertical bottom-up organization. This lacuna is a task for a new epistemology."[124] The lacuna is to be filled by a precise conception, "not without labour,"[125] of what I would call aggreformism, a version of Aristotle's hylemorphism, but such a version as can emerge in explanatory conception only in a mind which has explanatorily conceived and affirmed, for example, both the aggregate of chemical events within the genus Chlamydomonas and the correlations which inform the recurrence-schemes of botanical activity, or both the aggregate of neural events in the rabbit and the schemes of recurrence which systematize them, etc., etc. Without the aggreformist perspective mediated by the strange-memory of such a conception, systems theory will remain ill at ease and unable to "stack properly" the world with its many sciences and arts. On a smaller scale, linguistics will remain unable to "stack properly" the complex hierarchy which is the word (or even the spontaneous cough: the distinction between the two obviously adds a basic complexification) in the face of the growing body of neurolinguistics, biolinguistics, etc.[126] And I suspect indeed that the increasing number of people interested in systematic understanding such as is offered by Systems theory, in so far as they remain in dialogue, as open subjects,[127] with empirical studies, will eventually arrive at the larger systems theory which rests on critically-established aggreformism.

And here I take pleasure in admitting to the reader my deviousness. For, we have moved in this section from the initial question of adequate instruments of meaning, through the problem of the expression of a general heuristics of such instrumental acts as spoken words, to the source of basic solution to all these problems: open dialogue. Openness is an aspect of the solution we may pass over. The dialogue I have in mind here is that of the eighth functional specialty, the

dialogue of theology in its external relations, a
dialogue which statistically obviates dwindling on both
sides of the conversation.[128]

This topic of dialogue is enormously complex
and perhaps it is as well to conclude my ramblings
round[129] the problem of possible instruments and instrumental acts of meaning with such a large opening question.

I have touched, in the immediately preceding
paragraphs, mainly on the problem of interdisciplinary
dialogue. But the reader might ponder just what large
issues are involved, for example, in changing the
statistics of good sermons.[130] It is not enough to
advise preaching-students on the probability of their
adult-dwindling, on the folly of putting their thumbs
in the dyke of social work instead of putting their
minds systematically to their Faithful minds. For, the
students and the preachers and the teachers are within
schemes of schemes etc., etc. One needs then, also,
foundational reflection on categories for other probable
schemes and for possible schemes for persuading, or
gently replacing, the eminent, the influential and
those who plan or fail to do so.[131]

"As we said in another publication,
the keystone to Irish thinking is
summed up in the phrase, 'And where
will that get him?' when someone
refers to the achievements of a
great poet or thinker. Undoubtedly
it will get him nowhere if you don't
believe in the God of life, the
God of the grass, of the sun. What
kind of world would it be if there
was no hope, if we all felt and
said with the average Gael: 'where
will that get him?'

There would be no Shakespeare, no
Homer, nor a Saint Thomas Aquinas.
There would only be, as here, men
swilling themselves into forget-
fulness.

In our time the Welfare State is
doing all it can to produce some
sort of synthetic substance which
will take the place of a divine
purpose in the lives of the
people."[132]

I must conclude my unscientific prescript on the shaping of the foundations. It is evidently not an essay in foundations, and as methodology or procedural analysis it lacks precision. If it also is obscure, then there is consolation in the fact that it could have been more obscure, like the instrumental acts of meaning of Chesterton's Irishman.[133] I am content if I have seriously raised some questions and fruitfully fractured some psyches. I have avoided treatise-style in the chapter and the book, and in concluding this chapter I will also avoid any descriptive procedural analysis of it: what was going forward or round in my speaking and in your listening, and why? But I hope that, in memory and in fantasy, we have been and are somewhat in dialogue. Readers of different traditions will, obviously, resonate differently with me. For those of my own Christian tradition there is, for example, the relation of enlarged memory and fantasy to an adequate personal memoria passionis resurrectionisque Ejus. Again, readers of all traditions may feel that I have someway dodged issues: but it was a studied dodging. I did not think the time was ripe for an axial review of expression or self-referent linguistic feedback within procedural analysis: but, as is apparent, I do think that ongoing control of theological meaning requires more elaborate crutches in expression. The elementary science of space and time would be nowhere without the symbolism of n-dimensional differential geometry and the tensor calculus.[134] Much less can one hold the man Christ in explanatory heuristic perspective without heuristic expression, non sine artificio,[135] an expression for instance, manifesting his manhood in aggreformist hierarchy.[136]

Already in this book I have raised the problem of the need for artifices and strategies of expression. Most crudely, I drew attention in chapter one[137] to the range and specialization of journals in the field of botany in contrast to the unhappy state of theological journals and discourse. In the conclusion of that chapter I noted the need for embodiment in theological conversation.[138] In chapter three[139] I indicated possible strategies of suffixes manifesting different horizons and different levels of development of linguistic meaning, and when one ventures into the new fields dealing with the roots and rhythms of language one adds a need for further strategies of differentiated expression. So, when the questions of communications in theology is raised it is not enough to note the existence of the eight functional specialties. Even without the complexities noted here, it is evident, for example, that the exegete expresses himself differently to his colleagues, his pupils, his preaching community.[140] One is led then to think of communications in theology in terms of an 8x8 symmetrical matrix C_{ij}, i and j running over the numbers 1 to 8 in correspondence with the eight functional specialties. Moreover, the elements of the matrix would be conceived as submatrices to take in the complexities of internal and external relatedness, and most of the elements wouldhave reference to the six-levelled hierarchy that is the communicating temporal person. Have I moved into fantasy? Yes, and in my view a necessary concrete fantasy that may help to lift theologians in the culture of their lives and of their journals into a serious admission into consciousness and expression of Butterfield's Thesis that the scientific revolution "outshines everything since the rise of Christianity and reduces the Renaissance and Reformation to the rank of mere episodes".[141] The Shaping of the Foundations is only beginning. The Epilogue will indicate an ABC of that beginning.

Further details are not immediately important here. What is important is the raising, with some precision and fantasy, of the question of the need for modernity in symbol and diagram to control and expand the methodology of on-going process. Some such mesh of symbols would broaden the perspective of the dialectician towards a more massive effective and affective retrieval, and open the foundational theologian's possibilities of objectifying elements relevant to the last three specialties. For example, the shift from the fundamental theology of the fifties to the foundational theology of the nineties[142] is a massive task of anamnesis and prolepsis, involving communications in high and low places between churches, between department heads, between various incipient functional specialists. That shift is made more probable by the mesh of symbolic indications and a broad concrete normative heuristic, thus inclusive of fantasy as defined (bringing the Cardinal[143] to dinner is only a minor fantasy, but not irrelevant!).[144]

I have already made mention illustratively of the concrete intention of skin-colours and dialects on the part of the dialectic theologian.[145] It illustrates too the principle of subsidiary Selbstvollzug,[146] whereby members of subgroups would raise the issue of what is going forward and why, in the decades of our journals, in our classes, in our conventions, in our proceedings.

I would end by recalling that almost all of what I have written here was written for conferences

devoted to the thought of Fr. Bernard Lonergan, now in
his seventies, "perched on giant stilts".[147] Theology's
debt to him will only gradually emerge. My own indebted-
ness to him is evident. I recall now Stephen McKenna's
twenty years of work on the translation of Plotinus'
writings. His diary on his thirty-eighth birthday was
later found to contain the remark that this was "surely
worth a life". The same I think can much more surely
be said of the writings of Fr. Lonergan.

"Mick frowned, considering this.
-Questions of dogma you mean?
These can be involved matters.
-Straightforward attention to the
word of God, Joyce rejoined, will
confound all Satanic quibble. Do
you know the Hebrew language?
-I'm afraid I do not.
-Ah, too few people do. The word
ruach is most important. It means
a breath or a blowing. Spiritus
we call it in Latin. The Greek
word is pneuma. You see the
train of meaning we have here?
All these words mean life. Life,
and breath of life. God's breath
in man.
-Do these words mean the same thing?
-No. The Hebrew ruach denoted only
the Divine Being, anterior to man.
Later it came to mean the inflam-
mation, so to speak, of created
man by the breath of God.
-I find that not very clear.
-Well ... one needs experience in
trying to grasp celestial concepts
through earthly words."[148]

EPILOGUE:

AUTHENTIC SUBJECTIVITY AND INTERNATIONAL
GROWTH: FOUNDATIONS

> Mallarmé, don't you know, he said,
> has written those wonderful prose
> poems Stephen McKenna used to
> read to me in Paris. The one
> about Hamlet. He says: il se
> promène, lisant au livre de lui-
> même, don't you know, reading the
> book of himself."[1]

The issue throughout has been the shaping of
foundations, and the epilogue, predictably, does not
close off the issue, but rather opens it out. Moreover,
the opening out is not an undefined opening out but a
definite indication of an enriching direction of
foundational reflection. That enriching direction might
best be indicated at this stage in terms of two books
cited below: Heidegger's Being and Time and Voegelin's
The Ecumenic Age.[2] The first book helps to point to the
need for a recurrent reflective return to the lower
ground of Dasein's spatiality and temporality, to what
I call the ABC of foundations.[3] The second book calls
for a more profound eschatological reflection: "Through
the differentiations of consciousness, history becomes
visible as the process in which the differentiations
occur... Since the differentiating events are experienced
as immortalizing movements, history is discovered as the
process in which reality becomes luminous for the movement beyond its own structure; the structure of history
is eschatological".[4] One might say, then, that the
living of foundational authenticity requires continual
rediscovery of the bracketing residues - lower and upper
- of historical being.

The epilogue indicates a further movement towards
that foundational authenticity. It does so in six parts
which correspond to the six words in its title:
(1) subjectivity, (2) authentic, (3) and, (4) international, (5) growth, (6) foundations. It goes a stage
further in the search for an answer to the question
which has been with us from the beginning, the question
of the conception, affirmation and implementation of
what it is to grow old and wise.

1. Subjectivity

I restrict myself to the topic of human subjectivity.

By human subjectivity I mean the intelligible unity-identity-whole[5] genetically and dialectically integrative[6] of the six-levelled events of the life[7] of a man or a woman.[8]

What I am meaning here is a valued conception and affirmation of part[9] of the integral heuristic structure of the proportionate being that is a man or a woman. Let me indicate some elements of that conception.

We are obviously focusing here, in a manner to be explicated in the second section, on an instance in ourselves of the notion of a thing. Now just as "things are conceived as extended in space, permanent in time, and yet subject to change",[10] so are men and women. But let us not be too hasty about the meaning here of the space and time of men and women, or the meaning of change in their regard. The space and time of the six-levelled hierarchy of genetico-dialectically integrated aggregates of aggregates of aggregates of aggregates of aggregates that is a man or a woman is a six-levelled deeper complexity.[11] To take a simple[12] component of that heuristic conception of human space and time, there is the space and time of human physics and chemistry which has recently attracted attention under the rubric of brainwave and biofeedback analysis and which may be conceived of heuristically, within each level, as problems of primary relativity and secondary determinations,[13] and in its instrumental aspect[14] in terms of aggreformism,[15] of physical, chemical and neural demand functions[16] and of vertical finality.[17] The explanatory heuristic conception of human change meshes with and sublates that conception, and even in its biogenetic aspect it is already discouragingly complex. One of my favourite comments on this matter comes from the biologist Paul Weiss who begins his lengthy text book on the topic Development with the remark that the question, What is development?, seems trivial: "Does not everybody have some notion of what development implies? Undoubtedly most of us have. But when it comes to formulate these notions they usually turn out to be vague."[18]

Now Weiss was discussing a development whose operator is of the order of plant irritability or zoological consciousness. But in the human subject these operators are sublated by a hierarchy of three

operators - questions for intelligence, questions for
reflection, questions for deliberation - to yield four
levels of operation,[19] related upwardly in vertical
finality and downwardly in the transforming presence of
ultimacy at the apex animae.[20]   Moreover, just as the
heuristic conception of subjectivity is of a unity-
identity-whole, so the six-levelled person, never other
than one,[21] grows - within a tension of the limitation
and transcendence implied by the operators[22] - towards
being a more or less integral solution to the problem
of living, of surviving:[23] whatever the state of the
integration, the operators are inevitably meshed in
the concrete homo viator.[24] There is the obvious
dialectically-successful meshing of insight and phantasm, of evaluation and feeling, but there is the wider
dimension of dynamic meshing that becomes thematic when
the core of survival[25] is conceived in the context of
total process,[26] bracketed thus in finality between "the
unconscious, an irrepresentable totality of all subliminal
psychic factors, a 'total vision' in potentia"[27] and the
Eschaton.[28a]

One must conceive further that "the higher system
of intelligence develops not in a material manifold but
in the psychic representation of material manifolds,"[28b]
and that the heuristic conception of such development
involves the conception of sets[29] and sequences[30a] of
differentiations of consciousness.

Finally, "what the psychologist aims at understanding completely, the metaphysician outlines in
heuristic categories,"[30b] and contemporary psychology
would seem to be in dire need of such categories.

There is the need, for one thing, of a general
explanatory heuristic to make possible the transition -
which cannot but be slow and uncomfortably empirical[31]
- from conceptions of subjectivity in terms of id, ego,
persona, etc.,[32] or in the confused terms that mesh
reductionism with descriptive conjugation,[33] to a
heuristic conception that would exploit to the fullest
the potentialities of metaphysical equivalence.[34]
Perhaps a paragraph-pause on this last point would not
be wasted:

"Metaphysical equivalence possesses a special
significance in the human sciences. For man is a being
in whom the highest level of integration is, not a
static system, nor some dynamic system, but a variable
manifold of dynamic systems. For the successive systems
that express the development of human understanding are

systems that regard the universe of being in all its
departments. To that development the human organism
and the human psyche have to find appropriate adaptations. In consequence of that development, the range
of human skills and techniques, of economies and politics, of sciences and philosophies, of cultures and
religions is diversified. Only the broadest set of
concepts can provide the initial base and the field of
differences that will be adequate to dealing with a
variable set of moving systems that regard the universe
of being."[35]

There is, secondly, the need for a thorough
exploitation of genetic and dialectic method, so
briefly indicated by Lonergan,[36] to bring forth a normative account of adult growth.[37]

Thirdly, there is the root need for the transformation of the horizons of human scientists and scholars[38]
so that their correlating and hypothesizing would be
mediated by a explanatory thematic of interiority. For,
normatively speaking, the basic terms of psychology -
and they do not become irrelevant when one moves to
sociology, history, politics, economics or theology -
intend conscious operations of subjects, and the basic
relations intend conscious processes,[39] and what is to
be explained is what we have been naming in the previous
pages. At the risk of repetition, I note a useful
parallel. In zoology, "it is far easier to describe
organs and functions" than to trans rm one's constitutive heuristic by taking the stand that "an explanatory
account of animal species will differentiate animals not
by their organic but by their psychic differences."[40]
In parallel fashion - but with a positive infinity of
difference - it is far easier to describe the feeling
thinking actor child that is father to the man in terms,
however suggestive, that place that concrete <u>intentio
entis</u> in a space and time that subtly negate that
<u>intentio entis</u>, rather than to read the baby, bride,
godfather, grandmother, "loud and clear" from the perspective of one constituted adequately in the third
stage of meaning[41] as subjects growing into the many
species of worlds mediated by meaning.[42]

"...so the present discussion ends. It has all
been, of course, very general."[43]

2. <u>Authentic</u>

But has it? Or rather, what does "very general"
mean: which means, of course, in particular what does

it mean to the writer and reader? What would the meaning
be for one writing or reading "loud and clear" from the
perspective of one adequately constituted[44] in the third
stage of meaning, in the habit of the "very general"
categories named in Method in Theology?[45]

Here I would like to make my own the statement
that "the basic idea of the method we are trying to
develop takes its stand on discovering what human
authenticity is."[46] And the direction of my enterprize
might be intimated by focusing on the phrase "takes its
stand on discovering." But let us begin by a glimpse at
the general question of authenticity.[47]

I have in fact in the previous section been
categorizing the genus human authenticity, the self-
transcending realization of human potentiality[48] so often
written of by Fr. Lonergan in terms of the norms of attention, intelligence, reasonableness and responsibility
but now more recently meshed with his rediscovery[49] of
the surge of being and of finite subject in nerve and
apex animae.

But the categorizing of the previous section was
also a sign-posting: for the categories indicated were
the general categories of foundations, and the sign-
posting was not of general authenticity but of that
species of authenticity which would reach for a "contemporary, concrete, dynamic, maximal view that en-
deavors to envisage the range of human potentiality and
to distinguish authentic from unauthentic realization
of that potentiality."[50]

Such an authenticity is manifestly not essential
to human authenticity. It is a type of authenticity
that has no place in the subjectivity of such as are
called like Julian of Norwich: "Our good Lord showed
that it is the greatest pleasure to Him that a simple
soul come to Him nakedly, plainly and homely. This is
the kind yearning of the soul, through the touching of
the Holy Ghost."[51] Nor had this type of authenticity
any place in the human subjectivity of Jesus of
Nazareth. Whether it be in the process of prayer or of
problem-solving, "Jesus did not objectify the process,
neither did he make an inventory of the contents of
his mind."[52] To use a metaphor developed later here,
there are more ways to the Still Point and the mediation
of progress than the pilgrim way through the vortex of
method.[53] "And what is my way?" It is for each one to
answer out of the contingencies of one's nerves and
years, one's bread and butter, one's hopes, one's loves,

one's fears, within the concrete mesh of the universe's
need. My hope is that the reflection on the personal
contingencies and on the needs of the universe mediated
by Lonergan's challenge would change the statistics of
personal admission that "never has adequately differentiated consciousness been more difficult to achieve.
Never has the need to speak to undifferentiated consciousness been greater."[54] What is meant by "admission"
however has all the complexity of the subjects that you
and I are in the possibilities of concretely specifying
over the years the genuineness that is a continued,
precarious yet gentle, "admission of tension into consciousness."[55] What I will do, therefore, is briefly
indicate two limiting types of the admission that are
significant for progress. The two types have been
touched on in another context, and it seems worthwhile
to borrow substantially from that context: "Present
philosophers may argue that I spell out an impossible
task. In one sense I do, for, what I describe is the
possible philosopher of the future, a type of philosopher
not concretely communally possible at present. Yet, my
title indicates that I speak of the future of present
philosophers. That future is the task of cultivating
much-needed authentic methodologists. Undoubtedly such
a cultivation would require a transformation of education, not merely at university level, where a methodological component is now indispensible, but at all lower
levels. Still, each one can contribute in a basic
existential sense, by acknowledging the slow growth of
personal and communal understanding and by seeking to
win respect for remote meaning.[56] That respect must be
won above all within oneself, so that through a nurtured growth of awareness of this (I use awareness in
its widest sense), one becomes an incarnate acknowledgement of the mystery of man, where to the complexity of
the animal is added the elusive intelligibility of
human intelligence and the opaqueness of the absolutely
supernatural. In a certain sense, what matters for the
contemporary philosopher is not achievement but the
acknowledgement, intellectually and feelingly, that we
do not know what being is, nescimus quid sit ens."[57]

The possibile philosopher I had described was
one whose conversion to the world of theory was guaran-
teed by years of devotion to modern science, yet for
whom aesthetic differentiation of consciousness was a
foundational reality that could give categorical and
functional specialist meaning to that word "aesthetic."[58]
I elsewhere described that philosopher in terms of three
degrees of sympathy with critical realism: a sympathy
which appreciates that, say, chapter seven of Insight

was not about people already out there; a deeper sympathy
grown in a Proustian cultivation of the "memory of its
startling strangeness";[59] a sympathy growing within and
with these prior sympathies towards a capacity for
authentic foundational speaking and listening.[60]

Such is an intimation of the upper limit of
admission; and perhaps the lower limit is already sufficiently indicated in the previous lengthy quotation.
It is an admission of a tension into consciousness which
may perhaps only initiate a transition in, a transformation of, one's common sense: yet that transformation
may put to personal test the cast of one's pale
thoughts.[61] So the transition, however much bound to
common sense, is profoundly relevant: for, after all,
is not "the enemy within" common sense going beyond
itself to become common sense electicism, instead of
being "confined entirely to its proper realm of the
immediate, the particular, the concrete"?[62] There is no
point in repeating here the castigation of common sense
electicism of Insight,[63] nor to recall at length what
elsewhere I called "the menace of experiential conjugation",[64] the manner "in which the heuristic anticipation
of insight can pass muster for the occurrence of insight
and the partial insight for mastery."[65] What I wish to
note here, rather, is the possibility of the admission,
into the lower consciousness of academics, of the
realities of the human mind, with a concomitant transformation of academic talk,[66] and an orientation of
one's students to a higher level of admission.

But my paper has to do with the spectrum of
possible admissions, possible projects of authentic
subjectivity. It hopes to point towards further elements in the on-going development of general heuristics.
But within that pointing is an indication of an exercise in self-questioning with regard to experienced
extension and duration which can partly mediate, even
in its disappointingness, a transformation remedial to
common sense ecclecticism.

I return to the phrase which indicates the root
of anything that blossoms from this section's print:
"I (not it) take my stand on discovering."

A foothill to the stand is a vigorous rejection
of common sense ecclecticism. "Common sense ecclecticism
brushes aside the aim of philosophy. For that aim is
the integrated unfolding of the detached, disinterested,
and unrestricted desire to know. That aim can be pur-
sued only by the exercise of theoretical understanding

and, indeed, only by the subtle exercise that understands both science and common sense in their differences and in their complementarity. But common sense ecclecticism deprecates the effort to understand. For it, problems are immutable features of the mental landscape, and syntheses are to be effected by somebody else who, when he has finished his system, will provide a name for merely another viewpoint."[67]

But can we afford this rejection of truncated[68] subjectivity, or is it not rather to be accepted as an immutable feature of the mental landscape, of the campus? "Taking a stand on discovering" lies beyond that rejection, but without that communal rejection the stand will tend to constitute not persons, but only another view.

To take a stand on discovering is to be constituted in the pathos of Wonder.[69] Being is astounding, and what is discovered remains to be rediscovered. The authentic subjectivity of the philosopher is a patient cycling and recycling of a personal vortex in a strife to constitute him as an ever-fuller objectivity. "What makes a philosopher is a movement which leads back without ceasing from knowledge to ignorance, from ignorance to knowledge, and a kind of rest in this movement."[70]

3. And

It would seem odd to pause on a conjunction. Yet the conjunction indicates a possibility of completion, and the directions of completion to be noted here are four.

There is the immediate, existential, level of completion - not unrelated, obviously to the completion spoken of on the third line or the fourth last line of page 250 of Method in Theology - which I would associate with Gaston Bachelard's remark, "it is not until his eyes have left the page that recollections of my room can be a threshold of oneirism for him."[71]

I have signposted, with some frankness, some features of the life-long process of "discovering oneself in oneself".[72] "And": how do you feel about it, with eyes departing from the page?

There are three further, wider, but no less existential directions of completion.

I have written of a valued conception and

affirmation of a partial heuristic of particular
proportionate beings, and so there is the completion
that meshes this conception with that of an integral
heuristic structure of proportionate being,[73] and fur-
there to the valued critical method contextual to
"developments in the notion of God".[74] The shifts have
been abundantly sketched in the writings of Fr. Lonergan
but perhaps I might add to my indications by drawing
attention to the remote meaning of two diagrams: the
diagram in that neglected article "Finality, Love,
Marriage";[75] the diagram of the human good in Method in
Theology;[76] the diagrams name possibilities of transformed foundations for psychology,[77] sociology[78] and
politics.[79]

     The last two directions of completion raise more
acutely the issue of "implementation".[80]

     A valued conception and affirmation of the
integral heuristic structure of being includes the
heuristic conception of implementation: subjectivity was
not conceived as inactive. Moreover, that valued conception is not an abstraction: it is constitutive of
the existent authentic subjectivity which is our topic,
of originating value.[81] And the originating value
grounds the precarious implementation which is the man
or woman's living, a continually emergent and rediscovered subjectivity.

     The two directions I would note here are direc-
tions within the Wendung Zur Idee of the 8-fold method.
There is the direction which embodies the functional
specialties of doctrines, systematics and communications. That direction goes beyond my present interest,
but I would note that the reaching for the authentic
subjectivity of which I write here is not just the task
of fourth level functional specialists. So, for example,
the pastoral theologian, grappling with the problem of
communication within sets and sequences of differentiated
consciousness, grapples limply without a self-appropriation at the level of his problem.[82]

     My final direction of, pointing to, completion
is what I might name the proleptic direction. This
last direction of completion calls for a foundational
"creative minority"[83] who would conceive heuristically
and explanatorily and with constitutive adequacy of
the universe in terms of the emergence, in accordance
with successive schedules of probability, of a conditioned series of schemes and things in the assemblage,
however, heuristic, of secondary determinations of

relations.[84] That direction is a prolepsis: the species
of upper limit authenticity is only slimly probable[85]
in the 20th century, and the shift in its statistics
pivots on the possible spectrum of admissions within
various academic and ecclesiastical forms of neglected
and truncated subjectivity.

4. International

"Even if one could determine present contradictions - and Marx did so more successfully than anyone
else - their resolution will be in terms established by
the future, whose possibilities are so varied that historical prophecy is an exercise in intuition, even if
it is couched in the language of analysis. As Marx
predicted, 'new, higher relations of production' have
evolved. However, 'higher relations of production' do
not necessitate a higher, i.e., freer, social order.
And many of the undermining contradictions of capitalism,
such as the tendency to reduce free competition, are
among the strengths of the modern economy. The dialectic
is a powerful instrument of thought - the most fruitful
way to think about ideas and the historical process.
But it cannot predict its own movement, nor transcend
the possibilities of rational process which in society
are accompanied by the chaotic, non-Rational and the mad.
One can anticipate, with varying degrees of accuracy,
the effect of reforms within the existing structure.
But proposals for fundamental change, a manifesto for
revolution, is social prophecy. A purposeful alteration
of structure anticipates the entire social process."[86]

The quotation from Goodwin's book serves to
introduce the present topic in what might be called an
expected manner. But I quote it, not to comment on its
detailed evaluation of contemporary economics in its
relation to "the individual's loss of power over his own
social existence",[87] but to move from it beyond it in a
foundational manner. My interest, if you like, is "in
terms established by the future", but only in so far as
that future is present in the invariants of the dynamism
of history. My interest is in "proposals for fundamental change, a manifesto of revolution", where however
the fundamental in question is fundamental theology,
and the revolution in question is a revolution in
theology.[88] Moreover the quotation, in this context,
serves to make a particular point. The foundational
theologian is committed to conceive of the invariants
of progress, decline, and "our future destiny".[89] In
that conception he or she must live in the memory[90] of

"the inverse aspect of metaphysical equivalence",[91] remembering that metaphysics, or the fourth level functional specialties which sublate it, "derives from the sciences the content and enrichment that actual activity brings to a dynamic structure".[92] Without the living in that memory there is a shift in the personal statistics of events of that precariousness of authentic subjectivity which may be specified as "the ever-recurrent danger of discoursing on quiddities without suspecting that quiddity means what is to be known through scientific understanding".[93]

But is there not in what I say here an implicit demand for duplication of effort among functional specialists? I would make two points. In the first palce, the functional specialist's reading and speaking stance within the specialty can be quite well defined as correlative to a basic operator of human consciousness. Specialists are distinguished not by what they read and what they speak of, but how they read and how they speak.[94] Secondly, reading or writing within the orientation of functional specialization is at present as underdeveloped as was observing or theorizing in physics within the orientation of the integral or differential calculus at the time of Newton.

How then is the foundations person to conceive of what is international and of international growth? Since this is a sketch, a signposting, let me speak rather in mood than in metaphysical elements,[95] and in a quotation the total context of which is obviously relevant to our discussion of subjectivity.

"Millions of years of ancestral experience are stored up in the instinctive reactions of organic matter, and in the functions of the body there is incorporate a living knowledge, almost universal in scope, but not accompanied by any sort of consciousness. During the last few thousand years the human mind has laboriously made itself conscious, through its scientific knowledge of physics, chemistry, biology, endocrinology, and psychology, of some meager fragments of what the cells, functional systems, and organisms "knowingly" do in their adaptations and reactions. By reason of this incorporated knowledge the pleromatic phase of the uroboros is also intuited as one of primordial wisdom. The Great Mother has a wisdom infinitely superior to the ego, because the instincts and archetypes that speak through the collective unconscious represent the 'wisdom of the species' and its will."[96]

How is one to conceive, with adequate explanatory heuristic in the undertow of psychic resonance, of these millions of years, of the grounded dynamism of the Great Mother of history gestating the embryo of the Eschaton? Perhaps I weary the reader, but it is my personal stand: only by facing the slow decades-long personal task not only of conceiving the basic nest of terms and relations rooted in attention, intelligence, reasonableness, responsibility and love, but also of differentiating them with concrete explanatory non-deductivist authenticity in the manner described in pages 286-291 of Method in Theology, only through such an effort of existential conception can there emerge the adequate 21st century foundations for "a treatise on the concrete universal that is mankind in the concrete and cumulative consequences of the acceptance or rejection of the message of the Gospel".[97] Moreover, whatever the psychic trips of the Eschaton, that conception is in no way a drive towards imaginative synthesis.[98] How can the existential subject move, then, towards that conception, with less precariousness, without betraying subtly the growing objectivity that is the isomorphic fruit of authentic subjectivity?[99] How is one to re-member, to be mind-ful of, not to forget, Being? "He who attempts this sort of thing does not just 'busy himself' with 'merely verbal significations'; he must venture forward into the most primoridal problematic of the 'things themselves' to get such 'nuances' straightened out".[100] "And if the 'world' itself is something constitutive for Dasein, one must have an insight into Dasein's basic structures in order to treat the world-phenomenon conceptually".[101]

One may fruitfully note here a complexity in the defining of 'international' - does it not already call for a defining of 'growth'? - that parallels and indeed multiply includes the definition of subjectivity.[102] "While common sense relates things to us, our account of common sense relates it to its neural basis and relates aggregates and successions of instances of common sense to one another".[103] But the heuristic conception of international is the far larger achievement of relating aggregates and successions of instances of variously differentiated consciousness to one another,[104] within the matrix of generalized emergent probability. And it is within such a conception that one can tackle the problem of speaking in an explanatory fashion, in systematics, of "the fulness of time permitting the Word to become flesh and the mystical body to being its intussusception of human personalities and its leavening of human history".[105]

Let me put all this in another context, comple-
mented by a metaphor from economics that I find useful.

Moltmann, in his "Observations on the Eschatological Understanding of Christianity in Modern Society"[106]
points out the dangers of "this 'reflective philosophy
of transcendental subjectivity', as it was already called
by Hegel"[107] segregating the subject in a romanticist
way. "In harmony with this romanticist metaphysics of
subjecthood and this mental attitude of constant metaphysical reflection there then appears also the theology
which takes the cult of the absolute that has become of
no significance in our social relationships and culti-
vates it as the transcendental background of modern
existence. This is the theology which presents itself
as 'doctrine of the faith' and finds the place of faith
in the transcendental subjectivity of man. It is a
theology of existence, for which 'existence' is the relation of man to himself as this emerges in the 'total
reflection of man on himself'".[108]

In recent years I have been exploiting an analogy
between Lonergan's "longer cycle" and that long cycle in
the economy known as the Kondratieff.[109] I find it symbolically useful now to dissociate the two, and to consider "longer cycle" foundational thinking as Sargawit,[110]
the thinking forward beyond a million years, to consider
doctrinal or basic policy variations as analogous to
Kondratieff variations,[111] systematics as parallel to
Juglars, and finally communications as parallel to the
Kitchin cycles.[112]

To return now to Moltmann's problem, I would
consider the romanticist metaphysician of subjecthood,
whose "constant metaphysical reflection" is "of no
significance in our social relationships", purified of
the counter-positional elements noted partly by Moltmann,
to be the foundations person, seeking in concrete intentionality for Sargawit. I would consider his or her
primary relevance to be irrelevance. This is not to
say that there is not a wide field of secondary relevance: he or she may be fortunate enough to have
community of colleagues and students, and there is the
possibility of that mutually beneficial dialogue with,
for example, the doctrinal theologian, for whom "the
meaning of the dogma, in the context in which it was
defined"[113] is a remote personal quest requiring foundational mediation.[114]

Nor, obviously, is the foundations person
normally a solitary island: there is a personal life of

walk and talk, of tea and transport, of "reading the
universe" which to some extent - the ideal is remote -
is mediated by the full vigour of personal heuristic.
And a fuller mediation, it would seem, would be enhanced
by a transformation of perception which I will speak of
presently, a transformation, however remote personally
or communally, whose thematization would ultimately reach
the Kitchin, the kitchen, so as to make kitchen or subway
car more nearly "....a room filled with music".[115]

But whatever the colour of his, or her, personal
life - and here I would transform Moltmann's words - his
reflection places him "in a position of radical loneliness" with a freedom, balanced between discomfort and
serenity, "to stride confidently through darkness and
perplexity, and to venture and bear the responsibility
for action in the loneliness of his own decision".[116]

That darkness, that perplexity, is incarnately
bracketed between the veiled upper reaches of vertical
finality and the lower bounds of that finality in the
dispersedness of spatio-temporal being. But these
brackets are not extrinsic: they are intrinsic to the
thinker and the community of history and mediate genuine
growth through their presence, their thematization, their
psychic representation. The upper-binding Darkness can
be focused gropingly by an invariant element of ever-
growing "fructuosissima intelligentia":[117] but might it
not be foundationally underpinned by a growing grasp of
invariant elements of the lower bound, the prime potency
of history?

5. Growth

It is perhaps clear at this stage that my essay
is in various ways feeding on itself. But that feeding
is only mildly symbolic of the underlying problem of the
finite subject "reading the book of himself".[118]

Our question in this section is, how is the
foundations person to conceive of growth; more fully,
how is he or she to conceive of authentic subjectivity
and international growth; yet more fully, how is that
person not only to conceive but to become constituted in
that valued conception? Nor is this sequence representative of some logical[119] expansion: it is a naming of
parts of the skeleton of an existential dialectic, a
personal vortex.[120] Nor is the constitution a patterning
of a metaphysically-distinguished intellect: it is of
something akin to the romantic metaphysician earlier

referred to. There is a dynamic in finite historical
reality like the lines of a force field or the rhythm
of an unfinished symphony: fourth-level functional
specialists, more than others, must seek continually to
re-align themselves to that long-term magnetic rhythm,
with a subtle open passion reminiscent of Marcel's
"creative fidelity".[121] And I would note in this context that there are relevant lower aggregate demand
functions whose repression and inhibition[122] have not
yet been admitted[123] into academic consciousness. In so
far as "the persona of the dispassionate intellectual is
coupled with a sentimental anima"[124] the dispassionate
intellectual may consider that he needs a psychiatrist
but he may not consider that his philosophic efforts to
conceive of subjectivity or objectivity may be stunted.

My interest in these previous remarks is in
drawing attention to the possibility of a history, bio-
graphies, and prolepsis of the growth of authentic objectivity, one integrator-operator piece of which is expressed in chapter thirteen of Insight. Let me return
now to what may seem the more prosaic question of the
explanatory heuristic of growth. I quote at length a
passage from Insight with which, perhaps, the reader is
already familiar, but reading it here out of its context constitutes the possibility of a rediscovery of its
meaning.[125]

"Study of an organism begins from the thing-for-
us, from the organism as exhibited to our senses. A
first step is a descriptive differentiation of different
parts and, since most of the parts are inside, this descriptive preliminary necessitates dissection or anatomy.
A second step consists in the accumulation of insights
that relate the described parts to organic events, occurrences, operations. By these insights, the parts become
known as organs, and the further knowledge, constituted
by the insights, is a grasp of intelligibilities that
　　　　(1)　are immanent in the several parts,
　　　　(2)　refer each part to what it can do and,
　　　　　　　under determinable conditions, will do, and
　　　　(3)　relate the capacity-for-performance of
　　　　　　　each part to the capacities-for-performance
　　　　　　　of the other parts.

So physiology follows anatomy. A third step is
to effect the transition from the thing-for-us to the
thing-itself, from insights that grasp described parts
as organs to insights that grasp conjugate forms
systematizing otherwise coincidental manifolds of
chemical and physical processes. By this transition,

one links physiology with biochemistry and biophysics.
To this end, there have to be invented appropriate symbolic images of the relevant chemical and physical processes; in these images there have to be grasped by insight the laws of the higher system that account for
regularities beyond the range of physical and chemical
explanation; from these laws, there has to be constructed
the flexible circle of schemes of recurrence in which
the organism functions; finally, this flexible circle
of schemes must be coincident with the related set of
capacities-for-performance that previously was grasped
in sensibly presented organs.

The foregoing three steps of anatomy, physiology,
and their transposition to the thing-itself reveal one
aspect of the organism as higher system in an underlying manifold of cells, chemical processes, and physical
changes. Let us name that aspect the higher system as
integrator....

...However, the organism grows and develops.
Its higher system at any state of development not only
is an integrator but also an operator...."[126]

First, one must note that in the drive towards
explanation within an explanatory heuristic the growing
organism, so to speak, disappears. Images there are,
but they are appropriate symbolic images of the relevant
chemical and physical processes. "The tree, in so far
as it is considered as a thing itself, stands within a
pattern of intelligible relations and offers no foothold
for imagination".[127] And, as with the tree, so with the
growing unity that is the universe: the imagination
limps behind with symbolic images.[128] And in the growing
conception of the growing universe, the metaphysician,
the foundations person, also disappears. "So it comes
about that the extroverted subject visualizing extension
and experiencing duration gives place to the subject
oriented to the objective of the unrestricted desire to
know".[129] But who is the subject that gives place, in
transcendental method?[130] Is it you, or I, or some
subject in a not-yet Scienza nuova? And if it is a not-
yet subject, might we not prepare the foundational way,
in a manner whose indication once more turns us round
the question of growth, for, "like natural growth, it
goes forward without attracting widespread attention",[131]
making the time ripe for later times, when creative
fidelity can bring forth later genius? "For the genius
is simply the man at the level of his time, when the time
is ripe for a new orientation or a sweeping reorganiza-
tion".[132] Or is perhaps international growth, and core

foundational growth within it, a transcendental illusion,
and with it the Christian aspiration for a growing understanding of Faith?[133] Is there then, in cold fact, only
a uniform darkness in history, to be shattered by the
brightness of the Eschaton without any suspicion of a
prior reflected twilight?[134]

As I take my stand on discovering, I take my
stand on the ongoing dialectic discovering of spirit
beyond the realms of the limits of present fantasy.[135]
But my immediate interest is in present progress, and,
indeed, in one of the present physic's contribution to
the Ascent, the Ascension, of man: like the Ascension,
these tiny things that structure space and time can also
turn us "ad invisibilium amorem".[136] As we shall see,
however, the conversio which I wish to draw attention to
here is only that particular conversio through listening
to the Cosmic Word which will give to the foundations
person some answer to the question posed at the end of
the previous section.[137]

I have previously noted certain bridges to be
crossed in the search for differentiated subjectivity:[138]
there is the bridge noted by Langer leading to a non-
representational orientation in art;[139] there is the
bridge of "startling strangeness" noted by Lonergan.[140]
I would note now a further bridge, but I would note also
that these bridges do not form a sequence: in the vortex of personal growth they are mutually sublational.

It would seem, then, that the extroverted subject "gives way" to the subject adequately orientated
in the universe of being in so far as he or she questions
visual extension and experienced duration with sufficient
and regularly recurrent commitment not only to rediscover-
ingly conceive heuristically of extension and duration
but to mediatingly mesh that growing conception with a
psychic undertow.[141] That challenge to heuristic conception has already been given, but its wording may take
on new significance in the present context:

"For a variety of reasons, attention is now
directed to the notions of space and time. Not only are
these notions puzzling and so interesting, but they
throw considerable light on the precise nature of
abstraction, they provide a concrete and familiar context for the foregoing analysis of empirical science,
and they form a natural bridge over which we may
advance from our examination of science to our examination of common sense".[142]

I am, in fact, directing the reader's attention to chapter five of Insight. But I would ask of the reader an attention of the dimensions of Heidegger's care:[143] "In care is grounded the full disclosedness of the 'there',"[144] and only within the dynamism of a psychic undertow will the notion of space and time be of sufficient interest to bring forth in the reader a heuristic mediated by modern science and a conception of the concrete intelligibility of space and time.[145] The aim of the thinker is a valued conception that is an intending of the universe.[146] Is the conception an abstraction? "The intending that is conception puts together both the content of the insight and as much of the image as is essential to the occurrence of the insight; the result is the intending of any concrete being selected by an incompletely determinate (and, in that sense, abstract) content".[147] One can scarcely afford not to take seriously, if one cares about being, the offer of considerable light, even if it takes one a tenth of a thinking life.

Without that light any analysis of science, logic or mathematics rests on foundational obscurity. Without the transforming context of a contemporary heuristic of space and time, the following chapters of Insight read like popular psychology and sociology, and the discussion of "things" either obvious or needlessly obscure.

I am, of course, taking a stand that finds little welcome even in myself. I would note that "it is true that the development of explanatory science tends to eliminate the notion of 'body'".[148] But I would add that it is mythic to envisage that because one's colleagues in mathematical physics are struggling with transformation equations that one's own mind has disowned "any confusion or mixture taken both from the notion of thing and the notion of 'body'".[149] One must personally cross this natural bridge.

Without that crossing, that conception of space and time continually cared for, one gravitates precariously towards the "confusion or mixture", so that the real is only academically the universe of being: existentially it is a globeful of persons in calendar time and endless space with divinity everywhere or nowhere;[150] existentially one just does not admit that "what is first in the ontological constitution of a thing is not the experiential datum but, on the contrary, what is known in the last and most general act

of understanding with regard to it".[151]   So, it is,
perhaps, that "theologians, let alone parents, rarely
think about the historical process".[152]

     With the care for that conception goes the
openness of disclosedness cyclically generative of
further care, meshed in psychic undertow, underpinning
the ongoing precarious mindfulness of being.[153]   It is
with the question - and are not we the questions? - of
the genesis of that care and conception that I wish to
end.   It is a question that, cultivated at length,
would bring forth a transformed version of Heidegger's
Being and Time.   But all that I do now is point forward
to the possibilities of being-in-the-world within the
species that are forth-level functional specialists.
There is, for the thinker, a problem of withdrawal and
return which, more subtle than the traditional problem,
is a problem of self-constitution, symbolized perhaps
in the perceptible eye-difference between the thinker
"lost in thought" and the thinker looking you in the
eye.   Is there a remote possibility of a slow
interiorly-mediated transformation of sensibility so
that the elder thinker may look and listen in the constitutive anamnesis of history and the prolepsis of a
looking and listening of which "eye hath not seen nor
ear heard"?

     Whatever the answer,[154] the question can be
raised adequately only within positional categories,
only in so far as the question is constitutive of a
subject within an explanatory heuristic of historical
process that is neither utopian nor dystopian,[155]
but a creative envisagement of possibilities and probabilities of concrete schemes.   And, to bring to
mind a completeness[156] meshed through these last two
sections, the transformed sensibility cannot be adequately conceived or remotely achieved without recourse
to transformed versions of the diagrams earlier noted,[157]
by which the capacities of sensibility are related
through the sets of schemes of recurrence of intervening
terms to originating and terminal values, and natural
spontaneity has a many-branched linkage with an impossible dream.

     Or perhaps a dream of morning?[158]   At all events,
in the carefilled study of the tree of life in which we
are, and of the study itself in us, "the present must
be accepted as genuinely new (which is just what it
seems to be!) and we must seek to recognise integral
genetic development in a continuum of past-present-future,

in which the integrity of each allows us to penetrate ever more deeply the significance of each as processual". 159

The growing universe may well remain a seed or a sapling in its reaching for the blossoming and fruit of the Eschaton.   But it falls peculiarly to fourth-level functional specialists to bring forth continued fidelity to the Spirited and embodied intention of being in the listening to, and speaking of, the universe whose study, indeed, begins with the universe-for-us but ends in a world invisible, intangible, yet eschatalogically palpable.   In that study there is need for "appropriate symbolic images"[160] not only of physical and chemical processes but also "that release feeling and emotion and flow spontaneously into deeds".[161]   Instead of the flexible genetic circle of ranges of schemes of recurrence within the organism, there are the flexible dialectic meaning-filled circles of ranges of schemes of recurrence of the academy, the economy, the polity, the ecclesia, that call for ever-renewed categorical conception and embodiment, in a serene, repentant and pardoned acknow-ledgement that today's happy-faulted integrator is the concrete possibility of tomorrow's operator in a growth whose fruit is mystery.

6.   Foundations

My interest from the beginning has been in foundations, or more broadly in fourth-level functional specialization.   But have I not been writing as a methodologist?[162]   Already the central issue is here: where do they, dialectic, foundations, metaphysics, begin or end?   It is a large issue, and one that deserves more than some concluding remarks.   It is an issue involving a turning point in the history of meta-physics which leads me to recall Fr. Lonergan's remark of 1959:

"Evidently the question of a Christian Philoso-phy is not dead.   Nor will it die, for in substance it asks how a Catholic can attempt total reflection on man's situation.   But it will do no harm to recall that the twelfth century was steeped in Augustine, yet baffled by problems in method and concept-formation that were solved only in the thirteenth by the systematic and ontological distinction between the orders of Grace and Nature.   Further, this distinction is stretched to a separation of philosophy and theology, only when there

intervenes a further methodological component, namely,
that the one valid scientific ideal is an abstract
deductivism. Thirdly, against that ideal much contemporary thought, correctly, I believe is in revolt; but
to refute effectively, one must replace, and the replace-
ment must be better than a contrary exaggeration. So I
am led to suggest that the issue, which goes by the name
of Christian Philosophy, is basically a question on the
deepest level of methodology, the one that investigates
the operative intellectual ideals not only of scientists
and philosophers but also, since Catholic truth is
involved, theologians. It is, I fear, in Vico's phrase,
a _scienza_ _nuova_".[163]

     To that context[164] I would add the further
context of a decade of growth and of the specification
of the common origin in religious experience of philosophy of God and systematics, and of their common goal in
the development of persons.[165a] But "'person' is never
a general term. It always denotes this or that person
with all of his or her individual characteristics resulting from the communities in which he has lived and
through which he has been formed or formed himself.
The person is the resultant of the relationships he has
had with others and of the capacities that have developed
in him to relate to others".[165b] Dialectic, foundations
and metaphysics in the sense I have been indicating have
a common origin in one man's care of being of a decade
and several decades, and their adequate distinction has
the same origin. The writings of Lonergan are a possibility of a relationship,[166] a possibility of developed
capacity and of growth in this third stage of meaning,
a possibility,above all,of non-discipleship. The possibility becomes a probability within the schemes of
recurrence of concrete community, and my interest is in
the emergence of such schemes.[167] Perhaps my most
elementary contribution to that emergence is encourage-
ment to those younger than I: if you suspect in yourself
the capacity for metaphysics, dialectic or foundations then
you must cultivate[168] in yourself the suspicion[169] that
adult growth in this species of authenticity is a very
slowly accelerating vortex growth. Unless I am mistaken,
it calls for "years in which one's living is more or less
absorbed in the effort to understand, in which one's
understanding gradually works round and up a spiral of
viewpoints with each complementing its predecessor..."[170]
That growth is a personal vortex,[171] a dialectic symmorphosis
[172] to the roots of _imago_ _Dei_[173] in oneself, which is a
continued epiphany[174] of its own prolepticality in the mesh
of sin, repentance, suffering, pardon,[175] and a gentle
expectation of the slow growth of self with selves and universe.

And one must strive not to mistake the dimensions of the
words, underpinned by the root,[176] by which we reach
out to the other, "words as electrified cones, charged
with the power of tradition, of centuries of race consciousness".[177] The words, even these words about words,
name the project of Dasein, writer, reader, written about.

   Dialectic, foundations and metaphysics, then,
name something in a mind something in incarnate quest, on
some stage of the pilgrim way from implicit to explicit
dialectic, foundations, metaphysics. In Insight the
valued conception of proportionate metaphysics was named
"the conception, affirmation and implementation of the
integral heuristic structure of proportionate being",[178]
inclusive of the dialectic aspect of metaphysics".[179]
In Method in Theology there occurs a sublation and
differentiation of the metaphysical enterprize. The
sublation and differentiation are not simple, as one may
note if one asks; how much of Insight and Method in
Theology find their way into foundations,[180] or; do
Insight and Method in Theology not find their way into
the "final objectification of horizons"[181] of dialectic
procedure?   And, to end with the openness of the
question in a mind, are not these questions personal?

            "Why should we honor those
            that die upon the field of
            battle; a man may show as
            reckless a courage in entering
            into the abyss of himself".[182]

Notes: Introduction

1. Scribner, New York, 1948.

2. Ibid., 117.

3. See B. Lonergan, De Deo Trino, Pars Systematica,
    Gregorian Press, Rome, 1964, 255-6.

4. Claude Geffre, Un nouvel age de la theologie, Paris,
    Cerf, 1972.

5. In his "Aquinas Today: Tradition and Innovation",
    The Journal of Religion, 1975, 165-180, Lonergan
    discusses the two new ages.

6. I develop this point further in the Boston Lonergan
    conference paper of 1976, "The Psychological Present
    of the Contemporary Academic", particularly in the
    second of its three parts, which relates generalized
    empirical method to a general theory of Praxis.
    Parts 1 and 2 of the paper are to be published in
    a volume of the conference papers; part 3 is to be
    published in Festschrift in honour of Fr. F. E.
    Crowe, edited by T. Dunne, S.J., and J.-M. Laporte,
    Regis College Press, 1977.

7. B. Lonergan, Method in Theology, Herder & Herder,
    1972, 14.

8. See Method in Theology, 285-88.

9. Ibid., 290-91.

10. Ibid., 292.

11. Ibid., 298.

12. In his essay, "The Task of Foundemental Theology",
    The Journal of Religion, 1974, 13-34, Fr. David
    Tracy argues to the thesis that "the theologian
    should employ an explicitly transcendental or
    metaphysical mode of reflection." (29) The present
    book may be considered as a frankly uncompromising
    specification of the meaning of "employ".

13. I recall Descartes' emphasis on simple instances.
    The gap between technique and comprehension in the
    case of the square root is spelt out in my Wealth
    of Self and Wealth of Nations, Exposition Academic,
    New York, 1975, cp. 3, pp. 19-21.

14. _Method in Theology_, 286.

15. On the limitations of the treatise, see B. Lonergan,
    Insight, 573-5.

16. _Method in Theology_, 333.

17. _Ibid._, 272-6.

18. _Ibid._, 302-5.

19. _Ibid._, 308-9; _Insight_, Cp. 16. The metaphysics of
    course is in a new context: see _Method in Theology_,
    343. On contexts as psychologically present, see
    the paper referred to in footnote 6 above.

20. _Op.cit._, 120.

21. _Method in Theology_, 97-9.

Notes: Prologue, Part 1

1. James Joyce, _Two Tales of Shem and Shaun: Fragments
   from Work in Progress_, London, 1932, 35-6.

2. Stuart Gilbert: "Prolegomena to Work in Progress"
   Sameul Beckett and others, _Our Exagmination Round
   His Factification For Incamination of Work in
   Progress_, London, 1961, 50 (First Published in
   Paris, 1929).

3. Richard M. Kain, "Nothing Odd Will do Long: Some
   Thoughts on 'Finnegans Wake' Twenty-Five years
   later", _Twelve and a Tilly. Essays on the occasion
   of the 25th Anniversary of Finnegans Wake_, edited
   by Jack P. Dalton and Clive Hart, London, 1966, 92.

4. A. Walton Litz, _The Art of James Joyce: Method and
   Design in Ulysses and Finnegans Wake_, London, 1961,
   92-3.

5. William York Tindall, _A Reader's Guide to Finnegans
   Wake_, New York, 1969, 153.

6. Bernard Lonergan, _Gregorianum_ (40), 1959, 182-3,
   in a review.

7. James Joyce, Ulysses, London, 1958, 182.

8. James Joyce, Finnegans Wake, 20.

9. In the article cited in footnote 81 of chapter two, "Metamusic and Self-Meaning", Leo Treitler deals adequately with the a priori philosophy of history implicit in Stanley Kubrick's Space Odyssey of that year-title, 44-7.

10. Ulysses, 264.

11. The Tunc page of the Book of Kells containing the involved illumination of Matthew cp. 27, v. 38 (Tunc Cru-cifixerant-Xti-cum eo du-os latrones). cf. A. Walton Litz, op.cit., 98.

12. B. Lonergan, Insight, 274.

13. David Hayman, A First Draft Version of Finnegans Wake, London, 1963, 3.

14. Finnegans Wake, 614.

Notes: Chapter 1

1. James Joyce, Ulysses, London, 1958. 1. To be referred to hereafter as U.

2. From a letter of Edmund Husserl to Franz Brentano, October 15th, 1904; quoted in H. Spiegelberg, The Phenomenlogical Movement, Vol. 1, The Hague, 1965, 89.

3. In the sense of Insight, 562.

4. Randomness, Statistics and Emergence, Dublin and Notre Dame, 1970. Certain sections of the present essay do in fact go beyond the meaning of the previous work.

5. Method in Theology, p. 88, footnote 34.

6. U. 34.

7. Insight, 542.

8. Insight, 541.

9. I think immediately of Lonergan's study of Aquinas' development of thought in the Gratia Operans articles, Theological Studies (2) 1941, (3) 1942, later published as Grace and Freedom, ed. J. Patout Burns, Herder and Herder., New York, and Darton, Longman and Todd, London, 1971.

10. Insight, 484. Cf. 384, thirdly.

11. Op.cit., 121.

12. Insight, 391.

13. Insight, 685.

14. Insight, 260-1.

15. U. 273.

16. Insight, 555. One might recall here the views of Carl Stumpf on Phenomenology as prescience, illustrated by his Tonpsychologie, 1883.

17. Insight, 255; seee also 79.

18. U. 122.

19. Cf. B. Lonergan, Collection, London, 1967, 186.

20. Ibid.

21. Music That Is Soundless, Milltown Institute of Philosophy and Theology, Dublin, 1969; 2nd ed., University Press of America, 1977; cp. 4. In the growing literature on such things as other-directedness and alienation (Cf. the bibliography in V.C. Fergiss, Technological Man: The Myth and the Reality, New York, 1969) one finds authors continually returning to the question of self-neglect as central, yet being unable either to specify the possibilities of self-attention or to handle adequately the suspicion of selfishness that comes with it. On the present view of objectivity the relevant self-attention, be it in the purely intellectual pattern or in the fullness of incarnate meaning, is not an enclosing confrontation with the self but an expansive self-littling appreciation of limitless openness to all.

22. Cf. Insight, 334.

23. B. Lonergan, De Deo Trino, Pars Dogmatica, Rome, 1964, 274.

24. B. Lonergan, Verbum: Word and Idea in Aquinas, Notre Dame, 1967, 25.

25. Insight, 514.

26. Insight, 539.

27. Insight, 685-6.

28. Relevant here are the more recent writings of Fr. Lonergan on Religion, on Faiths and Beliefs, especially on the order of the conversions, religious, moral and intellectual. See also B. Tyrrell, Bernard Lonergan's Philosophy of God, Gill MacMillan and Notre Dame, 1974.

29. Cf. Insight, 498, 509.

30. Towards a Psychology of Being, New York, 1968, 204.

31. U. 501.

32. In the conclusion some further points will be made regarding the subject's return to the total "feeling" subject. Cf. footnote 147.

33. The following chapter will focus on this topic in a variety of ways.

34. "Are Our Publications and Conventions Suitable for the Personal Psychologies?" Appendix A of Towards a Psychology of Being, New York, 1968, 217.

35. U. 400-1.

36. Insight, 51.

37. One might recall here the large body of literature on random numbers or the long debate regarding Von Mises' axiom of randomness--both bearing witness to the oddness of specifying what specifically excludes certain conditions of intelligibility.

38. The process has in fact been computerized for 32 balls, and the account includes interesting comments on symmetry and randomness by the investigators. Cf. Edward Purcell, "Parts and Wholes," Parts and Wholes, edited by Daniel Lerner, London, 1963.

39. Insight, especially 48-51.

40. Some of my readers may find the following quotation
     suggestive of quasiparallels to points being made
     throughout this paper: 'To effect an agreement
     between general concepts and specific details is
     one of the most difficult tasks of human under-
     standing. In order to reduce the world of appear-
     ances to only a few concepts, knowledge must seek
     general truths. At the same time, one must examine
     the particular to the last detail, in all their
     secrets, if one wishes to grasp correctly these
     general concepts, which are, after all, supported
     by particulars. The task is difficult because
     generalities, however arrived at, easily mislead
     men into a premature satisfaction which spares any
     further effort concerning specifics. Through con-
     tinuous disregard for detail, knowledge of general
     truths is impaired; it does not ripen into truth,
     but remains limited to a scheme'. Heinrich Schenker,
     "Organic Structure in Sonata Form", Journal of
     Music Theory (12), 1968, 194-5. Consider, for
     example, the problem of appreciating two different
     Beethoven Sonatas, and compare this with the prob-
     lem of understanding members of two different species
     of the genus Chlamydomonas. In each case, differ-
     ent ideas are concretely realized. In each case
     'one must examine the particulars to the last de-
     tail' in order to appreciate fully the integration.
     Obviously there are differences. "Appreciation"
     is a thorny question in the field of music.

41. Insight, 50.

42. Insight, 17.

43. I recall here the four main aspects of understanding
     a text outlined by Fr. Lonergan. 'Understanding the
     text has four main aspects: (i) one understands the
     thing or object that the text refers to, (ii) one
     understands the words employed in the text, (iii)
     one understands the author who employed the words
     and (iv) it is not 'one', on, "man", that under-
     stands, but I do, as a result of a process of
     learning, and at times as a result of a conversion'.
     B. Lonergan, "Hermeneutics", a lecture delivered
     in July, 1962.

44. Insight, 16.

45. Insight, 205.

46. Etudes Blondeliennes. Directeurs J. Paliard et P.
     Archambault, Fascicule 1, Paris, 1951, 87-8.

47. U. 236.

48. Randomness, Statistics and Emergence, Cp. 9.

49. Stephen C. Pepper, "Emergence", Journal of
    Philosophy, (23), 1926, 244; P.E. Meehl and Wilfred
    Sellars, "The Concept of Emergence", Minnesota
    Studies in the Philosophy of Science, Minneapolis,
    1962, Vol. 1, 239.

50. Botanists will forgive my abuse of the genus-name
    Chlamydomonas. Chlamydomona may be roughly des-
    cribed as a tiny unicellular plant with two
    flagells; it swims about with a breast-stroke
    movement of about ten beats per second.

51. N. Rashevski, Mathematical Biophysics, New York
    (Dover), Volume 1, 7-372.

52. Ibid., 1.

53. Ibid.

54. "The Kinetic Structure of Organisms", Biological
    Organisation at the Cellular and Subcellular Level,
    edited by R. Harris, New York, 1963, 25.

55. U. 301.

56. Mathematical Biophysics, Vol. 1, 15, italics his.

57. Ibid., 16.

58. Ibid., 37-8.

59. Ibid., 37.

60. Cf. Mathematical Biophysics, Vol. II, 245-423,
    passim, and more recent references given there.

61. For example, in the line of H. Kaeser's "Some
    Physico-chemical aspects of Biological Organisation",
    The Strategy of the Genes by C.H. Waddington,
    London, 1957, 191-249.

62. Loewy and Siekevitz, Cell Structure and Function,
    New York, 1963, 56.

63. Ernest Mayr, Animal Species and Evolution, London,
    1963, 544.

64. A.M. Michelson, The Chemistry of Nucleosides and
    Nucleotides, London and New York, 1963, 580.

65. U. 101.

66. Insight, 256.

67. James Bonner, "Cell and Subcell", Plant Biochemistry, edited by James Bonner and J.E. Varner, New York and London, 1965, 12.

68. Allan Munck, "Symbolic Representation of Metabolic and Endocrine Systems", Mathematical Biosciences, (4), 1969, 367-394.

69. Quoted by H. Hermann, "Biological Field Phenomena, facts and concepts", Form and Strategy in Science. Essays in honour of Woodger, edited by J. Greeg and F. Harris, Holland, 1964, 351.

70. G.W. Wardlaw, Essays on Form in Plants, London and New York, 1968.

71. Insight, 385.

72. U. 378.

73. B. Lonergan, De Deo Trino, Pars Systematica, Rome, 1964, 86-92, is closely related to this point.

74. Cf. Insight, 393, 504-6.

75. Plant Biochemistry, edited by James Bonner and J.E. Varner, New York and London, 1963, 863.

76. U. 399.

77. Another illustration of this difficulty, the problem of handling the question, what is probability?, which occurs at the beginning of textbooks on probability, is discussed in Randomness, Statistics and Emergence, cp. 8.

78. London, 1965.

79. Op.cit., 1.

80. Ibid., 361.

81. "Activity" here should be understood in its technical sense. Cf. B. Lonergan, De Deo Trino, Pars Systematica, Rome, 1964, Appendix 1; De Ente Supernaturale (unpublished notes), thesis 5.

82. B. Lonergan, Collection, London, 1967, 223.

83. On all these cf. B. Lonergan, De Deo Trino, Pars
     Systematica, Rome, 1964, Appendix 1: more fully,
     the index of his Verbum: Word and Idea in Aquinas,
     Notre Dame, 1967.

84. Ia, q.18, a.2c.

85. Ia, q.18, a3c.

86. Ia, q.18, a2, ad 1um.

87. U. 70.

88. Cf. the references in the text in the following
     footnote.

89. B. Lonergan, Verbum: Word and Idea in Aquinas,
     Notre Dame, 1967, 136-7.

90. The word "uses" should be understood in the
     theoretic context which makes clear that 'actio est
     in passo' etc. For discussion and references cf.
     P. McShane, "The Causality of the Sacraments",
     Theological Studies, (24), 1963, 428-430.

91. Cf. Summa Theologica, Ia. q.79, a.2c; IaIIae, q.22,
     a.1; De Veritate, q.26, a.I.

92. Only after my choice of the terms did I find the
     terms autonomic and aitonomic used in Strasburger's
     textbook, referred to in footnote 115, for two
     species of irritability. Both of these are auto-
     nomic in my sense. My choice of terms was coloured
     by the statement in Insight, 73: 'To be alive,
     then, is to be a more or less autonomous centre of
     activity'.

93. David Riesman, The Lonely Crowd, Yale, 1961.

94. I have dealt in more modern terms with the forms
     of physics in relation to invariants of space-time
     geometry in Randomness, Statistics and Emergence,
     Dublin, 1970, 114-120.

95. Contra Gentiles, Bk. IV, Cp. 11.

96. Summa Theologica, Ia, q.18, a.2, ad 1um.

97. U. 394.

98. In Insight, cp. 8, the notion of thing is treated coherently but with an unavoidable density and lack of illustrative self-exercise that can leave the reader unchallenged.

99. Cf. F.C. Bawden, Plant Viruses and Virus Diseases, New York, 1964, I.

100. Ibid., 2.

101. Ibid., 12.

102. Ernest Baldwin, An Introduction to Comparative Biochemistry, Cambridge, 1964, 2.

103. B. Lonergan, Verbum: Word and Idea in Aquinas, Notre Dame, 1967, 25.

104. Cf. Insight, 459.

105. To treat adequately of genetic method here would double the length of both my labours and my paper. Note however that a distinction in method is a further and sufficient reason for asserting the autonomy of the science of botany. Cf. Insight, index under development, genetic. For a short discussion and references cf. my "Insight and the Strategy of Biology". Spirit as Inquiry, edited by F.E. Crowe, New York, 1964, 80-1; 85-7. The volume is identical with the winter number of Continuum, 1964.

106. Cf. Insight, 444-51.

107. Insight, xxviii.

108. U. 23.

109. J.W.S. Pringle, The Two Biologies, Oxford, 1963.

110. John C. Kendrew, "Information and Conformation in Biology", Structural Chemistry and Molecular Biology, edited by A. Rich and N. Davidson, San Francisco and London, 1968, 193.

111. The transformation I speak of, evidently, is not a transformation of the subject botany, but a trans-formation of the subject, the individual botanist. In this the crisis in botany parallels that in theology.

112. Insight, 464. The text goes on to the "operator" aspect of organic form, but, as already mentioned, I have tried to keep the paper within bounds by concentrating in an abstractive way on the "integrator" aspect.

113. On the difficulties of the scientist in the field of methodology, cf. Insight, 423-30.

114. In so far as textbooks include the cell in both these sections they tend to incorporate the beginnings of the third step, but a methodological discussion of this inclusion would lead us into too much detail.

115. Strasburger's Textbook of Botany, rewritten by R. Harder et alii, London, 1965, 404.

116. U. 628.

117. The question of recurrence-schemes is discussed in Randomness, Statistics and Emergence, cp. 10.

118. A. Frey-Wyssling and K. Mühlerethaler, Ultrastructural Plant Cytology, Amsterdam, London and New York, 1965, 1.

119. In his article, "Self-Assembly of Biological Structures", Bacteriological Reviews (33) 1969, 302-45, D.J. Kinshner gives 'a broad introduction to current research and thought patterns on the role of self-assembly in forming biological structures' (304), structures of the kind referred to above. One might fruitfully consider his article in relation to the significance of schemes of recurrence.

120. "Appropriate" in the sense, for example, that "DNA" is not a suggestive image but a helix-like diagram can be. Cf. Insight, 17-9.

121. Insight, 256.

122. Ernest Baldwin, Dynamic Aspects of Biochemistry, Cambridge, 1963, I.

123. Insight, 262-3.

124. One thinks spontaneously of the work of C.H. Waddington.

125. *Insight*, 250.

126. I think here of Lonergan's treatment of the two times of the temporal subject, *De Deo Trino, Pars Systematica*, Rome, 1964, 196-204.

127. *Insight*, 439.

128. The tendency towards such reductionism is of course much more a tendency of popularizers and philosophers of science. The specialists can normally be trusted for more clear-headed statements: "We do not believe that biochemistry represents a panacea for all systematic problems. If anything, the writing of this book has modulated our initial enthusiasm which even in the beginning did not lead us to conceive of present biochemical data as providing more than supplementary data for phylogenetic considerations. However, profound and far-reaching new insight into phylogenetic relationships is potentially available in biochemistry, ultimately we predict from intensive study of the comparative biochemistry of macromolecules'. R. Alston and B. Turner, *Biochemical Systematics*, New Jersey, 1963, 3.

129. Cf. footnotes 147, 148 below: also the concluding sections of "Metamusic and Selfmeaning". Total expansion of adult questing is an undeveloped area of reflection with a consequent lack in the mediation of lower-level expansions. Speaking of the paucity of research in this area, A.R. Arasteh remarks: "Unless the psychologist has himself experienced the state of quest of final integration in the succession of identifies he will hardly acquire an understanding or incentive for doing research on it'. *Final Integration in the Adult Personality*, Leiden, 1965, 18.

130. U. 420.

131. *Insight*, 170.

132. *Insight*, 505.

133. Cf. David Riesman, *The Lonely Crowd*, Yale, 1961.

134. *Insight*, 429.

135. Cf. for example, Paul Oppenheim and Hilary Putman. "Unity of Science as a Working Hypothesis", *Minnesota Studies*, II, Minneapolis, 1962.

136. One might instance the popularity of de Chardin, or
     to a lesser extent Whitehead.

137. A modern and extended version, one might say, of
     the works of Woodger, e.g. The Axiomatic Method in
     Biology, Cambridge, 1937.

138. U. 178.

139. Cf. B. Lonergan, De Ente Supernaturale (unpublished
     notes), thesis 4.

140. Cf. B. Lonergan, "The Natural Desire to See God",
     Collection, London, 1967, 96-113.

141. In a dual sense: there is both the mystery of the
     absolutely supernatural and the mystery of iniquity:
     the control of meaning in both requires the play of
     a central inverse insight.

142. Insight, 513.

143. Love and Will, New York, 1969, cp. 12. May does
     not break through to a metaviewpoint. Furthermore,
     his view of the present scene is somewhat negative.
     Technology and the growing awareness of the vast
     emptiness in life are positive possibilities of
     transformation.

144. Colin Wilson, Beyond the Outsider, London, 1965,
     175.

145. Insight, 581.

146. Cf. cp. 2, esp. the con lusion. I would note
     urgent need for a deeper liturgical theoretic.
     Stravinski remarked to Evelyn Waugh after the com-
     pletion of his Mass 1948 'Liturgical Music has
     practically disappeared, except of course, the
     third-rate academic kind. The tradition has been
     lost.' The emergence of a contemporary tradition
     would seem to require not only experimentation but
     also the mediation of "third stage meaning".

147. I think here of the application within philosophic
     discourse of such a work as R. Corlis and P. Rabe,
     Psychotherapy from the Centre, Pennsylvania, 1969.

148. To the work cited in the last footnote, which
      stresses enlargement of feeling, one may add
      Maslow's stress on "peak experiences" in Towards a
      Psychology of Being, New York, 1968, and P. Berger's
      discussion of "signals of transcendence in A Rumor
      of Angels: Modern Society and the Rediscovery of
      the Supernatural, New York, 1969.

149. Insight, 581.

150. From a talk on Art by Fr. Lonergan, during a summer
      course on Education, 1959.

151. U. 153.

152. Cf. George Simmel, "The Sociology of Sociability",
      Theories of Society, edited by T. Parsons et alii,
      New York and London, 1965, 157-63.

153. Incarnate meaning is one type of meaning touched
      on by Fr. Lonergan in the chapter on meaning in
      Method in Theology.

154. J.H. Newman, Sermon V. Oxford University Sermons,
      London, 1909, 75-98.

155. Cf. my Music That Is Soundless, chapter 6. I am
      indebted here to Fr. F.E. Crowe's forthcoming
      book on The Word of God.

156. From the talk on Art already cited, footnote 150.

157. Carl Stumpf. "Erinnerungen an Franz Brentano", in
      Oskar Kraus, Franz Brentano, Munich, 1909, 93.

158. T.E. Williams, in The Fugitive Kind.

159. Insight, 484.

160. Edmund Husserl, Phenomenology and the Crisis of
      Philosophy, translated by Q. Lauer, S.J., New York,
      1965, 189.

161. On language as a component of plausibility struc-
      tures Ch P. Berger, The Social Construction of
      Reality. A Treatise in the Sociology of Knowledge,
      New York, 1966, 21, 36, 140ff.

162.   'Relevance and timeliness are defined for the
       society at large primarily by the media of mass
       communication. These are afflicted with an in-
       curable hunger for novelty. The relevancies they
       proclaim are, almost by definition, extremely
       vulnerable to changing fashion and thus of generally
       short duration. As a result, the theologian (or,
       of course, any other intellectual) who seeks to be
       and remain "with it", in terms of mass communica-
       tion and mass-communicable relevance, is predestined
       to find himself authoritatively put down as irrele-
       vant very soon.' P. Berger, A Rumor of Angels, 29.

163.   U. 34.

Notes: Chapter 2

1.   James Joyce, Finnegans Wake (hereafter referred to
     as FW), 6.

2.   David Lewin, "Behind the Beyond": A Response to
     E.T. Cone, Perspectives of New Music (7), 1969, 61.

3.   B. Lonergan, "Functional Specialties in Theology",
     Gregorianum (50), 1969, 485-505, later published
     as cp. 6 of Method in Theology.

4.   E.T. Cone, "Beyond Analysis", Perspectives of New
     Music (5), 1967, 33-51.

5.   David Lewin, op.cit., 62.

6.   "Mr. Cone's Reply", Perspectives of New Music (7),
     1969, 70.

7.   Ibid., 71.

8.   FW 109

9.   Ernest Krenek, "Some Current Terms", Perspectives
     of New Music (4), 1966, 81.

10. Musical Quarterly (46), 1960, 246-59.

11. E. Krenek, op.cit., 84.

12. Lewin, op.cit., 69.

13. FW 8.

14. P. McShane, Wealth of Self and Wealth of Nations,
    Exposition Press, New York, 1975, cp. 9.

15. S. Langer, Feeling and Form, London, 1953, 100,
    footnote.

16. Wealth of Self and Wealth of Nations, 78.

17. FW 598.

18. A.P. Merriam, "Ethnomusicology Revisited", Ethno-
    musicology (13), 1969, 228.

19. A.P. Merriam, The Anthropology of Music, Northwestern
    University Press, 1964, 18. Readers familiar with
    the later writings of Lonergan will recognize these
    as central questions for him.

20. Merriam, The Anthropology of Music, 38.

21. The language here is mine. In Wealth of Self and
    Wealth of Nations, I discussed two general cases
    of such objectification: in logical symbolism and
    technology (chapter 8); in art (chapter 9). As
    we will note, development in the former is a
    possibility of novel transformation in the latter.

22. Merriam, The Anthropology of Music, cp. 6.

23. Ibid. cpp. 14, 15.

24. Bruno Nettl, Theory and Method in Ethnomusicology,
    London, 1964, 274.

25. B. Lonergan's Method in Theology, chapter 3, deals
    in some detail with levels of meaning. The work of
    Leonard B. Meyer, Emotion and Meaning in Music,
    Chicago and London, 1956, is extremely restricted
    by the lack of such an analysis as its context.

26. FW 614-5.

27. Leo Treitler, "On Historic Criticism", The Musical
    Quarterly (53), 1967, 188.

28. Arthur Berger, "New Linguistic Modes and The New
    Theory", Perspectives of New Music (2), 1964, 5.

29. Charles Rosen, "The Proper Study of Music",
Perspectives of New Music (1), 1962, 80.

30. Charles Wuorinen, "The Outlook for Young Composers",
Perspectives of New Music (1), 1963, 60.

31. Vance Packard, The Naked Society, London, 1964,
refers to the view of the audiologist Joseph Krimsky
that noise aggravates life's stresses and annihilates
privacy; it can produce pathological changes in the
auditory system and reduce 'sensitivity to the
nuances of sound and music', 209.

32. All along here parallels might be drawn with
popular music. So, for example, technological
transformation of musical possibilities is
obviously not a preserve of what is called 'serious'
music. Arnold Swah subtitles a chapter of The Rock
Revolution (London, 1969) "The Recording Studios
as Instrument". 'Songs are no longer written and
then recorded. They are most frequently conceived
in the recording studio, with the process of recording entering actively into the shape and form and
sound that the song ultimately takes'. 8. 'Music
is becoming a joint effort these days, and the composer is allied with the physicist, the expert in
film techniques, the electronic engineer'. 197.
Here we have all the problems of chance, creativity,
freedom of performance, etc., reflected in popular
music. In such things as atonality and serialization there is an inevitable lag.

33. Benjamin Boreth, "A Note on Discourse and Contemporary Musical Thought", Perspectives of New Music
(4), 1966, 76. Cf. also P. Boulez, "Son, verbe,
synthèse", Revue Belge de Musicologie (13), 1959,
5.

34. The word 'questing' was used in the first essay to
denote the total complex of intentionalities.

35. The policy is more properly operative in the more
elementary work, Wealth of Self and Wealth of
Nations. See, for example, pp. 19-21, where the
reader is invited to pause and grapple towards an
understanding of the rule underlying the technique
of getting square roots, in order to reach towards an understanding of that grappling. In the
present essay it is unfortunately much easier to
let the printed invitation pass, not to pause
seriously over such questions as "what exactly is
happening to the complexity, me, when I am greeted
by the symphonies of Mahler?"

36. FW 504.

37. Cf. B. Lonergan, Insight, 542.

38. Heinrich Schenker, "Organic Structure in Sonata Form", Journal of Musical Theory (12), 1968, 164-5. I have dealt in complementary fashion with this problem in the previous essay. Cf. footnote 40 and the text there.

39. B. Lonergan, Insight, 747-8.

40. Ibid., 498.

41. Ibid., 509.

42. A remark of Debussy made in relation to Stravinski's Le Sacre du Printemps, quoted in Donald Mitchell, The Language of Music, London, 1963, 22,

43. Igor Stravinski and Robert Craft, Conversations with Igor Stravinski, London, 1958, 18-9.

44. George Rochberg, "The New Image in Music", Perspectives of New Music (2), 1963, 6.

45. Leo Treitler, "The Present as History", Perspectives of New Music (7), 1969, 41.

46. Cf. McShane, Music That Is Soundless, Milltown Institute, Dublin, 1969, University Press of America, Washington, 1977, 33-6.

47. Benjamin Boreth, "A Note on Discourse and Contemporary Musical Thought", Perspectives of New Music (4), 1966, 78.

48. FW 12.

49. B. Lonergan, Insight, 393.

50. E. Varèse, "The Liberation of Sound", Perspectives of New Music (5), 1966, 16.

51. Milton Babbitt, "Edgard Varèse: A Few Observations on His Music", Perspectives of New Music (4), 1966, 18.

52. Henry Weinberg, "Letter from Italy", Perspectives of New Music (1), 1962, 193.

53. For Stockhausen's more general views of form and
    unity cf. K. Stockhausen, "The Concept of Unity in
    Electronic Music", (Die Einheit der musikalischen
    Zeit), Perspectives of New Music (1), 1962, 39.
    The rejection of the presence of any unity of form
    by some composers would seem to stem from deficient
    views on objectivity, on the dominance of the
    creative idea, however perverse, and on the nature
    of composition as subject-meaning. So, for example,
    even in aleatoric composition there is the prior
    idea of such of composition.

54. Pierre Boulez, "Sonate, Que me veux-tu?", Perspec-
    tives of New Music (1), 1963, 37.

55. Cf. for example, G. Rochberg, "The New Image in
    Music", Perspectives of New Music (2), 1963; G.
    Poole, "An Approach to Simultaneity in Twelve-
    tone Composition", Perspectives of New Music (3),
    1964.

56. Perspectives of New Music (5), 1966, 93-111.

57. "In Op Art instability is attained by the random
    eye movements and physiological reactions induced
    by the painted surface. There is something para-
    doxical in this. Instability is achieved by what
    at first sight might seem the most stable of all
    structures, periodic structures or systematic
    repetition of identical elements". Cyril Barrett,
    S.J., Op Art, London, 1970, 105-6. I quote, not
    only to draw attention to parallel developments
    in the arts, but also to point to the possibility
    of the transformation of 'listening and talking'
    in each particular area through the relevant meta-
    art.

58. Perspectives of New Music (7), 1969, 94-110.

59. H.H. Stuckenschmidt, Twentieth Century Music,
    London, 1969, 97.

60. A dictum of R.W. Gerard, quoted in motto-fashion
    by R.S. deRopp, Drugs and The Mind, New York, 1957,
    203.

61. Stuckenschmidt, op.cit., 114.

62. Lonergan, Insight, 439.

63. Cf. Merriam, The Anthropology of Music, cp. 6.

64. FW 184.

65.   Cf. for example, Richard Kostelaneth, "Modern Music
      Criticism and the Literate Layman", Perspectives of
      New Music (7), 1969, 119-33.

66.   Ibid., 128.

67.   Cf. Robert Morly, "Upset in Emotions", Journal of
      Social Psychology (12), 1940: 'Music, said to
      express emotion to an expert in music and emotion
      in western society, does not express emotion to
      auditors whose musical and social training is dif-
      ferent from that of the composer of the music'.
      (354). 'Western music is not recognized by the
      Loma of Liberia as expressing emotion', (342).

68.   G. Durand, Les Structures Anthropologiques de L'
      Imaginaire, Paris, 1963. Cf. p. 39 for references
      to Betcherevian reflexology. It is in some such
      context that one might begin to handle questions
      of 'upside-down' in art raised by Cone in the
      article cited, footnote 4.

69.   Hans Keller, "Problems in Writing about Music",
      Times Literary Supplement, September 9th, 1969,
      1149. The issue deals mainly with The New Language
      of Music.

70.   The expert in Methodology will recognize that I am
      touching here on the functional specialties of dia-
      lectic and foundations, with the possibility of
      conversions mediating their continual renewal.

71.   Cf. Stuckenschmidt, op.cit., cp. 9, especially 178.

72.   FW 407.

73.   Patterns of Discovery, Cambridge, 1965, chapter 4.

74.   H. Schenker, op.cit., footnote 38, 178.

75.   Perspectives of New Music (4), 1966, 20-36.

76.   Ibid., 20.

77.   The significance of this phrase is spelt out in B.
      Lonergan, Insight, especially chapter 8, and in
      Wealth of Self and Wealth of Nations, cp. 5.

78.   FW 176-7.

79.   Cf. chapter one, at footnote 75, above, pp. 27-8.

80. Gunther Schuller, "Conversation with Varèse",
    Perspectives of New Music (3), 1965, 36.

81. Leo Treitler, "The Present as History", Perspec-
    tives of New Music (7), 1969, 1-58.

82. The four books reviewed are Jacques Chailley, 40,000
    Years of Music (translation from French), London,
    1964; Walter Wiora, The Four Ages of Music (trans-
    lation from German), New York, 1965; Richard L.
    Crocker, A History of Musical Style, New York, 1966;
    Leonard B. Meyer, Music, The Arts and Ideas: Pat-
    terns and Predictions in Twentieth Century Culture,
    Chicago, 1967.

83. Treitler, op.cit., 2.

84. Ibid., 2.

85. Ibid., 4.

86. Ibid., 11-2.

87. Patterns of Discovery, Cambridge, 1958.

88. Personal Knowledge, London, 1958.

89. Treitler, op.cit., 20.

90. Ibid., 13.

91. Ibid., 23; cf. also Leo Treitler, "On Historical
    Criticism", The Musical Quarterly (53), 1967, 188-
    205.

92. David Lewin, "Inversional Balance as an Organizing
    Force in Schoenberg's Music and Thought", Per-
    spectives of New Music (6), 1968, 1-21.

93. Treitler, op.cit., 34.

94. FW 211.

95. B. Lonergan, Insight, 115-27.

96. Ibid., 260.

97. Ibid., cp. 17, sublated into different functional
    specialties.

98. A. Merriam, The Anthropology of Music, 38.

99.   FW 151.

100. Generically, in *Wealth of Self and Wealth of Nations*, cp. 9, and in the conclusion of chapter 1 above.

101. A. Silbermann, *The Sociology of Music*, London, 1963, 9.

102. P. Berger, *The Sacred Canopy. Elements of a Sociology of Religion*, New York, 1967, 8. An earlier book, *The Social Construction of Reality*, New York, 1966, provides a wider context.

103. Gibson Winter, *Elements for a Social Ethic*, New York, 1968, 138.

104. *Ibid.*, 135.

105. P. Berger, *A Rumor of Angels, Modern Society and the Rediscovery of the Supernatural*, New York, 1969, 128.

106. Silbermann, *op.cit.*, 177.

107. *Ibid.*, 173.

108. FW 284.

109. Pierre Boulez, "Sonate, Que me veux-tu?", *Perspectives of New Music* (1), 1963, 32.

110. Judith Becker, "The Anatomy of a Mode", *Ethnomusicology* (13), 1969, 272.

111. FW 430.

112. Becker, *op.cit.*, 267-8.

113. This is true of much less remote cultures. So, for example, the medieval mind is vastly foreign to ours and it requires a very precise hermeneutic not to stumble in its investigation. On the question of medieval musical syntax, cf. Leo Treitler, "Musical Syntax in the Middle Ages", *Perspectives of New Music* (3), 1965, 75-85.

114. That slow emergence and its linguistic expression in the early Greek period is discussed in detail by Bruno Snell. *The Discovery of Mind*, New York, 1960.

115. In Music That Is Soundless, 95-7, I made the same
     point in speaking of theology's tendency to dodge
     that mediation.

116. In the previous essay this was touched on in rela-
     tion to philosophic dialogue. As I noted there,
     that dialogue is not unrelated to the level of
     aesthetic expansiveness.

117. Cf. footnote 42. One might also consider the text
     referred to in footnote 52, above, in regard to the
     aesthetic objectification of man's mind-reach 'out
     of time' (the text, p. 58).

118. FW 373.

119. Wilfrid Mellers, Caliban Reborn, Renewal in Twentieth
     Century Music, London, 1968, 181.

120. Ibid.

121. B. Lonergan, Insight, 184-5.

122. Heinrich Schenker, "Organic Structure in Sonata
     Form", Journal of Musical Theory (12), 1968, 180.

123. Cf. the text at footnote 92 of cp. 1 (the text, p. 31).

124. Schenker, op.cit., 180.

125. Igor Stravinski and Robert Craft, Conversations
     with Igor Stravinski, London, 1958, 18.

126. P. Kavanagh, Collected Poems, London, 1964: the
     line recurs in the poem: "If ever you go to
     Dublin Town", and the sentiment in other contexts.

127. Here ends, or pretends to end, Finnegans Wake.

Notes: Prologue, Part 2

1. Hermann Hesse, Wandering, translated by James
   Wright, Farrar, Straus and Giroux, New York, 1972,
   51.

2. The famous Canto XLV of Pound's epic.

3. Robert Heilbroner, The Economic Problem, Prentice
    Hall, 1972, 352.

4. B. Lonergan, "Aquinas Today: Tradition and Innova-
    tion", The Journal of Religion, 1975, 178.

5. B. Lonergan, Method in Theology, xi.

6. Peter Russell (ed.), Ezra Pound, Nevill, New York,
    1950, in his Introduction, 19.

7. A marginal note in the "Triv and Quad" section of
    Finnegans Wake, 294, indicates "Sarga, or the path
    of outgoing". Sarga is the Sanskrit for 'process
    of world creation or emanation'. By Sargawit I
    mean that outgoing of subject which is also the
    foundational (with a prior dialectic) sublation of
    the Vorticism mentioned at footnote 11 below. The
    opposition in imagery here, of outgoing and inflow-
    ing, fades when one reflects on Aquinas' "Eo majus
    unum". (See B. Lonergan, Verbum: Word and Idea in
    Aquinas, University of Notre Dame Press, 1967, 197-
    201). In this context I recall the dialectic of
    procedures of Shem and Shaun, Joyce and Pound (see,
    on this, Forrest Read (ed.) Pound/Joyce, Faber and
    Faber, London, 1967, 262-6) which requires a sub-
    lation parallel to the sublation of Thomist Wisdom
    and Prudence. See footnote 6 on page 141, above.

8. See chapter 4, at p. 100; also footnote 94 of that
    chapter (below, p. 185).

9. Hermann Hesse, Narziss and Goldmund, Penguin, 64,
    quoted in a related context in Wealth of Self and
    Wealth of Nations, 195-6.

10. Harry Levin (ed.), The Essential James Joyce,
    Penguin, 12. See also Richard Ellmann, James Joyce,
    Oxford University Press, 1959; the index under
    Epiphany.

11. See Hugh Kenner, The Pound Era, University of
    California Press, 1971, 238-9; the context may be
    broadened from Kenner's index under Vortex,
    Vorticism.

12. See the conclusion to chapter 4 (though, as the
    reader will find, chapter 4 twists "round" to con-
    clude at footnote 129 of itself), p. 118 above.

13. See Method in Theology, the index under Gift.

14. Hermann Hesse, Wandering, 89.

Notes: Chapter 3

1. Konrad Lorenz, On Aggression, Methuen, London,
    1966, 185.

2. Cf. W.H. Thorpe's introduction to Lorenz's King
    Solomon's Ring, Methuen, London, 1964, where there
    is a good brief account of developments in animal
    psychology in the last century. The book itself
    is a classic of nature study.

3. Cf. in this context J.H. Newman, Oxford University
    Sermons, London, 1909, "Personal Influence, the
    Means of Propagating the Truth", 75-98.

4. F.E. Crowe, A Time of Change, Bruce, Milwaukee,
    1968, 151, 165, makes this point in a general
    fashion. On language as a component of 'plausibi-
    lity structures' cf. Peter Berger, The Social
    Construction of Reality. A Treatise on the
    Sociology of Knowledge, New York, 1966, 21, 36,
    140 ff.

5. See Chapter 1, pp. 10-1.

6. P. McShane, Randomness, Statistics and Emergence,
    Gill-MacMillan, Dublin, and Notre Dame, 1970, 29.

7. E.G. In The Lonely Crowd, Yale U.P., 1961. My
    original intention when I undertook this essay was
    to have it as a component of a book entitled Being
    and Loneliness. While man can be defined heuristi-
    cally as a six-levelled hierarchic complex, in
    relevant contemporary description he is the possi-
    bility of a range of temporal lonelinesses. See
    the epilogue, "Being and Loneliness" to my Wealth
    of Self and Wealth of Nations.

8. See Chapter 1, pp. 39 ff; the Epilogue, pp. 130 ff.

9. B. Lonergan, Insight. A Study of Human Understanding,
    Longmans, 1957, 468.

10. I have tried to develop the heuristic of that wider
    context in chapters 9, 10 and 11 of Randomness,
    Statistics and Emergence.

11. The Natural History of Aggression, edited by J.D.
    Carthy and F.J. Ebling, Academic Press, London,
    1964, 1.

12. B. Lonergan, Insight, 555.

13. Ibid., 542.

14. F.E. Crowe, op.cit., 138, 144.

15. On Aggression, xi.

16. Ibid., cp. 6, 72-92.

17. Ibid., 75.

18. Ibid., 73.

19. Ibid., 88.

20. Ibid., 89.

21. B. Lonergan, Insight, 464. See other contexts of this quotation: pp. 36; 133-4; p. 192, footnote 136.

22. The Natural History of Aggression, 65-72.

23. B. Lonergan, Insight, 505.

24. S.P. Grossman, op.cit., 396.

25. Animal Behaviour Volume 18 (1970), "Aggression and Gonadal Hormones in Captive Rhesus Monkeys (Macaca Mulatta)", 8-9.

26. Cf. B. Lonergan, Insight, 391 ff.

27. Ibid., 468.

28. Particularly in Chapter 1, p. 41. The topic will be developed further in Chapter 4, where it emerges more clearly as the central theme.

29. S.P. Grossman, op.cit., 396-7.

30. The title of an essay by Paul Oppenheimer and Hilary Putman, in Minnesota Studies, II, Minneapolis, 1962.

31. Cf. for example some of the essays in Computer Applications in the Behavioural Sciences, edited by Harold Borko, London, 1962, especially comments in W. Ross Ashby, "Simulating the Brain", 453-456; also in the essay "Do Computers Think?", 12-21.

32. B. Lonergan, Insight, 399. The same of course is true of present specialties in theology: cf. for example, Insight, 581, ff, on interpretation.

33. K. Jaspers, The Origin and Goal of History, London, 1953.

34. B. Lonergan, Insight, 398.

35. B. Lonergan, Verbum. Word and Idea in Aquinas, Notre Dame, 1967, 25. For a more developed view of the hylemorphic mind, see Chapter 4, p. 113 ff, where the aggreformist perspective is introduced.

36. Oxford, 1957.

37. Ibid., 112.

38. Ibid., 127.

39. B. Lonergan, Insight, 439.

40. Edited by H.S. Perry and I.L. Gawel, Norton and Co., New York, 1953.

41. "The Two Concepts of Probability", Readings in the Philosophy of Science, edited by Feigl and Brodbeck, New York, 1953.

42. On Meaning cf. Lonergan, Verbum, 2 ff; also the chapter under that title in his Method in Theology. The device in the text is obviously a simplification, nor does the complexification suggested immediately in this footnote take in all the dimensions of meaning. But within a scientific context one can easily see fruitful complexifications. The use of a_{1i} would signify different common sense meanings. Since there are different theories e.g. of the electron such notation as e_{2x} would be equivalent to the manner in which textbooks describe different theories in terms, say, of their authors. Again, there is room for superscripts to indicate where one is on the road to complete explanatory knowledge e.g. of aggression. So one would distinguish a_{3y}^{bcp} where b, c,p take on values 1,2,3, depending how one conceives animal aggression in relation to botany, chemistry, and physics. This is related to the "third step" mentioned in the citation from Insight at footnote 21 (the text at pp. 84-5).

43. B. Lonergan, Insight, 509.

44. Cf. Randomness, Statistics and Emergence, especially cpp. 3,5,9-11.

45. B. Lonergan, Insight, 460 ff.

46. N. Tinbergen, The Study of Instinct, Oxford, 1951, 103ff.

47. B. Lonergan, Insight, 265-6.

48. New York, 1966.

49. Ibid., viii.

50. Ibid., 110.

51. B. Lonergan, Insight, 265.

52. See Chapter 1, pp. 31 ff.

53. B. Lonergan, Insight, 265.

54. New York, 1967.

55. Ibid., 9.

56. Ernst Mayr, Principles of Systematic Zoology, New York, 1969, 79.

57. Ibid. 135. Cf. also Tinbergen, op.cit., 13; W.H. Thorpe, "Ecology and the Future of Systematics", The New Systematics, edited by Julian Huxley, 341-363. For detailed illustration cf., for example, P. Grover, "Newer Trends in Cecidomyiid Taxonomy", Symposium on Newer Trends in Taxonomy, National Institute of Sciences of India, New Delhi, 1966, 232-9; H.F. Barnes, "The Need for Biological Investigation in the Specific Determination of Gall Midges", Proc. 8th Internat. Cong. Ent., Stockholm, 1948, 106-110.

58. I have passed over the topic of development. It requires elaborate heuristic treatment in botany, zoology, etc. Cf. B. Lonergan, Insight, 451-479.

59. B. Lonergan, Insight, 468.

60. Ibid., 263.

61. Wyburn et alii, Human Senses and Perception, 337.

62. B. Lonergan, Insight, 263.

63. Ibid., 463.

64. Numerical taxonomy does not of course try to give
numerical value to characters; but in its method of
selecting an aggregate of characters and giving
them, normally, equal weight, it understresses what
one might call significant form, significant schemes.
For more particular taxonomic criticism, cf. H.
Khajuria, "An Assessment of Mathematical Approaches
to the Problem of Taxonomic Stability", Symposium
of Newer Trends in Taxonomy, National Institute of
Sciences of India, New Delhi, 1966, 269-274.

65. Specialization in particular philosophers, however,
should become transformed. But to develop this
point would require a discussion of the existential
nature of philosophy, and the significance of
Insight, cp. 17, and of Lonergan's Method in Theology
for this field.

66. B. Lonergan, Insight, 748.

67. It is a curiosity of our civilization that the order
of difficulty in the understanding of the levels of
being is inverted in more than the popular imagination. So, if one is very bright one may try physics
at the University; if one is a little slower botany
may be considered within one's competence; for the
less gifted there are of course the sciences of man!

Notes: Chapter 4

1. Flann O'Brien, The Dalkey Archive, London, Macgibbon
and Kee, 1964, 145.

2. Herbert Marcuse, Negations: Essays in Critical
Theory, translated by Jeremy J. Shapiro, Boston,
1968, 155.

3. Martin Jay, The Dialectic Imagination, A History
of the Frankfurt School and the Institute for Social
Research 1923-1950, Heinemann, London, 1973, 80.

4. A comment of Fr. Lonergan's in a lecture on art
during the summer-school on the philosophy of education, 1959.

5. Simone de Beauvoir, <u>The Coming of Age</u>, Warner Paper-
    back, New York, 1973, 805, 807. May I refer for-
    ward here to the quotations from Proust, regarding
    aging, in the second-last footnote of the paper?
    The present essay is, I fear, a little like
    <u>Finnegans Wake</u>: one begins where one ends.

6. See footnote 88 below, and the text there (p. 110, above

7. Francis of Assisi is surely acceptable as marking
    a problem area for the first four specialties (cf.
    M. Scheler, <u>The Nature of Sympathy</u>, London, 1954,
    on Francis' cosmic sympathy) but what of Marcel
    Proust's <u>A la Researche du Temps Perdu</u>? (The
    seven French volumes are contained in a two-volume
    translation, <u>Remembrance of Things Past</u>, Random
    House, New York, from which my quotations will be
    taken.) Which of the specialties searching things
    past will decide on his theological relevance?

8. <u>The Crisis of European Sciences and Transcendental</u>
    <u>Phenomenology</u>, translated by David Carr, North-
    western University Press, Evaston, 1970, 10.

9. I raise the issue in another context in the epilogue,
    "Being and Loneliness", to <u>Wealth of Self and</u>
    <u>Wealth of Nations: Self-Axis of the Great Ascent</u>,
    <u>Exposition Press</u>, New York, 1975. This book is an
    effort to initiate an anthropological turn in
    economics.

10. I am, of course, applying Maslow's view on the occur-
    rence of self-actualization "by my criteria, cer-
    tainly in less than one per cent of the adult popu-
    lation" (<u>Towards a Psychology of Being</u>, New York,
    1968, 204) to a particular subgroup. As a statistic
    for self-actualization among theologians it is not
    invulnerable: but the above paragraph raises a ques-
    tion, not of statistics, but of a self that the
    reader may be.

11. "...For it is not until his eyes have left the page
    that recollections of my room can be a threshold of
    oneirism for him." Gaston Bachelard, <u>The Poetics</u>
    <u>of Space</u>, Beacon Press, Boston pb, 1969, 14. This
    entire book of Bachelard's suggestions of incarnate
    remembering and reading of houses, drawers, gar-
    rets, etc., etc., belongs to the Way towards which
    this paper points.

12. <u>Insight</u>, 562-4.

13. <u>Method in Theology</u>, 88, footnote 34.

14. Two questions I was particularly anxious to raise
    at Florida were that regarding axiality and that
    regarding the danger of neglect of Insight. Fr.
    Lonergan's replies are relevant to the present con-
    text: cf. "An Interview with Fr. Bernard Lonergan,
    S.J.," Clergy Review, LVI, 1971, 428-9.

15. That cry comes extremely well from Roger Poole in
    his Towards Deep Subjectivity, Harper Torchbook,
    1972.

16. Anthony Burgess, The Novel Now, London, 1971, 79.

17. What I have in mind here is a point made already in
    chapter 1, page 19, when I quoted Blondel on the
    question of dangerous clarity.

18. James Joyce, Ulysses, London, 1958, 129.

19. Samuel Beckett, "Dante ... Bruno. Vico ... Joyce,"
    Our Exagmination Round his Factification for
    Incamination of Work in Progress. A New Directions
    Book, New York, 1972 (first published 1929), 13.

20. Walter Benjamin, Illuminations, edited with an
    introduction by Hannah Arendt, translated by Harry
    Zohn, New York, 1968, 258.

21. I refer here to the experience of Marcel Proust's
    hero, upon which the entire work pivots. For those
    unfamiliar with Proust I will quote extensively
    from the first volume of the work Swann's Way. In
    the seventh and final book, The Past Recaptured,
    Proust returns at length to the experience and the
    question of recapture (Vol. 2, pp. 990, ff-1124).
    We will return to the suggestiveness of Proust when
    we discuss memory (in the text, pp. 10, 107-111. I
    quote, then, from Vol. 1, pp. 34, 36: "Many years
    had elapsed during which nothing of Combray, save
    what was comprised in the theatre and the drama
    of my going to bed there, had any existence for me,
    when one day in winter, as I came home, my mother,
    seeing that I was cold, offered me some tea, a
    thing I did not ordinarily take. I declined at
    first, and then, for no particular reason, changed
    my mind. She sent for one of those short, plump
    little cakes called 'petites madeleines', which
    look as though they had been moulded in the fluted
    scallop of a pilgrim's shell. And soon, mechanical-
    ly, weary after a dull day with the prospect of a
    depressing morrow, I raised to my lips a spoonful

of the tea in which I had soaked a morsel of the
cake. No sooner had the warm liquid, and the
crumbs with it, touched my palate than a shudder
ran through my whole body, and I stopped, intent
upon the extraordinary changes that were taking
place. An exquisite pleasure had invaded my
senses, but individual, detached, with no suggestion of its origin. And at once the vicissitudes
of life had become indifferent to me, its disasters
innocuous, its brevity illusory - this new sensation having had on me the effect which love has
of filling me with a precious essence; or rather
this essence was not in me, it was myself. I had
ceased now to feel mediocre, accidental, mortal.
Whence could it have come to me, this all-powerful
joy? I was conscious that it was connected with
the taste of tea and cake, but that it infinitely
transcended those savours, could not, indeed, be
of the same nature as theirs. Whence did it come?
What did it signify? How could I seize upon and
define it?" (p. 34).

... "And suddenly the memory returns. The taste
was that of the little crumb of madeleine which on
Sunday mornings at Combray (because on those mornings I did not go out before church-time), when I
went to say good day to her in her bedroom, my aunt
Leonie used to give me, dipping it first in her own
cup of real or lime-flower tea. The sight of the
little madeleine had recalled nothing to my mind
before I tasted it; perhaps because I had so often ·
seen such things in the interval, without tasting
them, on the trays in pastry-cooks' windows, that
their image had dissociated itself from those
Combray days to its place among others more recent;
perhaps because of those memories, so long abandoned
and put out of mind, nothing now survived, everything was scattered; the forms of things, including that of the little scallop-shell of pastry, so
richly sensual under its severe religious folds,
were either obliterated or had been so long dor-
mant as to have lost the power of expansion which
would have allowed them to resume their place in
my consciousness. But when from a long-distant
past nothing subsists, after the people are dead,
after the things are broken and scattered, still,
alone, more fragile, but with more vitality, more
unsubstantial, more persistent, more faithful, the
smell and taste of things remain poised a long time,
like souls ready to remind us, waiting and hoping
for their moment, amid the ruins of all the rest;

and bear unfaltering, in the tiny and almost
impalpable drop of their essence, the vast structure of recollection.

And once I had recognized the taste of the crumb of
madeleine soaked in her decoction of lime-flowers
which my aunt used to give me (although I did not
yet know and must long postpone the discovery of
why this memory made me so happy) immediately the
old grey house upon the street, where her room was,
rose up like the scenery of a theatre to attach
itself to the little pavilion, opening on to the
garden, which had been built out behind it for my
parents (the isolated panel which until that moment
had been all that I could see); and with the house
the town, from morning to night and in all weathers,
the Square where I was sent before luncheon, the
streets along which I used to run errands, the
country roads we took when it was fine. And just
as the Japanese amuse themselves by filling a por-
celain bowl with water and steeping in it little
crumbs of paper which until then are without
character or form, but, the moment they become wet,
stretch themselves and bend, take on colour and dis-
tinctive shape, become flowers or houses or people,
permanent and recognizable, so in that moment all
the flowers in our garden and in M. Swann's park,
and the water-lillies on the Vivonne and the good
folk of the village and their little dwellings and
the parish church and the whole of Combray and of
its surroundings, taking their proper shapes and
growing solid, sprang into being, town and gardens
alike, from my cup of tea." (p. 36).

22.   Patrick Kavanagh, Collected Pruse, MacGibbon and
Kee, London, 1972, 155.

23.   The literature on the American scene is perhaps
familiar. The Dissenting Academy, edited by
Theodore Roszak, Random House, New York, 1967,
gives a general survey of the problem in literary
scholarship, economics, history, politics, anthropology, etc. Again, there are the writings of
Noam Chomsky, American Power and the New Mandarins,
Vintage Books, 1969; For Reasons of State, Vintage
Books, 1973. We will return to Chomsky later in
dealing with linguistics (see the text at footnote
117). The weaknesses indicated there apply also
to his political thinking, but most evident perhaps
to a student of Method in Theology (see e.g. p.
365) is the absence of procedural analysis and
distinctions between categories, policy, planning
and execution. Simone de Beauvoir puts flesh on

the problem of the French intellectual, "an intellectual no longer has any role to play" (The
Mandarins, Fontana Books, London, 1960, 540). We
will return briefly to these issues in the text at
footnote 128, pp. 114 ff above.

23a. A. Toynbee, Experiences, Oxford University Press,
New York and London, 1969, 356.

24. The concluding footnote to the previous chapter
gives body to the point. More on the problem of
hierarchization in the text, text, pp. 112 ff.

25. Robert Heilbroner, The Human Prospect.

26. A text relevant to my meaning here is Insight, 393,
398-9, 504-6, on the metaphysician as reorientating
his science and common sense. But also relevant,
as will appear gradually, is such comment as "when
one is endeavouring to explain, one is orientated
to the universe of being; one is setting up distinctions within being; one is relating distinct
beings to one another; and one is relegating all
the merely descriptive elements in knowledge to
particular instances of the case that arises when
some being with sense and imagination is related
though his senses and imagination to other beings."
(Insight, p. 505). It is a startlingly strange
perspective!

27. I used the term "perspective" in this paper initial-
ly in strict continuity with the meaning of per-
spectivism as far as I could glean it, in Method
in Theology (see index, under perspective, per-
spectivism), but as I move to a conclusion I fancy
my meaning is more incarnational than Fr. Lonergan
perhaps intended. It would take much more than a
footnote, however, to indicate the elements relating to feeling, sympathy, ecstasy, etc., of Method
in Theology I am developing. One would need to
go forward from the viewpoint indicated in the
text below (descriptively, the citation at footnote
33) backed by a transformed discussion of many-
levelled memory. The possibility of "reading" the
human past is not just the invariance of basic
mind, and the probability-schedules of more adequate interpreters may eventually include electro-
encephalographic conjugates relating to psychic
flexibility.

28. What I mean by fantasy will gradually be indicated.
     What I mean by probability schedules of emergent
     probability cannot be grasped sine artificio (see
     footnote 135 below) such as that suggested in my
     Randomness, Statistics and Emergence (Gill
     Macmillan and Notre Dame, 1970), p. 237, where I
     discuss F.M. Fisher's proposal of a multiple Markov
     matrix as giving a picture of history. Perhaps,
     too, the hard-headed foundations person, doing that
     part of metaphysics which falls to him (see Method
     in Theology, p. 287, at footnote 10; also footnotes
     44, 74, 140 below) had best think Kondratieff-wise
     towards the year 2040 when he or she is figuring
     out categories of innovation.

29. (My footnote). The mythology regarding Science
     present not only in the popular imagination but in
     the journals of philosophy is quite something in
     these times of 'man come of age'. For a good
     illustration of an economist struggling gallantly
     out of 'scientific economics' towards a procedure
     inclusive of what he calls micro-autonomy see
     Adolf Lowe, Economic Knowledge. Towards a Science
     of Political Economics, Harper and Row, New York,
     1965.

30. Op.cit., footnote 35 above, p. 30.

31. Insight, 733.

32. The text, pp. 10 ff.

33. Marcel Proust, op.cit., vol. 2, 874.

34. Note that I do not add 'temporal'. Although I ven-
     ture no view on procedural luminosity in angels,
     nor on their exceptional status in regard to instru-
     mental acts of meaning, (for a beginning in angelic
     dialogue see P. de Lanversin, "Le Concept de
     Presence", Recherches de Sciences Religieuse, 1933,
     58-80), I would not consider it (especially in
     these days of ESP enthusiasm) theologically irre-
     levant to pursue such questions. Again, there is
     the topic of procedural reflection in Christ: here
     one might take off from F.E. Crowe, 'Eschaton in
     the Mind and Heart of Jesus', The Eschaton: A
     Community of Love, Villanuova University Press,
     1974.

35. Relevant here is Insight, 573 ff. on the limita-
     tions of the treatise. Some of the reasons for my
     strategy will I hope gradually rise up in the
     reader's perspective.

36. J.-P. Sartre, Being and Nothingness, London, 1957,
21.

37. To be taken in the context of Lonergan's comment
on Schleiermacher's procedure (Insight, 678) on
Kant's view (Insight, 685; Collection, 86), and on
the paradox of finite intellect (Collection, 190).

38. Cf. footnote 14 above. The axiality may be described in terms of control, of Selbstvollzug
(Method in Theology, 363) and here one might consider the two times of the temporal subject as discussed by Lonergan, De Deo Trino II, Gregorian
Press, Rome, 1964, 196-204. Cf. also Collection,
256.: "changes in the control of meaning mark off
the great epochs in human history."

39. Add a context such as Lonergan, De Deo Trino I,
Gregorian Press, Rome, 1964, 274.

40. In the introduction to Language Truth and Meaning,
Gill Macmillan and Notre Dame, 1972, 5.

41. Method in Theology, 260.

42. The question of refined or opaque sensibility is
one around which this paper spirals. "The apprehension of values and disvalues is a task not of
understanding but of intentional response. Such
response is all the fuller, all the more discrimi-
nating, the better a man one is, the more refined
one's sensibility, the more delicate one's feelings" (B. Lonergan, Method in Theology, 245). I
quote from Lonergan's introduction to the issue
of dialectic. An American may think more concretely of this issue in terms, for example, of extended research in American dialects (for a phantasm see Webster's New World Dictionary, 1970,
inner cover: non sine artificio: see footnote 135
below), the problem of an evaluative interpretation of Growth Games (the title of a book by H.R.
Lewis and H.S. Streitfeld, Bantam, New York, 1972),
a dialectic of the history of the conflict of white
and red sensibilities (I think of the Indian Vine
Deloria's critique of Christianity e.g. God is Red,
1973; Custer Died for Your Sins, 1968).

43. Cf. footnote 24, and the corresponding text, p.
100. The higher sciences appear elementary because
of their lack of development. The potential methodologist should bear this in mind in tackling the

first five chapters of Insight with their five-finger exercises.

44. Howard H. Pattee, (ed.), Hierarchy Theory: The Challenge of Complex Systems, Braziller, New York, 1973, in his preface, xi.

45. From the Preface of the Nativity of the old Latin Mass.

46. Flann O'Brien, op.cit., footnote 1, 88.

47. "All we know is somehow with us; it is present and operative within our knowledge; but it lurks behind the scenes" (Insight, 278). And all we know and are is somehow in what we say. But who will hear it? Fleshed analysis of Process is an eternal and surprising process: but that view requires an amount of self-digestive listening towards which the present paper points. Is the paper not rather dealing with fourth level functional specialization? On the overlap of dialectic and foundations with procedural analysis, see footnotes 55 and 74 below. The question of reading with "all we know somehow with us" will be followed through the paper, with counterpointing especially at footnotes 53 and 129.

48. Cf. Method in Theology, 270: "what is paramount is control of process."

49. I refer to the work of Jerzy Grotowski in his experimental theatre. Cf. the collection of articles and interviews, Jerzy Grotowski, Towards A Poor Theatre, A Touchstone Book, 1968. According to Peter Brook, Director of the Royal Shakespeare Company in England, "No one since Stanislavski has investigated the nature of acting, its phenomenon, its meaning, the nature and science of its mental-physical-emotional processes as deeply and completely as Grotowski" (ibid., preface, p. 13). Obviously one must allow for possible exaggeration, but what I wish to point out to the reader is the interest in 'hyphenated' process indicated.

50. Grotowski, op.cit., 40.

51. Grotowski, op.cit., 57.

52. Samuel Beckett, Endgame. I recall here Beckett's remark "I think anyone nowadays who pays the slightest attention to his own experience finds it

the experience of a non-knower." (Quoted in the
Introduction to Beckett in Masters of Modern Drama,
edited by H.M. Block and R.G. Shedd, Random House,
New York, 1972).

53. See footnotes 47 and 129. Can you imagine, fanta-
size, the transposition being done with some spontaneity? A century ago Ruskin accused Whistler of
"flinging a pot of paint in the public's face" ...
Whistler's mother, for instance, had become an
"Arrangement in Grey and Black" (1871). Now
Mondrian is old hat. Could there not be a shift
in the "realism" of reading? So that the expression on the page might be like the text of a Chopin
Ballade sight-read by a Van Cliburn? But one must
begin with five-finger exercises.

54. See the text at footnote 137, p. 116.

55. This is not easy to conceive adequately. The reader
may raise the question, for example, How much of
Insight and Method in Theology recur in the categories of foundations. See also footnotes 74, 140,
141.

56. The reader may pursue the question of the sense in
which such aggregates can be integrated in a
reader, and mesh this question with the sociology
of address (Berger's "we become what we are addressed
as by others").

57. A central topic which we will come round to below,
in the text, pp. 107-111.

58. I am indebted here to an unpublished doctorate
thesis of the University of Toronto, The Transcendental Vindication of the First Step in Realist
Metaphysics, According to Joseph Marechal by J.M.
Vertin, of the Department of Philosophy, St.
Michael's College, University of Toronto, for light
on Marechal and Fichte. The latter's recognition
of pure self-determining activity as an a priori
dynamic condition of possibility was for Marechal
the major post-Kantian step. Dr. Vertin's thesis
may be indicated by considering the four following
disjunctive questions (see his thesis pp. 316-26).

1. Are the constitutive transcendental conditions
(i.e. of the descriptive object-of-consciousness)
merely formal, static, or also active, dynamic?

2. Are the active, dynamic constitutive transcendental conditions merely synthetic or also
finalistic?

3. Is the metaphysics implied by the finalistic,
active, dynamic constitutive transcendental condition idealist or realist?

4. Is primitive transcendental self-awareness
intrinsically reflexive or intrinsically non-
reflexive?

On Marechal's interpretative reading of the history
of modern philosophy, the first three issues are
manifested in the criticisms of Hume by Kant, of
Kant by Fichte, and of Fichte by Marechal. Marechal
in each concludes to the second alternative. The
fourth issue is not explicitly treated by Marechal.
His tendency, however, is to assume intrinsic re-
flexiveness. It is the tendency of a large group
of contemporary theologians. If one clearly takes
the position on this issue, the second alternative,
one brings forth categories, the fall-out from
which, for example, in trinitarian and christo-
logical systematics are unacceptable to that group.

59. The reader should have no difficulty in finding
illustrations, even in relation to Lonergan's work,
of such debates - Lonergan and Collins, Lonergan
and Dewart, Lonergan and Ogden, etc., etc., - which
need location and transformation to fit into the
new context. But there is a deeper issue which
the reader might raise by putting the question,
Why indeed, should the specialty history tie in
with the level of truth? See, in this connection,
the text below, p. 107, at footnotes 69 and 70.

60. Chapter 2 gives some indication of the complexity
of the problem and of the relevance of functional
specialization in this area. It is quite another
matter to spell out with precision the special
tasks of music history, music criticism, music
theory, etc. And it is a further matter to indicate the symbiotic relationship between this methodological spelling-out and foundations of musicology.

60a. Insight, xxviii.

61. Brendan Kennelly, "Good Souls, to Survive",
Selected Poems, Allan Figgis, Ltd., Dublin, 1969,
37.

62. George Armstrong Kelly, "Notes on Hegel's 'Lordship
and Bondage'", Hegel: A Collection of Critical
Essays, edited by Alasdair MacIntyre, Anchor Books
New York, 1972, 191. The essay is reprinted from
The Review of Metaphysics, XIX, 1966.

63. I would refer the reader here, as I do at footnotes
    11 and 103 to Bachelard's work on The Poetics of
    Space, his consideration of "houses in which the
    human beings' certainty of being is concentrated"
    (p. 33). He expresses very beautifully a direction
    I am trying to give in the following sections:
    "the space we love is unwilling to remain permanent-
    ly enclosed. It deploys and appears to move else-
    where without difficulty; into other times, and on
    different planes of dream and memory" (p. 53).

64. Lionel Trilling, Sincerity and Authenticity,
    Harvard University Press pb., 1973, 8.

65. I am drawing a parallel here between Insight and
    the first book of Proust's Remembrance of Things
    Past, Swann's Way, which pivots on the little
    phrase from Vinteuil's sonata: "The little phrase,
    as soon as it struck his ear, had the power to
    liberate in him the room that was needed to contain
    it; the proportions of Swann's soul were altered".
    "Deep repose, mysterious refreshment for Swann, -
    for him whose eyes, although delicate interpreters
    of painting, whose mind, although an acute observer
    of manners, must bear for ever the imprint of the
    barrenness of his life, - to feel himself trans-
    formed into a creature foreign to humanity, blinded,
    deprived of his logical faculty, almost a fantas-
    tic unicorn, a chimaera-like creature conscious of
    the world through his two ears alone" (op.cit.,
    Vol. 1, p. 182, also Vol. 2, pp. 1000ff). An ade-
    quate re-reading of Insight should pivot on the
    little phrase (quoted at footnote 60a, page 105)
    of the Introduction. But pivot to what dimensions?
    With the power eventually to liberate in the reader
    the room, the philosophic space, to hear with
    altered flesh and soul all instrumental acts in
    each and each in all. See, in this present chap-
    ter, the sequence of footnotes 47, 53, 129, and
    add the sequence 82, 106.

66. Cf. the comments above, in the footnotes 24, 43,
    and corresponding texts, pp. 100, 102.

67. The reader should find it interesting to listen to
    Lonergan in dialogue about the dog, so I quote here
    two significant passages: "A useful preliminary
    is to note that animals know, not merely phenomena,
    but things: dogs know their masters, bones, other
    dogs, and not merely the appearance of these things.
    Now this sensitive integration of sensible data

also exists in the human animal and even in the
human philosopher. Take it as knowledge of reality,
and there results the secular contrast between the
solid sense of reality and the bloodless categories
of the mind. Accept the sense of reality as criterion of reality, and you are a materialist,
sensist, positivist, pragmatist, sentimentalist,
and so on, as you please. Accept reason as a
criterion but retain the sense of reality as what
gives meaning to the term 'real', and you are an
idealist; for, like the sense of reality, the
reality defined by it is non-rational. In so far
as I grasp it, the Thomist position is the clear-
headed third position: reason is the criterion and,
as well, it is reason - not the sense of reality -
that gives meaning to the term 'real'. The real
is what is; and 'what is' is known in the rational
act, judgement." (Verbum, Word and Idea in
Aquinas, Notre Dame, 1967, 7).

"Suppose that on this table there is a small but
very restless dog, moving about, demanding attention, whimpering, making a nuisance of himself.
However, that supposition merely provides an
ontological cause. What is first in our knowledge
is a stream of sensible presentations. That stream
might be organized or unorganized in a variety of
manners. It might give rise to the reaction described by Sartre in La Nausee, or to a vital adapta-
tion if the dog suddenly barked or snapped at one,
or to any degree of seeing without noticing, noticing without attending, or attending that issues
forth into any of a wide variety of psychological
processes. However, you are philosophers. The
presentations to you are organized by detached intellectual inquiry. You verify that they cannot
be classed as illusory or hallucinatory. You attend
to them, not as kinds of individual data, despite
their spatial and temporal multiplicity, you grasp
an intelligible unity, a single whole, an identity
that unites what in space is here and there and
what in time is then and now. From that insight
there proceeds the concept of a thing. You revert
from the concept to the data to conceive the particular object of thought, this thing. In fact,
all this supposing has yielded merely an object of
thought. But if the supposing all were true, then
all of you would be certain of the dog's real,
concrete, actual existence. Why?" (Collection,
Herder and Herder, New York, 1967, 161.)

I recall my own personal experience of first

reading the passage from Verbum in, I think, the
Winter of 1958, and getting my first intimation of
the position of startling strangeness. Reading-
stance is of course all important. How, for instance, did you read the word 'you' in the above
passages? Are you perhaps a materialist? A transformed dialogue would have to round the delicate
corner of conventions at conventions and conventions of address so that there would be sharing
without resentment of the strangeness of you and I,
the human animals in question.

68. "Jack and Jill" are of course borrowed from Lonergan's
'Cognitional Structure', Collection, 232-7.

69. We indicate an enlarged view of memory and fantasy
in the remainder of the paper.

70. Method in Theology, 253.

71. Fichte's Sun-Clear Statement was printed, in the
English translation of A.E. Kroeger, in The Journal
of Speculative Philosophy, Vol. II, 1868. The same
Journal prints Kroeger's translation of Fichte's
introduction to the Science of Knowledge written
in 1797, three years after the first publication
of his full system. A piece of it is worth quoting in the present context, and in relation to the
concluding remarks of this essay: "The author of
the Science of Knowledge was soon convinced, through
a slight acquaintance with the philosophical literature since the appearance of Kant's Critiques, that
the object of this great man - to effect a total
reform in the study of philosophy, and hence of all
science - had resulted in a failure, since not one
of his numerous successors appeared to understand
what he had really spoken of. The author believed
that he had understood the latter; he resolved to
devote his life to a representation - totally independent from Kant's - of that great discovery,
and he will not give up this resolve. Whether he
will succeed better in making himself understood
to his age, time alone can show. At all events,
he knows that nothing true and useful, which has
once been given to mankind, is lost, though only
remote posterity should learn how to use it."

72. Cf. footnote 34, above. Against the background of
Fr. Crowe's article and Fr. Lonergan's work on
Christ's mental life (De Verbo Incarnato,
Gregorian Press, Rome, 1964, esp. 335-416), it
would seem clear that Christ did not have "a
house for the position."

73. The beginning of Brian Moore's novel, I am Mary Dunne, McClelland and Stewart, Toronto, 1966.

74. See footnotes 55, 140, 141. The fourth level specializations are intrinsically procedural and intentionally concrete in a manner which sets them apart from the other six, and leaves them with problems of expression proper to them that this present paper is but an "opening out to".

75. Insight, 502-9.

76. Insight, xxviii.

77. I think here of the poem "Transcend" in Hermann Hesse's novel, Magister Ludi (Bantam, New York, 1970), 421, the poem written by Joseph Knecht "on one of those special days on which he had experienced that spiritual shock which he called 'awakening'" (p. 345). Later he changed the title to "Stages" (see footnote 90 below and the text, p. 110). The poem includes a verse which one may link with Bachelard's remark of footnote 103, and with the text below at footnote 88:

    "Serenely let us move to distant places
    and Let no sentiments of home detain us.
    The Cosmic Spirit seeks not to restrain us
    But lifts us stage by stage to wider spaces.
    If we accept a home of our own making,
    Familiar habit makes for indolence.
    We must prepare for parting and leave-taking
    Or else remain the slaves of permanence."

78. Marcel Proust, op.cit., Vol. 2, 984.

79. They Speak by Silences by a Carthusian, Longmans, 1959, 5-6.

80. Cf. footnotes 11, 63, 77, 103.

81. Herbert Marcuse, Eros and Civilization, Beacon Press, Boston, 1966, 232.

82. My stress here, of course, is on understanding or "reading" the object, as in contrast with the other features of interpretation (see Method in Theology, 155-62), an aspect of basic importance in dialectic interpretation (the intending subject is, too, an object to be read).

83. Recall footnotes 11 and 65.

84. Andre Maurois, From Proust to Camus, Doubleday Anchor, 1968, 8.

85. See footnote 104 and the corresponding text, page 111; also footnote 53.

86. Insight, 542.

87. A remark of Debussy, made in relation to The Rites of Spring, quoted in Donald Mitchell, The Language of Music, Faber, London, 1966, 22.

88. A. Maslow, The Further Reaches of Human Nature, Viking Compass, pb., 1972, 349.

89. Cf. footnote 27.

90. The matter is technical and requires elaborate systematics. Popularly, cf. the quotation from Beckett, footnote 52, or Aquinas' remark, "It is all straw." Adult Growth, in procedural analysis or in other suffering, pati (cf. Verbum, index, and note that the dispute which Lonergan deals with runs right through the present paper) is a revela- tion of open nescience knitted where probable (aggreformically - see footnote 125 and the text there - and the hierarchic mix is individual) with lower level harmonics. Its stages (see footnote 77) merit indeed a Rite of Passage, a Sacrament of the Way, in any community which is not radically alienated.

91. Insight, 469-79, adds a context. My stress here is on genetic rather than dialectic development of the person's position and feelings - a therapy therefore of the normal (but which of us is nor- mal? or which of us can lay claim to growth without darkness?)

92. I would refer the reader here forward to footnote 143, with Proust's comments on growth and non- growth. The comments are part of a lengthy subtle account of a reception, and the reader probably needs little fantasy in envisaging a like contem- porary reception. The metaphor of "stilts" is telling. Our spontaneous materialism leads us to measure growth in the terms of the lowest science.

93. This is a very large question, going beyond the issue of ordinary common sense reaction to art to the problem of art criticism, its nature and ade- quacy. I am no enemy of serious criticism, of the

mediation of mind. But functional specialization
puts its problems in a new context, and would, for
instance, point up more clearly the place of aesthetic conversion.

94. Reading of this passage in the mode indicated in
footnote 129, would, I expect, be psychedelic,
whatever tradition of ultimacy one is in. The axial
turning and spiralling is of surprising dimensions.
"Sandhyas! Sandhyas! Sandhyas! Calling all downs.
Calling all downs to dayne. Array! Surrection!"
begins Finnegan's Awakening, "The smog is lofting"
Finnegans Wake, 593). Sandhyas is a Sanskrit word
meaning "twilight, the period between aeons, period
of junction"). No one, you may say, can beget the
habit of thinking all the mesons of, thinking all
the oxygen of, thinking ... of, say Frederick the
Great's horse, or of Bucephalus. No one? Can?
"A way, the Margan, from out astamite, through
dimdom done till light kindling light has led we
hopas but hunt me the journey on, iteritinerant..."
(ibid., 594). Time, the second millions years, is
on our side.

95. Obviously what I am asking for, pointing towards,
is in the reader (whether potentia prima, proxima
or habitualis is for the reader to self-question),
and the entire paper points. The self-digestion
includes, of course, all the usual facets of
therapy: dream-absorption, etc.

96. Insight, 385.

97. Insight, 741-2.

98. I refer again to Roger Poole's work (cf. footnote
15, above). He concludes his final chapter, on
"Philosophical Space", with the remarks: "Deep
subjectivity emerges finally then as a concern for
objectivity, for a full, real and adequate objectivity. In order to express this concern, it has to
discover (first of all) and then to trust to (even
harder) a space of personally won philosophical
commitment.

Deep subjectivity operates from within this philosophical space with the tools of subjective analysis
and critique. It thus affects and challenges the
world of objectivity and sets up a more acceptable
standard of objectivity beside it.

Everything remains to be done, and time is growing
short."

99. I think of work in continuity with that of Durand
     (see footnote 116 below). See Lonergan's comments
     on inner communication, "An Interview with Fr.
     Bernard Lonergan, S.J.", Clergy Review LVI (1971),
     422; Method in Theology, 66-7.

100. While this sensitivity may be taken in a secular
     context I recall St. Ignatius's sentire et gustare
     and St. Theresa's Mansions, and I repeat in this
     context footnote 38 of the Epilogue to the Wealth
     of Self and Wealth of Nations: "The problem is
     closely related to the development of a new
     spirituality, meshing such streams as the Francis-
     can, the Carmelite, the Ignatian and negative
     mysticisms of East and West into a new objective
     interiority." See also footnote 106, below.

101. A question within systematic eschatology.

102. Insight, 700, gives an added context.

103. Gaston Bachelard, op.cit., footnote 11, above.
     See also footnote 63.

104. Quoted in W.I. Thompson, At the Edge of History,
     Harper Colophon book, 1971, 152, 170.

105. Fiction, of course, falls within the arts, and
     with it science fiction. But I feel that there is
     an overdose of "mollycules" in a great deal of the
     latter: my preference is for something either like
     C.S. Lewis' Narnia books for children, or for big-
     ger children the vegetation of Perelandra. The
     contemporary Bloom alias Henry Flower suffers from
     stifled botanical conjugates, "Language of flowers.
     They like it because no-one can hear" (Joyce,
     Ulysses, London, 1952, 70). Fiction is an art
     to fantasy in my present sense, which includes in
     its heuristic a thinking of this (see Insight, 249).

106. This quotation, from the same talk on art by Fr.
     Lonergan indicated in footnote 4, raises many issues.
     The issue of horizon-maintenance central to this
     paper is there: Julian of Norwich has parallel
     expression (The Revelations of Divine Love, trans-
     lated by James Walsh, D.J., London, 1961, 63).
     The issue of history as revelation is there, and
     there is the possibility of acknowledging the total
     Histocosmos as primary word of God. (I am in-
     debted here to an unpublished course of F.E. Crowe
     on The Word of God.) The issue, finally, of self-

digestion in faith-perspective is there, of open-
sensed absorption of the instrumental acts of God,
of the world as mime: "mime is not an empty
chattering but a quiet tragedy, a lyrical recital,
the echo of silence, which specifies with its mute
measures the rhythm of time" (Marcel Marceau, Die
Weltkunst der Pantomime, Zurich, p. 56).

107. J. Brennan, Three Philosophical Novelists, 45.

108. Consider, in this context and in relation to our
circular ramblings, Lonergan's remarks on the reading of Aquinas: "Inasmuch as one may suppose that
one already possesses a habitual understanding similar to that of Aquinas, no method or effort is needed to understand as Aquinas understood; one has
simply to read, and the proper acts of understanding and meaning will follow. But one may not be
ready to make that assumption on one's own behalf.
Then one has to learn. Only by the slow, repeti-
tious, circular labor of going over and over the
data, by catching here a little insight and there
another, by following through false leads and pro-
fiting from many mistakes, by continuous adjustments and cumulative changes of one's initial sup-
positions and perspectives and concepts, can one
hope to attain such a development of one's own
understanding as to hope to understand what Aquinas
understood and meant." (Verbum, 216).

109. Recall Blondel's remarks as cited in chapter 1, page
p. 19.

110. Cf. Method in Theology, the index under Post-; include also post-aesthetic, post-mystical, etc., etc.

110a. J.H. Woodger, The Axiomatic Method in Biology,
Cambridge, 1937.

111. See Don Davis Roberts, "The Existential Graphs and
Natural Deduction", Studies in the Philosophy of
C.S. Peirce edited by E.C. Moore and R.S. Robin,
University of Massachusetts Press, 1964, 190-21.

112. I have developed this in other contexts: cf. the
epilogue to Wealth of Self and Wealth of Nations,
and the previous chapter here, in footnote 42.
The points are resumed in the concluding pages of
this chapter.

113. "A concrete plurality of lower entities may be the material cause from which a higher form is educed" (B. Lonergan, 'Finality, Love, Marriage', Collection, 20). This article is an obvious candidate for sublation into general heuristics.

114. The question of "filling out" is of extreme importance. As a context take the comments in Insight on "division of labour" (p. 498) and "loss of contact" (p. 509), then look back at the history of philosophy and theology in its books and locations, and look forward to the future of a theology blossoming from Method in Theology. Could it happen that the categories of foundations become new words in old battles? This is the question round (cf. footnote 129, below) which my paper rambled. If I have wandered about in seeming unconcern for division of labour, it was not with the intention of denying that division, but with the hope that such a tour would spark a quite different glimpse of future and Future, so that, in the tenement-address that we so liberally add to the cosmic word, the reader's "soul too might not harden in the end into the neat, self-contained shape it is desirable souls should take," (Patrick White, The Tree of Man, Penguin, 42), so that we might have a more adequate Shaping of the Foundations.

115. I refer here to an old Thomist thesis regarding the variability of materia for a higher form, but obviously the thesis is to be sublated in aggreformism (cf. the text here at footnote 125).

116. G. Durand, Les Structures Anthropologiques de l' Imaginaire, Paris, 1963, cf. p. 39 for references to Batcherevian reflexology.

117. "The correspondence between Freud's terms and system and the structures discovered by modern linguistics is so close and so striking that Dr. Lacan was led inevitably to what is perhaps his most startling conclusion, that the structure of the unconscious is the structure of language." Jan Miel, "Jacques Lacan and the structure of the unconscious," Structuralism, edited by Jacques Ehrmann, Doubleday Anchor, 1970, 98, (italics his). If the thesis to follow in the text above holds, then Lacan's synthetic advance also carries forward weaknesses in both Freud and Chomsky.

118. In II de An., lect. 18, parag. 477.

119. Insight, 555.

120.   For an indication of aggreformism, cf., below,
        especially the references at footnote 125. Regard-
        ing perspective, what I said at footnote 27 holds.
        So, for example, one does not develop a spontaneous
        hierarchic aggreformist vocabulary for psychology
        or politics without a new level of incarnate mean-
        ing. Again, consider the problem of musical ex-
        pression. However strange they may seem to Western
        ears, the songs of Ramnad Krishnan, mediated main-
        ly by an incarnate tradition, are aggreformist
        hierarchic, whereas music such as that of Xenakis,
        mediated by higher mathematics, may well have the
        weaknesses of some of contemporary linguistics talk
        of "deep structure", and may eventually be heard
        no more. But the point is that mediation of mind
        occurs and increases in all fields. If that media-
        tion is itself mediated by a fertile or an infertile
        thematic heuristic this fertility or lack of it
        terminates in concrete human subjects' spontaneous
        orientation or disorientation.

121.   J. Piaget, Structuralism, London, 1971, 90.

122.   Ibid., 60-6.

123.   Later, writing of the problem of the relation be-
        tween language and thought, Piaget remarks: "We
        can obviously not begin to solve the problem here;
        all we mean to do is to indicate what, from a
        structuralist perspective and taking recent develop-
        ments into account, the state of the question is."
        (Ibid., 92).

124.   Albert Wilson, "Systems Epistemology" in The World
        System, edited by Ervin Laszlo, Braziller, New York
        1973, 125-6.

125.   B. Lonergan, Verbum: Word and Idea in Aquinas,
        Notre Dame, 1967, 25. Lonergan is writing here in
        an Aristotelian Thomist context of the difficulty
        of conceiving the philosophic concepts of form and
        matter. I have spelt out the difficulty in the con
        text of modern science in Randomness, Statistics
        and Emergence, Gill Macmillan and Notre Dame, 1970,
        especially in chapter 9 on "Randomness and Emer-
        gence". In chapter 1 I indicated the need for
        hylemorphic vocabulary in botany (above, 25). In
        chapter 3 I have a similar indication with regard
        to zoology (above, 9). Perhaps the word "aggre-
        formic" indicates better than the word "hyle-
        morphic" the contemporary need. At the level of

the lowest science aggreformism becomes hylemorphism.

126. For a survey see John Lyons (ed.), New Horizons in
      Linguistics, Pelican, 1970.

127. "What goes forward" in the usual journals and con-
      ventions of philosophy of science is worth con-
      sidering in this context. See A. Maslow, Towards
      a Psychology of Being, New York, 1968, Appendix A:
      "Are our publications and conventions suitable for
      the personal psychologies?"; also his The Psychology
      of Science, Gateway pb., Chicago, 1969, especially
      chapter 3 where he discusses "The Cognitive Needs
      under Conditions of Fear and of Courage".

128. I have been trying, throughout, to put more flesh
      on the introductory words of Method in Theology, "A
      Theology mediates between a cultural matrix and the
      significance and role of a religion in that matrix."
      A theologian is a person of ultimate concern con-
      tributing to the mediation of survival, supervivere,
      through a commitment to reflection in his or her
      own life with others: that reflection lives in
      symbiotic mediation with concrete adult growth,
      whether his or her specialization is in putting in
      question the patterns of the past or in putting
      forth signs of probable invariants of the future.

129. "bagdad, sir, yond would be for a once over our all
      honoured christmastyde easteredman. Fourth posi-
      tion of solution. How johnny! Finest view from
      horizon. Tableau final." (Finnegans Wake, 590)
      And in this final footnote I would like to thank
      my wife Fiona for her many-faceted support in
      these five years, as well as the friends who saw
      me through the many changes from Joyce's Jesuit
      Dublin to the New World Academic Discord. Most
      especially I wish to thank Fr. Lonergan both for
      friendship and light. Nor could I pass over in
      thanksgiving my friendly Nova Scotia typist, Miss
      Mary Joyce.

      Might I now be so foolish as to put the message of
      the paper, indeed of the book, in a few words?
      The problem is to change the statistics of those
      capable of what I call Vertical Reading (recall
      the composer O'Riada's Vertical Man - it has a
      nice Ascensional symbolism! - recall also the sus-
      picion of verticality in some contemporary music:
      see p. 58, above). Recall, too, previous

footnotes on reading, on five-finger exercises, etc., etc. Advanced exercises consist in applying one's incipient heuristic perspective to each word of a text, say, "...offense, repentance, apology, forgiveness..." (Method in Theology, 65), so that each word disappears into the best you can do in specifying the heuristic history of the hierarchy of aggregates of aggregates of aggregates ... of the objects referred to. Progress is slow: like a beginner trying to mesh right and left hand in reading Chopin's Fantasie Impromptu in C# Minor. But a decade or two could see you reading louder and clearer and capable of new speech. "In that earopean end meets Ind ... And your last words todate in camparative accoustomology are going to tell stretch of a fancy through strength towards joyance..." (Finnegans Wake, 598).

130. We have the context of footnotes 128 and 129. A developed dialectic theologian hears a sermon, not only with piety but with his heuristic ear to the cosmos. A foundational theologian may not be competent to preach or instruct preachers, but he will not be without perspective on what might go forward. So, for instance, the distinctions between intellectual, moral and religious conversion have a fallout down through doctrines and systematics yielding new normative skeleton-schemes for preaching and counselling. See also footnotes 140, 141.

131. Cf. Method in Theology, 366-7.

132. P. Kavanagh, Collected Pruse, Macgibbon and Kee, London, 1972, 151.

133. "A Dublin tradesman printed his name and trade in archaic Erse on his cart. He knew that hardly anybody could read it: he did it to annoy. In his position I think he was quite right." G.K. Chesterton, George Bernard Shaw, Bodley Head, London, 1961, 16.

134. An artistic example may help for it is a question of the mediation of transformed instruments. Think of the history of the piano and what a blues pianist or a Rubenstein can do with the contemporary piano. Then think in fantasy of the second million years of music and theology that we are beginning.

135. I would recall here Lonergan's remark in the twenty-fourth point of his discussion of the hypostatic

union: "Quae quidem omnium per modum unius
apprehensio vel formalis esse potest vel virtualis.
Et virtualis quidem est inquantum quis habet
habitum ut prompte, faciliter et saltem sine
tristitia ad quamlibet quaestionem usque ad ultimum
"cur" respondere possit. At formalis non est sine
quodam artificio; hac enim in vita nihil intelligere
possumus nisi per conversionem ad phantasma; at in
quaestione longiori atque difficiliori phantasma
conveniens haberi non potest nisi per diagramma
quoddam adiuvatur ipsa imaginatio; et ideo qui omnia
per modum unius apprehendere velit, diagramma quoddam
faciat in quo et elementa quaestionis omnia omnesque
inter elementa nexus symbolice repraesententur."
(De Constitutione Christi Ontologica et Psychologica,
Gregorian Press, Rome, 1961, 80).

136. The reader would probably find it a useful expansion of heuristics to read here Insight, 464, "study
of the organism...", replacing "organism" by "Manhood of Christ", then continuing through the chapter with this perspective.

137. Above, p. 35.

138. This is related both to the need for internal communication (Method in Theology, 66), literary language's relation to lack of mutual presence (ibid.,
72), and of course the mediation in all this of
self-appreciative understanding of modes of meaning (ibid., 172-3). Chapter two above, on Metamusic and Self-Meaning, is only an indication of
one area of the latter needed mediation.

139. Footnote 42 of chapter three. See also Wealth of
Self and Wealth of Nations, in the Epilogue, 113-4.

140. Method in Theology, 170-1.

141. H. Butterfield, The Origins of Modern Science,
London, 1965, vii.

142. See Lonergan's contribution to the dialogue,
"Variations in Fundamental Theology", one of a
series of lectures given in the University of
Toronto, 1973, under the general title "Revolution
in Catholic Theology?".

143. Or whatever "hard-headed practical men" need convincing "that by God's grace intelligent and

reasonable solutions can work and, on the other
hand, that the desertion of intelligent and reasonable solutions for 'realist' policies is the operative principle in the breakdown and disintegration
of civilizations", (Insight, 747).

144. As I have indicated already, I am not advocating
that the generals rush to the trenches, though I
see no reason why a foundational theologian should
not have an occasional good dinner at an influential person's expense. There is a larger problem
here of placing the definition of metaphysics (see
Insight, 391; and Method in Theology, 287, under
(6)) correctly in the new context. What I am advocating is that the foundational theologian conceive adequately the categories of implementation.

145. See, for example, footnote 42 as loosely indicative
of concrete intention, but not as a normative procedural indication: that is already indicated in
Method in Theology, 249-50. I would note however
the spiralling possibilities intrinsic to functional specialization - a Finnegans Wake image or even
a snowball image can help. There is an ideal-type
circulation from first specialty to last and back
again, and that ideal type contains within it the
goal of the concrete category of globo-historical
statistics of aggreform persons anonymously in
Love - the ideal foundations persons' basic theological speech - becoming every dialectic theologian's genetic concern. See footnote 94.

146. Method in Theology, 363.

147. Various authors have been mentioned who deal with
questions of adult-growth and aging, but I do recom-
mend for digestion the subtle observations of
Proust's hero in the context of the reception of
the Princess of Guermantes (Vol. 2, pp. 1029-1124).
"Ski, for example, as little altered as a flower or
a fruit that has dried, one of those connoissuers,
'celibates of art', who go through life useless
and unsatisfied. Ski had thus remained like an
embryonic attempt, confirming my theories on art.
Others followed him who were not in any way con-
noisseurs of art, society people who took an interest in nothing, and they, too, had not been
ripened by age but their still rosy-cheeked faces
retained the cheerful expression of their early
youth, even though bordered with the first fringe
of wrinkles and crowned with a wreath of white

hair. They were not old folk but young people of
eighteen, very much faded" (p. 1042). Contrast
this with the man who "had wavered as he made his
way along the difficult summit of his eighty-three
years, as if men were perched on giant stilts, sometimes taller than church spires, constantly growing
and finally rendering their progress so difficult
and perilous that they suddenly fall. I was
alarmed that mine were already so tall beneath my
feet; it did not seem as if I should have the
strength to carry much longer attached to me that
past which already extended so far down and which
I was bearing painfully within me!" (p. 1123).

148. Flann O'Brian, op.cit., footnote 1 above, 197.

> "....the memories of the past and
> the hicnuncs of the present em-
> belliching the musics of the
> future....This is not the end by
> no manner means...."
> (Finnegans Wake, 407-373).

Notes: Epilogue

1. James Joyce, Ulysses, The Bodley Head, London,
1954, 175.

2. See the comments on Voegelin's book in footnotes
42, 134. For Heidegger, see footnotes 100, 101,
153.

3. See footnote 168, below.

4. E. Voegelin, The Ecumenic Age, Louisiana State
University Press, 1974, 304.

5. Insight, 245, 319, 459, 514-20.

6. Take-off points in Insight are 187-206, 467 ff.,
535, 558-62, 607 ff., 642 ff., 696 ff.

7. How broadly one defines life depends on one's
foundations. Here, then, I would add reference
to Method in Theology, index, under Gift, and to

"The Natural Desire to See God", Collection,
Darton Longman and Todd, 1967, 84-95.

8. Here I would recall a definition of life given by
    Lonergan in his discussion of the life of Christ
    (De Verbo Incarnato, Gregorian Press, Rome, 1964,
    344):
    "Vita: sumitur concrete; eam denotat realitatem
    totam quae per biographiam describitur; dicit ergo
    non solum substantiam sed etiam subiectum, non
    solum potentias et habitus sed maxime totam actuum
    seriem. Sicut ergo in Christo distinguimus Deum
    et hominem, comprehensorem et viatorem, ita in
    eodem distinguimus vitam divinam Christi qua Dei,
    vitam aeternam Christi qua hominis comprehensoris,
    et vitam humanem et historicam Christi qua hominis
    viatoris". The definition relates forward to the
    Christological references below in footnotes 52 and
    154.

9. The meaning of 'part' comes from the context of
    Insight, 350 ff.

10. Insight, 246.

11. I recall how "the famous experiments on sea ur-
    chins reveal the immanent direction of the aggre-
    gation of aggregates of aggregates of aggregates"
    (Insight, 267). Intelligence adds the complexity
    of integrating "coincidental aggregates of sensible
    contents" (ibid.) and of reaching also for "the
    point of intersection of the timeless with time".

12. I refer here to the fact that physics is the most
    elementary science, chemistry less so, etc.

13. See Insight, 39-69; 84-102; 490-7; on related
    problems here. These heuristic problems link up
    eventually to a basic question towards which this
    paper moves: the question which concludes the
    section on "International", p.128, which is dis-
    cussed further in the section on "Growth".

14. There are broad issues involved here, but on an
    elementary level "a concrete plurality of lower
    activities may be instrumental to a higher end in
    another subject". "Finality, Love, Marriage",
    Collection, 19.

15. The word 'aggreformism' relates to the complex
    problem of conceiving of the form-matter relation-
    ship above the level of physics.

16. I extend here Lonergan's notion of neural demand function (Insight, 190). There is a possible precising here of the older notion of the range and limits of disposed matter.

17. See "Finality, Love, Marriage", Collection, 18 ff.

18. P. Weiss, Principles of Development, New York, 1939, 1.

19. In the discussion of the topic of human development in Insight these operators were grouped under the generic operator, the question (Insight, 469 ff.).

20. B. Lonergan, "The Response of the Jesuit as priest and apostle in the modern world", A Second Collection, Darton, Longman and Todd, 1974, 173, focuses on the downward dynamism which is a central topic in Method in Theology (see index, under Gift). The upward dynamism is a central topic in "Finality, Love, Marriage". But in each treatment there is a balance of the dynamisms with a difference that longer analysis would bring out. Lonergan's viewpoint would seem to provide a transforming context for the "cybernetic model" in the study of Religion (see Robert N. Bellah, Beyond Belief, Essays on Religion in a Post-Traditional World, Harper and Row, New York, 1970, 9-12.

21. See the comment in Insight, 456, on multiple personality. The problem of unity here obviously draws in the discussion of the definition of person found in Lonergan's theological works.

22. Insight, 472-9.

23. The plant or the animal is "an intelligible solution to the problem of living in a given environment" (Insight, 265), to the problem of surviving, and significantly different solutions give different species. Man is an intelligent source of solutions, and in that sense "genus is coincident with species" (Insight, 267). I go on later to speak of differentiation of consciousness in terms of speciation: but the issue is altogether more complex.

24. I have been influenced in what follows by Fr. Lonergan's comments on the dynamism of lower and upper quasi-operators at the Boston Workshop of June 1974. He has not, however, published on the topic yet.

25. In the final chapter on "The Notion of Survival" in Wealth of Self and Wealth of Nations, Exposition Press, 1975, I introduced a broad notion of survival as "you at core, but also you in kilos" where the core referred to the notion of being and of value. There is a problem here relating to Paul Ricoeur's topic of "The Myth of the Exiled Soul" (The Symbolism of Evil, Part II, cp. 4).

26. I include here Eternal Processes. On the inadequacies of process philosophy see B. Lonergan, Philosophy of God and Theology, Darton, Longman and Todd, 1973, 64-5.

27. C.G. Jung, Psychology and Religion: West and East, translated by R.F.C. Hull, London, 1958, 551; add the context of Insight, 444-51, on potency and finality.

28a. See footnotes 134 and 154 below.

28b. Insight, 469.

29. Method in Theology, 271-6.

30a. E.g., Method in Theology, 302-5.

30b. Insight, 470.

31. The primary problem here of course is the dialectical and foundational discomfort on which this book centres. But the problem of interest here is the dialogue between Communications and human science, between the human scientist and the "object" of his science, and in this context I find extremely suggestive the discussion of creative dialogue by Maria-Barbara Watson-Franke and Lawrence C. Watson, "Understanding in Anthropology: A Philosophical Reminder", Current Anthropology, June, 1975, 227-54. I quote a relevant passage: "In the dialogue it ideally becomes possible to leave the familiar context of our preunderstanding; this, however, is a difficult process that requires the exercise of 'imagination'. For Gadamer (Die Universalitat des hermeneutichen Problems", in Kleine Schriften I, Philosophie Hermeneutik, Tübingen, 1967, 108), imagination (Phantasie) is not an undisciplined rambling, but a creative force which enables one to find the questions worth asking (das Fragwürdige) in the new context. Thus, the ultimate goal becomes finding the question" (p. 251).

32. I refer forward here to the quotation from Insight
    at footnote 126: it is a slow empirical process
    determining the various integrations of aggregates
    of aggregates in the human organism; but beyond
    that there is the generalized empirical investiga-
    tion which is intrinisc to psychology.

33. One may think most immediately of the Skinner-type
    psychology, but there is a larger issue here of
    what I call generalized common sense eclecticism.

34. On the nature and significance of metaphysical equi-
    valence, see Insight, 502-9.

35. Insight, 509.

36. See footnote 6 above and add the contexts of foot-
    notes 31, 37 and of the interlocking set of foot-
    notes 164-75.

37. Obviously our reflections bear directly on the
    foundations for such normative psychology. The
    present state of discussion of what are regularly
    regarded as "the years of attrition" appals me.
    For a recent gloomy survey, see Leon Rappoport,
    Personality Development, Scott, Foresman & Co.,
    Illinois, 1972, 368-400. There is a task here for
    functional specialists in communications (Method
    in Theology, 132, 136, 364-5; Insight, 745), but
    since there is a problem of absence of samples of
    growth among both theologians and psychologists,
    ("Unless the psychologist has himself experienced
    the state of quest of final integration in the suc-
    cession of identities he will hardly acquire an
    understanding or incentive for doing research on
    it", A.R. Aresteh, Final Integration in the Adult
    Personality, Leiden, 1965, 18) the task involves a
    great deal of Kondratieff thinking and living (see
    footnote 109 below, and the corresponding text,
    page 131.

38. I am using Lonergan's distinction, Method in
    Theology, 233-4.

39. See the citation, p. 136 (note 147), on the nature of
    conceptual intending. Like Aquinas, Lonergan has
    treated these terms and relations very basically
    in the context of trinitarian theology.

40. Insight, 265.

41. Method in Theology, 93-9.

42. I would like to add two points here for creative
    reflection. The first point relates to the study
    of the growth of the subject: think of the trans-
    formation of Piaget's work that will become prob-
    able through the mediation of interiority that
    gives a positional perspective on objectivity and
    on the operators of that growth. The second point
    relates to the study of international growth, the
    topic of the second half of this paper. Think of
    the transformation of Voegelins's work that will
    become probable through a similar mediation, in-
    clusive of a thematic of sets and sequences of dif-
    ferentiated consciousness. I am indebted here to
    Fr. Lonergan for bringing Voegelin's latest volume,
    The Ecumenical Age, and certain aspects of it, to
    my attention. It is the fourth of his series on
    Order and History, but breaks with the program in-
    dicated in Volume I. A long introduction (1-58)
    discusses the change in perspective, and among the
    "dominant lines of meaning that became visible" was
    "the fundamental advance from compact to differen-
    tiated consciousness and its distribution over a
    plurality of ethnic cultures" (ibid., 57-8).

43. Insight, 478.

44. I refer here to the constitutive function of mean-
    ing (Method in Theology, 78).

45. Method in Theology, 286-7: habit in this context
    points towards an ideal: if you like, Aristotle's
    virtuous philosopher of the future. As we note in
    footnote 52, Jesus was not in the habit of such
    general categories. The present essay seeks to
    win the reader's sympathy for the personal vortex
    project required to heuristically specify that
    ideal.

46. Method in Theology, 254.

47. I would note here two more recent discussions by
    Lonergan of authenticity which provide a context
    for the present topic: A Second Collection, Darton,
    Longman and Tood, 1974, 165-70 (part of "The
    Response of the Jesuits as priest and apostle in
    the modern world") and "Dialectic of Authority",
    Boston College Studies in Philosophy Vol. III, M.
    Nijhoff, The Hague, 1974, 24-30.

48. A Second Collection, 166.

49.   What I mean by "rediscovery" will emerge to some
      extent in the paper, but its full discovery, re-
      discovery and thematization is central to an ade-
      quate theory of adult growth.

50.   A Second Collection, 165.

51.   Julian of Norwich, The Revelations of Divine Law,
      translated by James Walsh, S.J., London, 1961, 54.

52.   F.E. Crowe, "The Mind of Jesus", Communio, 1974,
      382, see also the references in footnotes 8 and
      154.

53.   The notion of vortex was introduced in the pro-
      logue to the second part; see p. 102.

54.   Method in Theology, 99.

55.   Insight, 477. Note also the problem of weighing
      one's place in one's time, or one's age against the
      ending of the twentieth century: "What is authen-
      tic for a lesser differentiation of consciousness
      will be found inauthentic by the standards of a
      greater differentiation. So there is the sin of
      backwardness, of the cultures, the authorities,
      the individuals that fail to live on the level of
      their times", ("Dialectic of Authority", 27).

56.   That cultivation, seeking and respect are to be
      determined by the reader through some such personal
      vortex as is indicated by the interlocking foot-
      notes 164-175, below.

57.   The conclusion to chapter three, "Zoology and the
      Future of Philosophers", above, p. 95.

58.   Method in Theology, 286.

59.   Insight, xxvii.

60.   See above, pp. 105 ff.

61.   There are problems here of anxiety and dread in
      facing the "existential gap" between, say, one's
      language in a tradition and one's constitution in
      it, a topic treated by Lonergan in his lectures on
      Existentialism in 1957.

62.   Method in Theology, 329.

63. Insight, 416-41. I note here that I incline to
speak of generalized common sense eclecticism in
relation to "generalized empirical method" (Insight,
72).

64. A notion I introduced in the paper "Image and
Emergence: Towards an Adequate Weltanschauung", p.10.

65. Insight, 542.

66. I recall here Heidegger's view of talk and Jasper's
view of the decay of the academy.

67. Insight, 418.

68. A Second Collection, 73. I refer to the article
on "The Subject".

69. The reference is to Heidegger's Was ist das - die
Philosophie, Günther Neske Pfullingen, 1960, 37-40.
For this and the following reference I am indebted
to Fr. Conn O.'Donovan, S.J., "On the Discomfort of
Being a Philosopher", Horizons, Milltown Institute,
Dublin, 1974, 105-14.

70. Merleau-Ponty, Éloye de la Philosophie, inaugural
lecture at the College de France, January 19 3.
Translated by John Wild and James Edie, Northwestern
University Press, 1963, p. 5.

71. Gaston Bachelard, The Poetics of Space, Beacon
Press, Boston pb., 1969, 14.

72. Method in Theology, 260.

73. Insight, 391.

74. Insight, 686.

75. Collection, 42.

76. Method in Theology, 48.

77. See, in particular, the text above, pp. 116 ff.
The basic text from Lonergan's theology is worth
recalling.   "....in quaestione longiori
atque difficiliori phantasma conveniens haberi non
potest nisi per diagramma quoddam adiuvatur ipsa
imaginatio; et ideo qui omnia per modum unius
apprehendere velit, diagramma quoddam faciat in

quo et elementa quaestionis omnia monesque inter
elementa nexus symbolica represententur", (B.
Lonergan, De Constitutione Christi Ontologica et
Psychologica, Gregorian Press, Rome, 1961, 80).

78. The diagram of the human good, bracketed by dia-
grammatic crutches relating to psychology, generalized emergent probability, and functional specialization, needs to be brought into a dialectic with
equivalent efforts in sociology. A convenient survey for such an exercise is Charles P. Loomis and
Zona K. Loomis, Modern Social Theory, Van Nostrand,
1965, where the various theories are diagrammed
with some degree of isomorphism. Add the context
of Gibson Winters, Elements of a Social Ethic,
New York, 1968, and that of footnote 169 below:
sociologists in general seem to have less "suspi-
ions" of generalized empirical method than psy-
chologists.

79. Eugene J. Meehan, The Foundations of Political
Analysis, Empirical and Normative, The Dorsey
Press, Illinois, 1971, certainly raised foundational
issues, but he is locked within the schemes of recurrence of a contemporary American academically-
respectable truncated subjectivity (see his select
bibliography, 257-67). The question I wish to
raise here in the reader's mind is the complex
foundational problem, not merely of formulating
invariants of praxis, but of including in that
formulation foundations for the emergence of alternate schemes. See footnote 167, below.

80. Implementation is included as a component of metaphysics, as far as I know, twice (391, 493) in
Insight. See the text below, after footnote 178.

81. Method in Theology, 51; add the context of page
116, and contrast the earlier context of Insight,
601.

82. "The use of the general categories occurs in any
of the eight functional specialties", Method in
Theology, 292. I feel that the specialist in
communications will, more than others, suffer from
the temptation to regard self-constitution in
these categories as not vital for him. I recall
Fr. Lonergan's lecture at the Boston Workshop of
1974, "A New Pastoral Theology", where he noted
that pastoral theology or any other specialty in
theology, "should spring from roots that are alive,
intersubjective, communal and historical,

ecumenical, universalist and eschatological": that
categories are an on-going explanatory heuristic of
these roots.

83. B. Lonergan, "Dialectic of Authority", Boston
College Studies in Philosophy, III, Nijhoff, The
Hague, 1974, 29.

84. See Insight, 490-7; also the appendix, "De
Relationibus", in De Deo Trino, Pars Systematica,
Gregorian Press, Rome, 1964.

85. The context is the discussion of probable seria-
tion, Insight, 119.

86. Richard N. Goodwin, The American Condition,
Doubleday, New York, 1974, 391.

87. Ibid., 149.

88. I recall the title and content of the series of
lectures given by Lonergan in Toronto, November
1973: "A Revolution in Catholic Theology?".

89. Method in Theology, 291. See also 292.

90. I use "memory" here in a full Proustian constitutive sense.

91. Insight, 509.

92. Insight, 509. See also 498, and place in this context Method in Theology, 284, footnote 8.

93. Insight, 509.

94. Relevant here is an extension of the discussion of
"stating the meaning" (Method in Theology, 167 ff.)
within interpretation to all the functional specialties. See Insight, 398 ff., 553 ff.

95. The mood I would associate with the problem of
total self-appropriation. On the metaphysical
elements, see Insight, 497 ff.

96. Erich Neumann, The Origins and History of Consciousness, Harper Torchbooks, 1962, 284.

97. Insight, 743.

98. See Insight, 91-3.

99. See B. Lonergan, <u>Philosophy of God and Theology</u>,
     Darton, Longman and Todd, London, 1973, 12-3, 49,
     51, 61, 66.

100. M. Heidegger, <u>Being and Time</u>, Harper & Row, New
     York, 1962, 127; the context is a discussion of
     Dasein's spatiality and the 'aroundness of the
     environment' - a context, as we shall see, relevant
     to our problem.

101. <u>Ibid</u>., 77.

102. A context here is <u>Insight</u>, 510, on "The Unity of
     the Proportionate Universe"; a fuller context is
     the discussion of Justitia Dei in <u>De Verbo
     Incarnato</u>, Thesis 17, Gregorian Press, Rome, 1961,
     1962, 1964.

103. <u>Insight</u>, 244.

104. Including the subtly differentiated consciousness
     of Christ, instances of non-temporal finite con-
     sciousness, and the simple consciousness of the
     tri-subjective divinity.

105. "Finality, Love, Marriage", <u>Collection</u>, 21.

106. The subtitle of the concluding chapter of his book,
     <u>The Theology of Hope</u>, SCM Press, Edinburgh, 1967.

107. <u>Op.cit</u>., 313.

108. <u>Ibid</u>.

109. For Lonergan's "longer cycle" see <u>Insight</u>, 226 ff.
     The economic cycles were named after economists
     associated with their investigation. The Russian
     economist Kondratieff gave his name to the long
     cycle of about 60 years. The Juglar was somewhat
     over eight years long. A shorter cycle of about
     three years was named after the Englishman,
     Kitchin.

110. A marginal note in the "Triv and Quod" section of
     <u>Finnegans Wake</u>, 294, indicates "Sarga, or the path
     of outgoing". <u>Sarga</u> is the Sanskrit for 'process
     of world creation or emanation'.

111. The analogy is not altogether farfetched. The Old
     Testament transitions are certainly long
     Kondratieffs of mind and heart; on the pace of the

New Testament shifts see Fuller, <u>The Foundations</u> <u>of New Testament Christology</u>, Scribner, New York, 1965. The Conciliar shifts are well known.

112. I enjoy, of course, the related puns. The systematic theologian seeks to keep, so to speak, all the concrete elements in the air, with the heuristic dexterity of the juggler. The communications cycle is shorter, not because it is a type of table-talk, but because of present-day turnover of science and art, of cultural and class interests, of communications' techniques: see above footnote 82.

113. <u>Method in Theology</u>, 325.

114. The mediation and the doctrine as thus thematized should be constitutive of the doctrinal theologian. See <u>Method in Theology</u>, 318.

115. <u>Method in Theology</u>, 290.

116. <u>Op.cit.</u>, 314; the last part of the quotation is in fact from Bultmann, <u>Glauben und Verstehen</u>, III, 1960, 196.

117. DS 3016.

118. My initial quotation. I would put my feedback procedure into the context of Lonergan's comment on linguistic feedback, <u>Method in Theology</u>, 88, footnote 34.

119. In more recent years Fr. Lonergan has rediscovered "The limitations of the treatise" (<u>Insight</u>, 573-7) in his criticism of logic as the habitat of the static mind (see the indices to <u>A Second Collection</u> and <u>Philosophy of God</u> and Theology, under logic).

120. See footnotes 53 and 171.

121. G. Marcel, "Creative fidelity", <u>Creative Fidelity</u>, Farrar, Straus and Giroux, New York, 1964, 147-74. I think of Marcel more in terms of mood than of content. The basic issue here is the apparent impossibility of foundations for <u>praxis</u>, a sublation of "The Possibility of Ethics" (<u>Insight</u>, cp. 18).

122. See <u>Insight</u>, 192-4.

123. The meaning of 'admission' is that indicated earlier,124 ff. On the basic tension, see <u>Insight</u>, 385.

124.   Insight, 194.   The topic raised here is related to
       a present popular movement - of which Sam Keen's
       Apology for Wonder (Harper and Row, 1973) is repre-
       sentative - which calls for some integration of
       Apollonian and Dionysian attitudes.   I would note
       a deeper relationship to the two types of philo-
       sophy of religion of Tillich, thc cosmological
       approach which begins from the world and the ontolo-
       gical approach which begins with the self's experi-
       ence of self.   On the manner in which intentionality
       analysis sublates Tillich's typology see John C.
       Robertson, Jr., "Tillich's 'Two Types' and the
       Transcendental Method", Journal of Religion, 1975,
       199-219.

125.   See footnote 160 and the corresponding text, p.138.

126.   Insight, 464-5.

127.   Insight, 250.

128.   There is, of course, the limping of mind: "The
       intelligible unity of the existing world order may
       be known in three ways, imperfectly by philosophy,
       less imperfectly by theology, but satisfactorily
       only as a result of the beatific vision".   B.
       Lonergan, "The Natural Desire to See God",
       Collection, 89.   A context worth adding here is
       the discussion of the necessity of an inner word
       in human knowing: See Verbum, 192-3; De Deo Trino,
       Pars Systematica, Rome, 1964, 105, 289.

129.   Insight, 514.

130.   See Method in Theology, 14.

131.   Insight, 419.

132.   Ibid.; again, "the individual of genius appears no
       more than the instrument of human solidarity", B.
       Lonergan, "Finality, Love, Marriage", Collection,
       39.

133.   The question requires detailed foundational treat-
       ment mediated by a rediscovery, not unrelated to
       the bridge indicated in the text below, of the dis-
       cussion of inverse insight (see Insight, 19-25,
       687, 689; De Deo Trino, Pars Dogmatica, Rome, 1964,
       274).   There is question here of focusing the dark-
       ness in that "orientation to transcendent mystery
       which is basic to systematic theology" (Method in
       Theology, 341).

134. "There is a process of the Whole of which In-Between reality with its process of history is no more than a part, though the very important part in which the Whole becomes luminous for the eschatological moment beyond its own structure": Voegelin, op.cit. supra, footnote 4, p. 333: this entire concluding chapter on "Universal Humanity" (300-35) provides a relevant context. The meaning of "luminous" requires the determination indicated in the previous footnote 133.

135. Recall footnote 37.

136. From the Preface of the old Latin Mass for the Nativity of Our Lord. I would like to note in this context another contribution of science to The Coming Convergence of World Religions, Whitson notes in the book of that title (Newman Press, New York, 1971) the emergent need "to analyse systematically the creative process in any religious tradition" (p. 56) as well as "man in the process of knowledge". Later centuries will see a global presence of science, a global shift in the statistics of emergence of the analysis of its creative processes.

137. Supra, p. 18.

138. Wealth of Self and Wealth of Nations, chapter five and chapter nine at footnote 5.

139. Susanne Langer, Mind: An Essay on Human Feeling, I, Baltimore, 1967, 97, footnote.

140. Insight, xxviii.

141. There is a principle of correspondence between the levels in man involved here. See Insight, 471-2; Method in Theology, 66-7.

142. Insight, 140.

143. A care sublated by the subjectivity and objectivity of Insight, and by the appropriation of serenity and concern: on the latter pair see F.E. Crowe, "Complacency and Concern in the Writings of Aquinas", Theological Studies (20), 1959.

144. M. Heidegger, Being and Time, Harper & Row, New York, 1962, 402.

145. Insight, 170-2.

146. On the importance of the perspective of <u>omnia simul</u> see "Finality, Love, Marriage", <u>Collection</u>, 38.

147. <u>Method in Theology</u>, 10-1.

148. <u>Insight</u>, 254.

149. <u>Ibid</u>.

150. See <u>Insight</u>, 385, 388, 379-80, 513-4.

151. "Finality, Love, Marriage", <u>Collection</u>, 47, footnote.

152. <u>Ibid</u>., 48.

153. I have been dealing with one aspect of the return to self and sources continually regenerative of authentic tradition in oneself. I recall Heidegger's remark: "Tradition takes what has come down to us and delivers it over to self-evidence; it blocks out access to those primordial 'sources' from which the categories and concepts handed down to us have been in part quite genuinely drawn. Indeed it makes us forget that they have had such an origin, and makes us suppose that the necessity of going back to these sources is something which we need not even understand", <u>Being and Time</u>, 43.

154. "A man who understood everything might proceed...." <u>Insight</u>, 513. I have no doubt that care for this question is intrinsic to developed foundations, just as is care for the question, What is being? (<u>Insight</u>, 642, 2nd last line). The resulting categories are, for instance, clearly relevant to the systematics of the mind of Christ. For a masterly use of such categories see F.E. Crowe, "Eschaton and World Mission in the Mind and Heart of Jesus", <u>The Eschaton: A Community of Love</u>, edited by Joseph Papin, The Villanova University Press, 1971, 105-44. Recall footnotes 8, 52, <u>supra</u>.

155. John Passmore surveys both in <u>The Pefectibility of Man</u>, Duckworth, London, 1970. Another relevant context here is <u>Theology meets Progress</u>, edited by Philip Land, Gregorian Press, Rome, 1971. I would note especially the essay by Paolo Tufari, S.J., "The Church between Ideology and Utopia", 249-88, as crying out for an advance into functional specialization. This latter volume tempts me into what is no doubt an imprudent frankness.

I do not find a vast number of contemporary theologians "arriving on the scene a little breathless and a little late" (Insight, 733): more signs of the breathing pattern of the dreams of morning would be welcome.

156. Cf. supra, p. 11.

157. At footnotes 75 and 76, the text at p.127.

158. R.E. Whitson, The Coming Convergence of World Religions, Newman Press, New York, 1971, speaks of the significance of "dreams of unity", 17-9.

159. Whitson, op.cit., 145.

160. I refer back to the text quoted at footnote 126 in the hope that the reader might rediscover it by replacing "universe" for "organism".

161. Insight, 547; see also 741-2.

162. I have not, however, prescinded from my particular tradition, and in this I would hope that I come under Whitson's norm: "the theologian does not exist in a vacuum and hence must identify himself clearly in terms of his actual religious tradition. His creativity derives from that tradition and he must recognize this and express it unambiguously. But from the nature of what he is attempting to do he must also recognize that he is moving resolutely from any negative narrowness of separatism. Always present in his commitment and conviction must be the consciousness of the authenticity of his tradition as not determined by isolation." (op.cit., 167-8).

163. B. Lonergan, Gregorianum (40), 1959, 182-3, in a review.

164. Here I mean context as constitutive of the subject, the actual "interweaving of questions and answers" (Method in Theology, 163).

165a. B. Lonergan, Philosophy of God, and Theology, Darton, Longman and Todd, London, 1973.

165b. Ibid., 59.

166. "Incidentally, I am sure that I don't have to explain that by the term 'conceptualization' I don't mean something unchanged, permanent, nor

simply an idea that pops out of somebody's head;
rather, it is the final result of a long process
that begins with the relationship between one
human being and another". The citation is
from Peter Karvas, a Slovak playwright, The
Politics of Culture edited by Antonin J. Liehm,
with a preface by Sartre, "The Socialism that
came in from the Cold", Random House, New York,
1973, 333. The book also adds a relevant context
to the problem of mandarinism. It focuses on
the dialectic of power and authority in Czechos-
lovakia in the late '60s. There is a politics
of culture, too, in America, which requires
functional specialist consideration.

167. "Not Utopia, but creativity, is that for which
men should strive": a remark of Fr. Lonergan
during a lecture in Montreal on "Healing and
Creativity in History", as reported in The Gazette,
Montreal, Friday May 16, 1975, 26. The creativity
required, I would surmise, is one which, especially
in the second four functional specializations can
collaboratively bring forth in idea the complex
of probable schemes of recurrence the times demand,
including the adequate idea of ongoing implementation and renewal. Cf., B. Lonergan, "The
Dialectic of Authority", Boston College Studies in
Philosophy, III, The Hague, 1974, 29-30.

168. I have focused here mainly on the possibility of
cultivation that lies in a return to which I would
call the ABC of Foundations (The reference is to
the triangle ABC of Insight, 27, 504). But one
must note the priority of prayer and poetry.

169. In his Boston Workshop paper of 1974, "The Modern
Philosophic Differentiation of Consciousness, or
What is Enlightenment?", Fred Lawrence discussed
the debate between a"Hermeneutics of Suspicion"
and "Integral Hermeneutics", Habermas being representative of the former, Gadamer of the latter.
The paper adds an enriching context to the present
one. My interest is in continual creative self-
constitution, and by "suspicion" I mean a complex
six-levelled reality of the constituted self.

170. Insight, 186. Note However, that I have
indicated a wider context of cultivation of,
and fidelity to, that intellectual pattern of
experience. But no one, I hope, will mistake
my indication as an indication of a softening
of the intellectualism of Lonergan.

171. To previous discussion and reference to "vortex"
I would add Gerhard Adler's comment: "This movement of the spiral - here reinforced by the
dynamic action of the vortex - is characteristic
of the 'indirect approach by means of the
circumambulatio'. It is as if an unknown centre,
which we can define only as the psychological
self, produces a constant centripetal movement,
or in Jung's words 'acts like a magnet on the
disparate materials and processes of the unconscious ... Often one has the impression that
the personal psyche is running round this central
point like a shy animal, at once fascinated and
frightened, always in flight, and yet steadily
drawing nearer'". The Living Symbol, A Case
Study in the Process of Individuation, Pantheon,
New York, 1961, 183. The inner quotation is
from Jung's Alchemy.

172. The reference is to Paul Ricoeur, The Symbolism
of Evil, Beacon Press, Boston, 1967, 274: his
discussion of "conformed to the image of the
Son" (Rom. 8:29).

173. See B. Lonergan, Verbum: Word and Idea in Aquinas,
University of Notre Dame Press, 1967, especially
90-94, 183-220, for the retrieval of Aquinas'
view. Lonergan's development represents a
sequence of sublations of this view, which in
fact intimate further possibilities of rediscovery.

174. I recall here both my notion of transformed
sensibility (above, 40ff., 107ff., 137) and Joyce's
notion of the ballast office clock (a clock near
Dublin's main street) as epiphany: recall the
Prologue to Part 2, above, 75-77, and the references there, 163-64.

175. The context is B. Lonergan, De Verbo Incarnato,
Gregorian Press, Rome, theses 15-17, with an
additional context supplied by Paul Ricoeur,
op.cit.

176. <u>Insight</u>, 376ff., with the addition of <u>Method in Theology</u>, 101-03: "the spark in our clod, our native orientation to the divine", (103).

177. Ezra Pound, quoted in Hugh Kenner, <u>The Pound Era</u>, University of California Press, 1971, 238.

178. <u>Insight</u>, 391. Recall footnote 80 above.

179. <u>Insight</u>, 531.

180. The take-off point here is a comparison of the tables of content of <u>Insight</u> and <u>Method in Theology</u> with pages 286-87 of <u>Method in Theology</u>.

181. <u>Method in Theology</u>, 250.

182. A remark of W. B. Yeats quoted in Richard Ellmann, <u>Yeats: The Man and the Masks</u>, Dutton, New York, 1948, 5.

... completed as it happens on my 45th birthday, like Husserl a beginner (see above, 6), seeking now to point a brick (cf., Bachelard, above, iii) of <u>Praxis-Weltanschauung</u>: Lonergan's analysis of the normative rhythms of economic process. Present economic pseudo-theory-praxis (Joan Robinson, <u>Economic Heresies, Some Old-Fashioned Questions in Economic Theory</u>, Harper, New York, 1973 provides some background) resembles an effort to achieve steady acceleration in first gear of a gear-shift car, with little understanding of the cycles of the engine, or of the nature of the multicoloured passengers.

Philip McShane
February 18th 1977